# THE POLISH COUNTRY KITCHEN COOKBOOK

Expanded Edition

# THE POLISH COUNTRY KITCHEN COOKBOOK

Expanded Edition

Sophie Hodorowicz Knab

Illustrations by

Elliott Hutten

**HIPPOCRENE BOOKS, INC.**
*New York*

*Also by Sophie Hodorowicz Knab*:

Polish Customs, Traditions and Folklore

Paperback Expanded Edition 2012.



Book design by Susan Ahlquist, East Hampton, NY

For more information, address:
HIPPOCRENE BOOKS, INC.
171 Madison Avenue
New York, NY 10016
www.hippocrenebooks.com

Previous edition ISBNs: 978-0-7818-0882-8; 0-7818-0882-0

ISBN-13: 978-0-7818-1294-8
ISBN-10: 0-7818-1294-1

For my brothers Michał, Andzej, and Mieczysław

We ate *skwarki*, *kapusta*, *pierogi,* and bread and butter with sugar sprinkled on top. We drank beer soup when we had colds, ate milk soup during Lent, and chicken soup for Sunday dinner. We mixed the blood of geese with vinegar for *czarnina*, picked wild blackberries for *sok* and jam, and did our homework in the kitchen next to a barrel of fermenting sauerkraut.

This book is for you, with much love, in memory of our Polish American childhood.

Zosia

## ACKNOWLEDGEMENTS

First, I'd like to thank the people who shared ideas and recipes for this book: Maria Pysikiewicz, Christine and Robert Gorny, Johnette Skrypeck, Jean Tuohey, Katie Wrobel, Florence Wandel, Arlene Zawadski, Sophie Krysa, and Judy Krauza.

Next, I express thanks to Jadzia Dziegielewska and Bronislaus Trzyzewski who helped me translate arcane Polish words; to Mark Mistriner and Carl Heintz of the Culinary Arts Department at Niagara County Community College for cooking and baking consultations; to the fabulous librarians and staff of Niagara County Community College who give unstintingly—Fran Angelleti, Diane Balcom, Karen Ferington, Liz Fullwell, Catherine Gibbs, Kathleen Greenfield, Beth Hodgeson, Lilliane Passanese, Jean Tuohey and Nancy Verstreate. I wish you to know how much I admire all of you.

In Poland I am especially indebted to Krystyna Bartosik who is constantly on the lookout for books and photographs to help me write my books and to the Panstwowy Muzeum Etnograficzne (National Ethnographic Museum) in Warsaw for allowing me to access their collections; to Władysława Muras, the artist who created the wonderful paper cut out for the cover of this book and to Katarzyna Raczkowska of the Bibliotecka Narodowa (National Library) in Warsaw who helped me locate material that was not available in the United States.

My deepest thanks to Elliott Hutten, gifted artist and friend, who did the illustrations for this book.

To my sister-in-law Sheryl Knab for preparing the index.

To my husband Ed. Where would I be without your love and encouragement?

Lastly, a very special thank you to my editor Carol Chitnis-Gress, who is a joy to work with, and all of the folks at Hippocrene Books who helped (once again!) make this book a reality and who are helping it reach its audience.

*Bóg zapłać.*

# Contents

*Do kraju tego, gdzie kruszynę chleba*
*Podnoszą z ziemi przez uszanowanie*
*Dla darów nieba . . .*
*Tęskno mi, Panie.*

For the land where a crumb of bread
Is raised from the ground with reverence
For the gifts of heaven . . .
I yearn, O Lord.

Cyprian Kamil Norwid (1821–1883), *Moja Piosnka*

# POLAND

Primary Regions and Major Cities

# Introduction

In the years since the release of my first book, *Polish Customs, Traditions and Folklore* I have repeatedly been asked for a book that combines traditional Polish foods along with customs and traditions. Readers have also asked about the history of Polish cooking and the kind of kitchens and kitchenware that their grandmothers and great grandmothers were likely to have used. They want to try and reconstruct the lives of their ancestors, seeking answers about their day-to-day life. What types of utensils did they use for cooking? What kinds of stoves did they have? When did the use of matches become common? How did they bake bread? What is the meaning of the butter lamb at Easter? What foods should I put in the Easter basket?

It is my hope that the most pressing questions will be answered through this book. It explores the life of the peasant as he strives to grow, consume, and preserve food throughout the cycle of the seasons and the role of that food in his customs and traditions. For that reason, I have chosen to write this cookbook according to the cycle of the seasons—potato dishes in the fall when they are freshest, cucumber dishes in the summer when they are plentiful, and buckwheat groats in the winter when other staples have run out. This is the way our forefathers lived and ate. This is also the way many Poles who immigrated to America at the turn of the century lived and ate. So much of what is written in this book is certainly the way my mother lived and prepared food in Poland and here in America all the years of my growing up.

Born in 1911 and raised in Nisko, a small town in southeastern Poland, my mother was the daughter of Polish peasants. Their parents were also Polish peasants, as were their parents and grandparents before them. She always said with great pride "*Jestem chłopska córka*" (I am the daughter of a Polish peasant). She was proud of who she was and the fact that the labors of the Polish peasant had been the backbone of the Polish nation. The region she lived in was called Galicia, that part of Poland controlled by the Austro-Hungarian Empire during the partitions of Poland. It was a poor, overpopulated region where every *hectare* of tillable land was under cultivation and people still went to bed hungry. I grew up listening to stories of life in Poland. As I watched her crush leftover pieces of dried bread with a rolling pin to make bread crumbs, she told me of the sacredness of bread and how it must never be treated lightly or wasted, not even a crumb. When it happened to fall to the floor she would raise it to her lips and kiss it in reverence and taught my brothers and I to do the same. As she cut out large circles of dough for pierogi she told me about the lives of my grandmother and grandfather, gave me images that made me know them even though I never had the opportunity to meet them. We ate the foods and dishes that she had eaten in Poland only now there were more of them and no one went to bed hungry. Each summer her garden yielded fresh parsley, radishes, lettuce, tomatoes, and cucumbers for the kitchen table and enough green beans to put up for the cold time. She sent us to the woods to seek blueberries, raspberries, and blackberries to make thick jams and jellies and fruit juice to sweeten our tea and to pour over ice cream. Every summer and fall was a frenzy of activity to prepare for the winter. She canned apples, pears, peaches, and the sweet cherries of summer for compote. In the fall, Mr. Burek, a Polish American farmer, would deliver eight to ten bushels of cabbage which we converted to a large barrel of sauerkraut to last us through the winter months. He also brought sacks and sacks of potatoes with black clods of earth still clinging to their skins. The wood stove, heated with a combination of wood and coal, was the site of a pot of soup gently simmering throughout a winter's day. Even though my mother took advantage of the conveniences of life in America she still maintained a Polish kitchen and a home filled with Polish customs and traditions. There were *chruściki* just before Ash Wednesday. We shared *opłatek* before our Christmas Eve meal and then ate mushroom soup and pierogi. In the spring we hunted pussy willows in the woods and cranked out our own sausage to place in our basket for blessing on Holy Saturday. I know that these experiences and variations on these experiences are also true for millions of other Polish Americans. Our lives, our traditions are closely linked with food and the memories of our mothers and grandmothers in the kitchen wearing their aprons. May the memories stay with us. May they never be forgotten.

# THE COUNTRY KITCHEN

## Kuchnia Wiejska

*Market in a small town. Original drawing by J. Konopacki. Woodcut from Tygodnik Ilustrowany, 1886.*

## EARLY POLISH COOKBOOKS

The earliest documented Polish recipes date back to the 16th century. They consist of fragments of a work printed in Kraków in 1530 about making vinegar. In that same century, Szymon Syrenski (1540–1611), a graduate of Kraców Academy with degrees in philosophy and medicine, wrote a 1540 page book titled *O przyrodzeniu i użycie ziół* (About the Properties and Uses of Plants). The book was dedicated to physicians, pharmacists, and veterinarians as well as gardeners, chefs, cooks, and farmers. Besides entire sections on herbs and plants, the book offered recipes for vegetarian foods "which will please both the healthy and the sick." He offers: "Prepare mushrooms with pepper or lovage or coriander, rue or with fat, a little oil, honey and a little wine and bring it to the table while hot."

The oldest extant Polish cookbook was published during the reign of King Jan Sobieski (1674–1696). Its author was Stanisław Czerniecki, master chef of the fabulously wealthy Aleksander Michał Lubomirski. As chief administrator of the Kraków province, there were only a dozen individuals in all of Poland with Lubomirski's type of wealth. He lived in a beautiful castle in Łancut, entertained frequently, set a very lavish table, and had his own chef.

Czerniecki's cookbook first appeared in Kraków in 1682 and was titled *Compendium Ferculorum.* The book, consisting of dishes and recipes that were prepared at the tables of the nobility, was separated into three major sections and offered 300 recipes: 100 each for meat, fish, and dairy, and it contained thirty appendixes. The book gives insight not only into the gastronomical appetites of the rich and famous but how foods were prepared at the time. For instance: "Take a live capon, pour some wine vinegar into its throat with the help of a funnel and hang for a good five hours, pluck nicely, season well—and bake or cook as you wish."

A section of the book was devoted to preparing meat from wild animals: "Take a fresh auroch or elk or deer or stag or goat or whatever you prefer from the forest. Chop into pieces but don't soak, don't rinse. Place in a clay pot with drawn butter. Fry a lot of onions with apples, mix together and make a thick mush. Dice a goodly amount of parsley, salt to taste and pour the broth over the vegetables and when half cooked, pour in wine vinegar and cut a lemon, raisins along with pepper, cinnamon, cloves, nutmeg, sweeten well and take to the table." In today's terms the recipe leaves many gaps and questions but was, perhaps, understood by cooks of that particular time period. It does, however, highlight the dependency on herbs, spices, and vinegar.

The book also offered numerous recipes for desserts including crepes filled with ground almonds, sugar, and egg whites; macaroons also made from almonds, sugar, and egg whites; and a gruel made with milk, sugar, almonds, and raisins. His book also gave insights as to the types of vegetables that were available to the wealthy such as cauliflower, artichokes, asparagus, cardoon, broccoli, spinach, and various lettuces. Mr. Czerniecki also stressed the importance of the many necessary items needed in a well-equipped kitchen such as copper molds. *Compendium Ferculorum* remained Poland's main cookbook for over a hundred years reaching as far as Lwów and Wilno and enjoyed several reprints.

In 1793, a new author emerged by the name of Wojciech Wielądko with his cookbook entitled *Kucharz Doskonały Pożytecznego dla Zatrudnienia się Gospodarstwem* (The Cook's Best Guide for Home Use). It was a thoroughly complete cookbook filled with recipes for preparing soups, meat and wild game, domestic and wild fowl, fresh and saltwater fish, vegetables, patê, sauces, syrups, how to make vodka and ratafia, as well as marzipan, cakes and sugar cookies. Three years later it was reissued and then again in the years 1800, 1808, 1812, and 1823. Both books, Czerniecki's *Compendium Ferculorum* and Wielądko's book, eventually became important sources of information for Adam Mickiewicz when writing about food and banquets in his epic poem *Pan Tadeusz.*

In the second half of the 1800s, help for the kitchen came in the various women's magazines: *Bluszcz* (Ivy) in 1865, *Dwór Wiejski* (Country Manor) in 1882, *Kalendarz Gospodarski dla Kobiet* (Woman's Household Calendar) in the 1870s, and *Dobra Gospodyni* (Good Housewife) published in Poznań in the early 1900s. One came in the form of a regularly published column entitled *Listy do córki o zarządzaniu gospodarstwem domowym z dodaniem praktycznych przepisów* (Letter to Daughters on Running a Home with Practical Recipes) that was published in Warsaw in 1828. Specific magazines were geared towards the rural housewife. These included *Poradnik dla Gospodyń Wiejskich* (Handbook for the Rural Housewife) published in Warsaw, as well as *Gospodyni Wiejska* (Country Housewife), *Ziemianka* (Country Woman), and *Głos do Kobiet Wiejskich* (Voice of Country Women).

In 1842, a cookbook devoted solely to the preparation of potatoes was published. The anonymous author described its uses in feeding horses, oxen, sheep, goats, and chickens; how potatoes can be used to make homemade starch, flour, bread, and cheese as well as beer, wine, soap, and candles. There were also numerous dishes to prepare purées, salads, pastry, potato dishes topped with cheese and/or breadcrumbs more familiarly known today as "au gratin," puddings, tortes, and even dishes utilizing potato peelings.

In 1845, *Ulżenie kłopota młodym gospodyniom w dysponowaniu obiadów* (Simplified Cooking for the Young Housewife) was published in Warsaw. Also from Warsaw was a book in the form of an encyclopedia titled *Encyklopedia potrzeb domowych i rad do nich stosowania jako podręcznik dla pań domu zawierający 1560 ważnych wiadomości* (An Encyclopedia of 1560 Helpful Hints). Another book that enjoyed a great deal of popularity was *Kucharz Polski dla młodych gospodyń—podręcznik obejmujący 1553 przepisy kucharskie* (Polish Cookbook for Young Housewives with 1553 Recipes) that was published in 1856 and was reissued seven times from 1856 to 1901. From Kijów came *Poradnik dla Młodych Gospodyń* (Helpful Hints for Young Housewives) written by Maria Krzywkowska Marciszewska that was published in 1856 and then reprinted in 1861 and 1885. *Polska Kuchnia i Spiżarnia* (Polish Kitchen and Pantry) was written by Jadwiga Izdebska in 1894. She

*The market near Żelazna Brama in Warsaw. Sale of crockery. Illustration from Kłosy (magazine), 1884.*

*"In a small town." Woodcut from Tygodnik Ilustrowany, 1888.*

was a well-known author of many other handbooks for young women including *Młodej Gosposi* (Young Housewife). Another book was *Skrzętnej Gospodyni* (The Resourceful Housewife) by Paulina Szumlańska and *Najnowsza Kuchnia Wytworna i Gospodarska* (The Newest, Most Stylish Kitchen and Household).

One of the most successful writers of Polish cookbooks was Lucyna Ćwierczakiewicz. Writing before the turn of the century, she was a prolific writer who turned her pen to numerous books and projects. Her *365 obiadów za 5 złotych* (365 Dinners for 5 Cents), directed at the middle class of Poland, was first published in Warsaw in 1860. By 1901, 90,000 copies of her books were circulating in Poland. Her books were second in popularity only to Henryk Sienkiewicz's *The Trilogy*. The popularity was understandable. Unlike Czerniecki's 17th-century guide to cooking which directed one to "take a grouse hen or partridge, bird or pigeon, capon or calf or whatever you want . . . ," Lucy's *365 Dinners* offered much clearer and concise directions. She writes:

> "A good omlet rests on three important conditions: Do not make it out of more than three or four eggs. You should have a separate thin iron skillet, not too deep and use it only to make omlets. Thirdly, do not heat the eggs too long unlike what many believe that it makes the omlet bigger. Beating them for a long time only makes the eggs watery."

In her book Lucyna offers recipes for long forgotten Polish dishes such as beer soup, lobster patê, sausage in beer, and buckwheat groats with milk. The 20th reprinting of *365 Dinners* took place in 1910 in Warsaw and brought publication of the book to 100,000. In the introduction, the editors testify that each recipe was kitchen tested by Lucyna herself. The author also wrote a brief preface, letting her readership know she had updated and modernized her recipes to fit current trends in cooking. "I always tell housewives," she writes, "that a well prepared dinner is the foundation of a happy home and contented husband."

Lucyna Ćwierczakiewicz was a multitalented woman. She taught home economics at several famous boarding schools in Warsaw. She was the initiator of a major food exhibit in Warsaw in

1885 where she exhibited her cakes and conserves. For twenty-eight years she wrote a column titled *Wskazówki i Rady Gospodarskie* (Guide and Helpful Hints for the Home) in *Bluszcz* (Ivy), a popular women's magazine. She also wrote for other journals directed specifically at women such as the fashion magazine *Tygodnik Mód* (Fashion Weekly). Her articles focused on a variety of culinary issues as well as mixing anecdotes with recipes. She hosted a "salon" as was popular in those days, where the wealthy and famous could mingle with those involved in literature and art. The less well-known were also invited. Every Thursday during the winter months she invited ten tinkers for dinner. Her second book titled *Jedyne Praktyczne Przepisy dla konfitur, różnych marynat, wędlin, likierów, win owocowych, miodów oraz ciast* (Only Practical Recipes for Conserves, Marinades, Meat, Liquor, Fruit Wines, Honeycakes and Baked Goods), printed in Warsaw from 1858 to 1921 had twenty-one printings. Lucy was also the author of various books on keeping house and household hints and tips such as removing spots and organizing a home titled *Poradnik porządki i różnych hygienicznych wiadomości potrzebnych kobiecie* (Guide for Housekeeping and Various Health News for Women) *Podarunek Ślubny* (Wedding Gift), and *Kurs Gospodarstwa Miejskiego i Wiejskiego dla Kobiet* (Housekeeping Course for City and Country Women) published in Warsaw in 1885. She also wrote a book on making artificial flowers. Some of Lucy's household hints are interspersed throughout the book.

Numerous cookbooks have been published since 1945 but the most thorough and complete was *Kuchnia Polska* (Polish Kitchen). Its 800 pages featured scientifically prepared recipes compiled by eight nutrition experts and two physicians. The book enjoyed nine printings and sold millions of copies.

Once the province of the rich and middle class who could read, cookbooks eventually traveled down country lanes to small villages and cottages. The increasing industrialization of the late 1800s brought about not only the opening of new factories and then stores to sell goods, but it also saw an increased emphasis on education for the masses, the development of village schools, and increasing literacy. With that came the printing of more pamphlets, books, and periodicals. Traveling salesmen and craftsmen, with their books and goods strapped to their back or loaded on a pony cart, peddled their wares from hamlet to hamlet. One of the strongest influences for change in a small village came from the parish priest. The work of the clergy was such that it often required traveling to larger towns and cities to meet with superiors to deal with church matters. The country priest was often the first to bring back something new and intriguing to the delight of his mother or sister who often acted as his housekeeper. This could be a small cookbook or a new cake pan. Since many a poor young country girl earned her first money working at the rectory to do general cleaning, helping in the kitchen, or serving at table, the link to the cottages was inevitable. The young girl would describe the new dish to her mother. What woman could resist trying the latest recipe from the big city? Or, if it was a baking pan, the girl described it to her father or an uncle who was handy and could replicate the item in stoneware or tin. This was also true of young girls employed at the big manor houses. Things like cookbooks or the newest pans or molds were bought by the lady of the manor on a buying trip to the nearest large city and quickly copied. Another opportunity for change in the country villages came when young girls temporarily left home seeking work in town to earn money for a dowry. When they returned home to settle down they often brought back new ideas and if literate, a new cookbook, to help them be good housewives. Some young women traveled to nearby cities to culinary art schools to learn the fine art of cooking and baking.

Besides the help of formally printed cookbooks there were also private, family-type cookbooks. There were many women who documented their own recipes, many of them hard-won through trial and error or obtained from a neighbor or family member. There were also secret formulas for Auntie's best pickles or Grandmother's plum jam, or how to make the lightest, highest Easter *baba*, the housewife's culinary pride and joy. Any such notebook would have had not only recipes but tips for various problems such as how to care for linens and clothes, cleaning, running a dairy, keeping chickens, sewing—all the items that made the round of a woman's day. When a young woman married she received, along with her mother's blessings, a collection of these recipes. Most often it was handwritten copy book filled with recipes, secrets, or advice that had been passed down in the family through the years. In the 19th century when they became available and affordable, a young bride might receive a new cookbook, along with her mother's or grandmother's handwritten notebook. When magazines and periodicals became popular many women cut and pasted household tips and recipes to their own handwritten ones and created their own family cookbooks.

One of the more frustrating things about old recipes and cookbooks is that they invariably list ingredients in terms of weights. Unlike the kitchens of grandparents or great-grandparents, most households today do not have a scale for weighing ingredients. The following tables may be helpful in converting older recipes into today's standard measures.

## WEIGHTS AND MEASURES

| Item | Weight | Approximate Quantity | Yield |
|---|---|---|---|
| Apples | 1 pound | 6 medium | 3 cups, chopped |
| Beans, Green | 1 pound | 4–6 medium | 2⅔–3½ cups, chopped |
| Cabbage | 1 pound | 1 small head | 3½ cups, shredded |
| | 2 pounds | 1 medium head | 7–8 cups, shredded |
| Cauliflower | 1½ pounds | 1 medium head | 4 cups flowerets |
| Cucumbers | 1 pound | 2 large | 2 cups, sliced |
| | 6 pounds | 12 large | 1 gallon |
| | 6 pounds | 50 medium | 1 gallon |
| Onions | 1 pound | 3 large | 2–2½ cups, diced |
| Peaches | 1 pound | 3–5 | 2–2½ cups, peeled and sliced |

| Item | Weight | Approximate Quantity | Yield |
|---|---|---|---|
| Pears | 1 pound | 4–5 medium | 2⅔ cups, peeled and sliced |
| Peppers | 1 pound | 4 large | 2 cups, chopped |
| Plums | 1 pound | 12–20 | 2 cups, sliced |
| Pumpkin | 1 pound | | 2 cups raw chunks |
| Raisins | 1 pound | | 3 cups |
| Strawberries | 1 quart | | 3 cups |
| Tomatoes | 1 pound | 4 medium | 3 cups, sliced |

***Miscellaneous***

| | |
|---|---|
| 1 pound pickling (canning) salt | 1⅓ cups |
| 1 tablespoon fresh herbs | ½ teaspoon dried herb |
| 1 pound granulated sugar | 2¼ cups |
| 1 pound brown sugar | 2¼–2¾ cups |
| 1 pound butter | 2 cups |
| 1 pound honey | 1½ cups |

1 package active dry yeast (¼ ounce) = 1 cake fresh yeast (0.6 ounce)

***Liquid Weights***

| | |
|---|---|
| 15 ml (milliliters) | = 1 tablespoon or 3 teaspoons |
| 30 ml | = 2 tablespoons |
| 60 ml | = ¼ cup |
| 80 ml | = ⅓ cup |
| 120 ml | = ½ cup |
| 160 ml | = ⅔ cup |
| 180 ml | = ¾ cup |
| 240 ml | = 1 cup |
| 480 ml | = 2 cups |
| 1 liter = 1 quart | = 4 cups |

## Early Cooking Methods

During the Middle Ages, cooking in a Polish peasant hut consisted of a hollow in the ground surrounded by stones. There were no openings in the hut for the smoke to escape except through the front door. As a result, the smoke hung within the room stinging the eyes and making it very dark. By the 16th century, cooking was done on an open fire on a hearth made of bricks or stone against a center wall or a corner. Today, we call this a fireplace. The women of the house cooked in clay pots that were placed on three-legged trivets directly

A
A
A
A
A
B
C
A• CAST IRON SKILLETS
AND POTS
for open fire cooking
B• FIRE POKERS
C• TONG

TRIVETS—
for holding pots
over open fire.

over an open fire, hung over the fire, or were simply set next to the flames. Overhead there was a hood made of wood covered with clay to help direct the smoke from the fire up to the ceiling where the smoke finally found a small opening in the roof to escape. Next to the hearth there was often a dome-shaped oven used for baking bread. These early cooking fireplaces can still be seen in *skansens* throughout Poland. These are open-air museums or reconstructed villages much like Williamburg in Virginia or Sturbridge Village in Massachusetts here in the United States. The fireplace was an improvement over the old method but smoke and soot still lingered about the room causing the walls to become dark and often black. These old smoke-filled rooms were called *czarna izba*, *dymna* or *kurna izba*.

A major advance in heating and cooking came with the building of chimneys. By the 18th century, most cottages in western and central Poland were equipped with a chimney made out of a mixture of straw and clay to direct the smoke up to the attic or all the way through the roof and out of the house. Over time, the straw and clay chimneys were replaced by those made out of stone or brick with the additional luxury of building an oven into the back of the fireplace. The Carpathians and surrounding regions were slower in building stoves with chimneys.

The next phase in cooking began when the hearth, initially low and close to the ground, was raised to waist or hip level. This raised hearth took the shape of a large square block made from bricks or stone covered with clay. An open fire was made on the top of the raised hearth. This was still an open fire cooking method but the raised hearth eliminated the stooping that was necessary for the earlier ground-level hearths. Clay pots were still placed over the open fire with the help of three-legged trivets, hung over the fire from poles or simply set next to the flames which required it to be turned repeatedly to keep the food from scorching.

The 1830s saw yet another advance in stove building whereby pots and pans were placed over a concentrated heat source. Fires were no longer made on top of the hearth. The top of the hearth was changed and became a large metal plate. Initially, the metal plate was one solid piece but later had lids. Wood was fed through an opening

*China cabinet. Ostrołęka region, 1936.*

in the front of the raised hearth. A fire was lit that would then heat up the metal plate. Clay pots were no longer appropriate since they cracked frequently. Iron and metal pans began to be used on top of the metal plate. Smoke was funneled out of the house through a chimney that went all the way to the roof or was built with a hood that blocked sparks and carried smoke as far as the attic. It was, in essence, the forerunner of the wood-burning stove. By the 1860s even smaller villages could boast about having closed stoves.

## The Stove

Whether a country cottage had four rooms or consisted of one large room, the heart of every Polish cottage was the stove. The stove has long been identified with home fires—the symbol of family life and closeness. It was around the fire that two, and sometimes three generations of families gathered at the end of the day. The children played and teased the family cat. The elders warmed their old bones and listened to the pops and crackles of the fire on a cold day. Everyone absorbed the smells emanating from the pots on the stove. The stove always stood in the corner to the left or right corner of the wall that gave entrance to the room from the hallway. On the opposite corner was the *święty kąt* (God's corner). The diagonal placement was almost universal.

Over the centuries, cooking had evolved from a simple fire on the floor into a multipurpose stove with separate devices for cooking, heating, and baking and was even used as a sleeping berth. They were massive affairs with large spark hoods, ovens for baking, a separate cooking area, drying niches for food, and niches for young rabbits, chicks in spring, or a brood hen. There were often stairs leading to a sleeping platform on top or off to the side of the stove called a *zapiecek*. This area was one of the warmest and toastiest places in a country cottage during the colder months. It was often a sleeping place for a grandparent or sick family member or where the children slept and played during the cold winter months. The style of stoves in peasant homes

• COOKING STOVES •

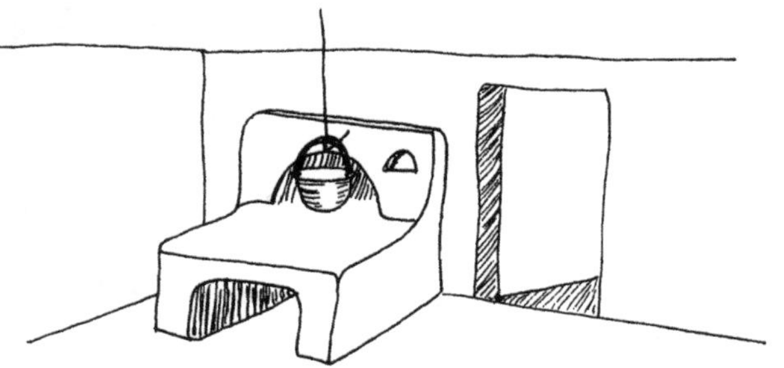

EARLY COOKING STOVE - without chimney

LATER STOVE from OSTROŁĘKA REGION (1887) with copper pot hanging from movable rod.

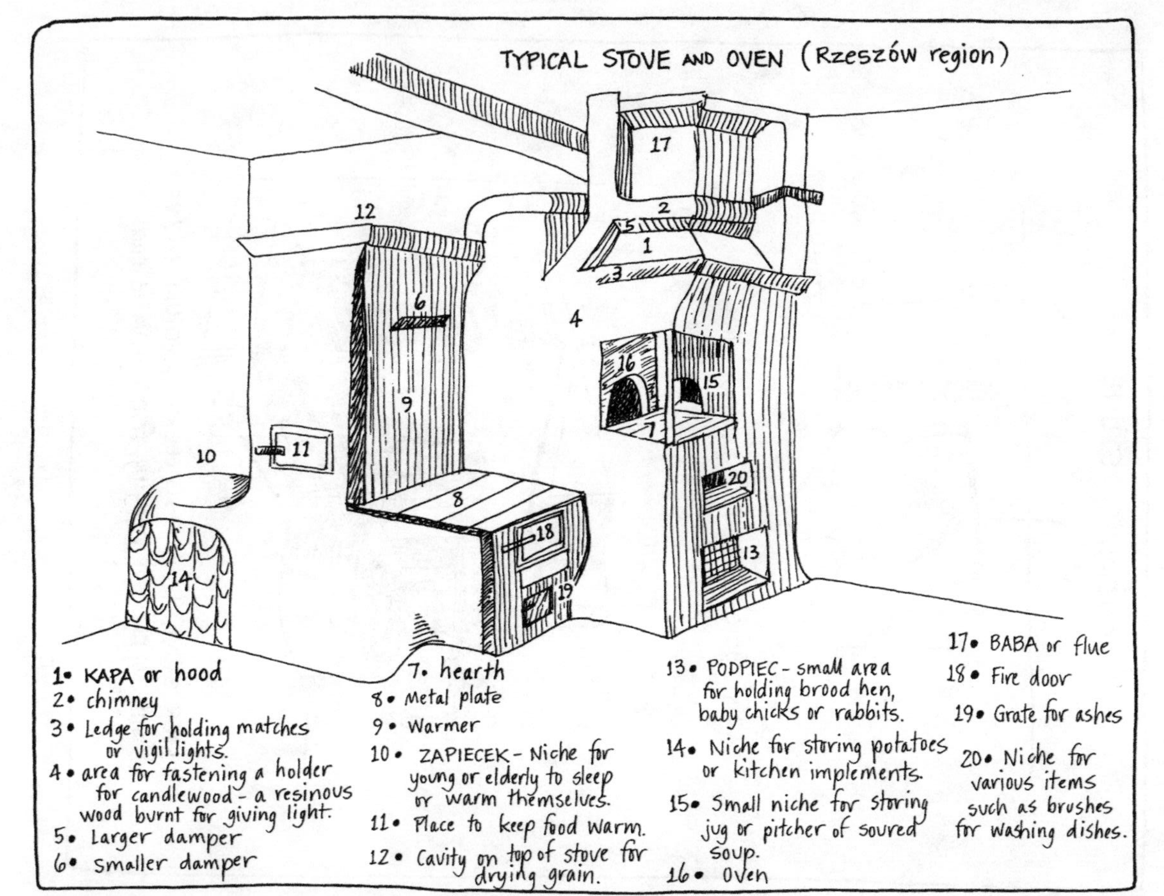
TYPICAL STOVE AND OVEN (Rzeszów region)
1 2 3 4 5 6 7 8 9 10 11 12 13 14 15 16 17 18 19 20
1• KAPA or hood
2• chimney
3• Ledge for holding matches or vigil lights.
4• area for fastening a holder for candlewood - a resinous wood burnt for giving light.
5• Larger damper
6• Smaller damper
7• hearth
8• Metal plate
9• Warmer
10• ZAPIECEK - Niche for young or elderly to sleep or warm themselves.
11• Place to keep food warm.
12• Cavity on top of stove for drying grain.
13• PODPIEC - small area for holding brood hen, baby chicks or rabbits.
14• Niche for storing potatoes or kitchen implements.
15• Small niche for storing jug or pitcher of soured soup.
16• Oven
17• BABA or flue
18• Fire door
19• Grate for ashes
20• Niche for various items such as brushes for washing dishes.

varied from region to region but often occupied the bulk of the room commensurate with its central role in the life of the people.

## LIGHTING THE STOVE

Up until the middle of the 19th century, most homes started their fires by obtaining sparks from striking flint against steel. Since this took some time and effort, fires were generally kept going all through the year. Embers were banked with ashes to keep a few sparks alive until morning when it was built up again. If the fire went out, someone was sent to a neighbor to borrow a few hot coals or use the flint and steel method. Matches did not come into widespread use until after 1870.

Fires were chiefly fueled by wood but in some parts of Poland such as Gdańsk, peat was also used as fuel. Entire families would go out to dig their own bricks or squares of peat using an iron spade-like tool with a long handle. When cut, the peat was stacked in such a way as to permit ventilation between the pieces. An average-size family needed six or seven wagonloads a year. There were also individuals who were in the business of digging peat and sometimes families just bought their peat. Later, a combination of wood and coal became the chief source of fueling the stove.

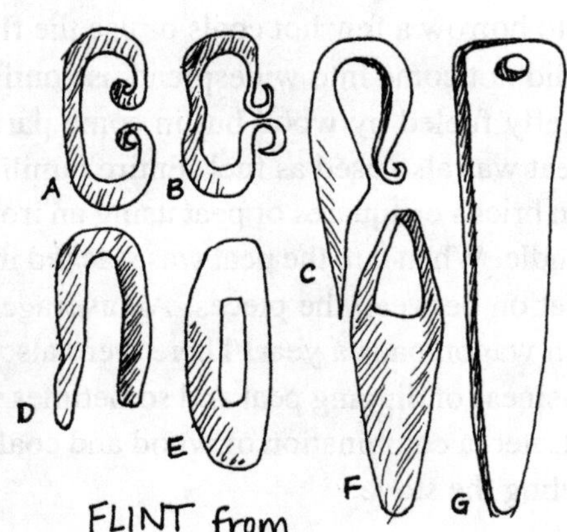
A
B
C
D
E
F
G
FLINT from
A• Małopolska B• Mazowsze C• Pokucie D• Podlasie
E• Małopolska F• Podhale G• Polesie

## Changing Times

With the progress that comes with the passage of time, the Polish peasant cottage grew. No longer a single room dwelling, the cottage had other new rooms which took on some of the roles of the former single multipurpose kitchen. The floor plan included a narrow entry hall called a *sień*. Hanging on the walls were scythes, sickles, and other small tools needed for the everyday management of a small farm. The room also contained such items as a grinding quern, cheese press, butter churns, barrels for sauerkraut or fermented beets, wooden buckets, wooden tubs for washing clothes, baskets, milk pails, and various sundry items needed for day-to-day household management. Wood for the fire was also kept here.

The room containing the cook stove still remained the center of the house. It was an all-purpose room, both kitchen and living area, laundry room, dining room, bedroom, and during bad weather a shelter for small domestic animals. The popularization of chimneys and absence of smoke led to the whitening of walls with the use of lime and sometimes painting the walls with folk art. The floor was made out of hardened clay or of unpainted wood and left bare. Sometimes, cheap rag rugs, woven at home or bought from country peddlers called *szmaciaki*, brightened the floor. Within the confines of this room, two or three generations of people lived, slept, carried on cottage industries while the woman of the house cooked, rocked her children in their cradles, and entertained visitors.

Besides the stove, this central room contained other simple furnishings. Primitive cupboards for storing dishes were common by the end of the 19th century. Inventories of deceased individuals reveal such items as "one kitchen cupboard for placing dishes with doors at the bottom with shelves," "kitchen cupboard stained walnut," or "kitchen cupboard with four doors." They were often made of plain wood or gaily decorated with painted flowers and fit neatly in corners or against a wall. Some of the cupboards contained open shelves decorated with strips of cut paper or handmade lace displaying the best dishes while the bottom portion was enclosed with doors. At the turn of the century, we see cupboards enclosed in glass. Initially they were just showpieces but gradually became more useful. The cupboard also contained drawers for holding forks and spoons. The fork was supposedly introduced into Poland by Queen Bona. In 1562, Katarzyna Jagiellonka, daughter of Bona, on her marriage to Jan Waza, received a complete set of silver forks. The use of forks, however, did not become commonplace until the 17th century and even then, used mostly by the nobility.

Wooden utensils and cooking implements were the norm. Many items were made or whittled by the man of the house, a local craftsman at the marketplace, or an itinerant peddler. These included spoon racks, potato mashers, whisks, ladles, dippers, lids, peels for placing food into ovens, and carved items such as plates, bowls, spoons, mortar and pestles for breaking up pepper and salt, wooden tubs for butter, and dough troughs in various sizes. These dough troughs were 70 to 90 cm long, 30 to 40 cm wide, and 12 to 16 cm deep. Flatter ones were used for making noodles and deeper ones for making dough for bread. The larger dough bins were made of linden or poplar and less often from alder or aspen. The dough bins were round and had wooden tops. Cheese hoops and butter paddles were also made at home. Wooden spoons were eventually replaced by metal ones by the end of the 19th century. By the second half of that century, wooden plates were also becoming rare. Many families couldn't even boast having individual serving plates. Most meals in very poverty stricken homes were eaten from a large common bowl. Some bowls received so much use they were reinforced around the rim by a wooden band made of juniper and hazelnut.

As artists and craftsmen traveled through Poland, many ended up settling down and introducing items from their own countries to the rural population. These included strainers, colanders, graters, various pans for baking bread, and molds for making desserts. By the middle of the 18th century Warsaw shopkeepers were selling rolling pins and metal baking forms in the shape of animals and lambs. Hanging on the walls were coffee mills and salt cellars. By the end of

SPOON RACKS

GOOSE-FEATHER PASTRY BRUSH

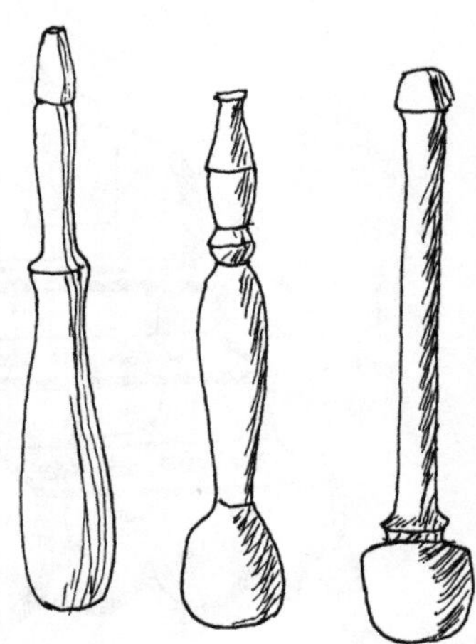

POTATO MASHERS

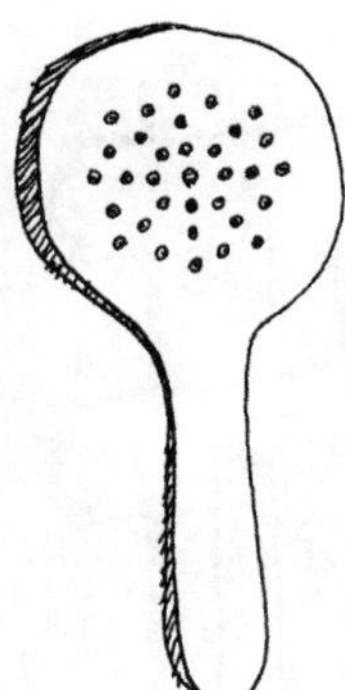

STRAINER FOR NOODLES OR POTATOES (Made from poplar)

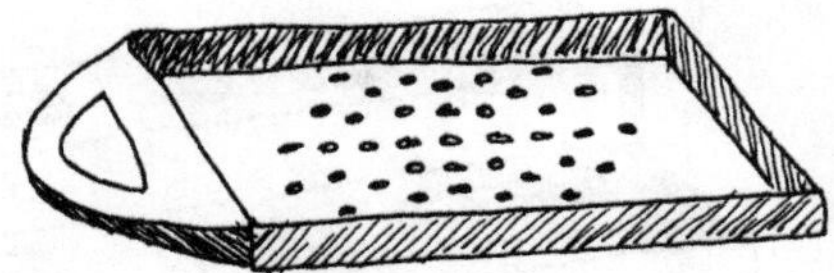

OLD WOODEN COLANDER

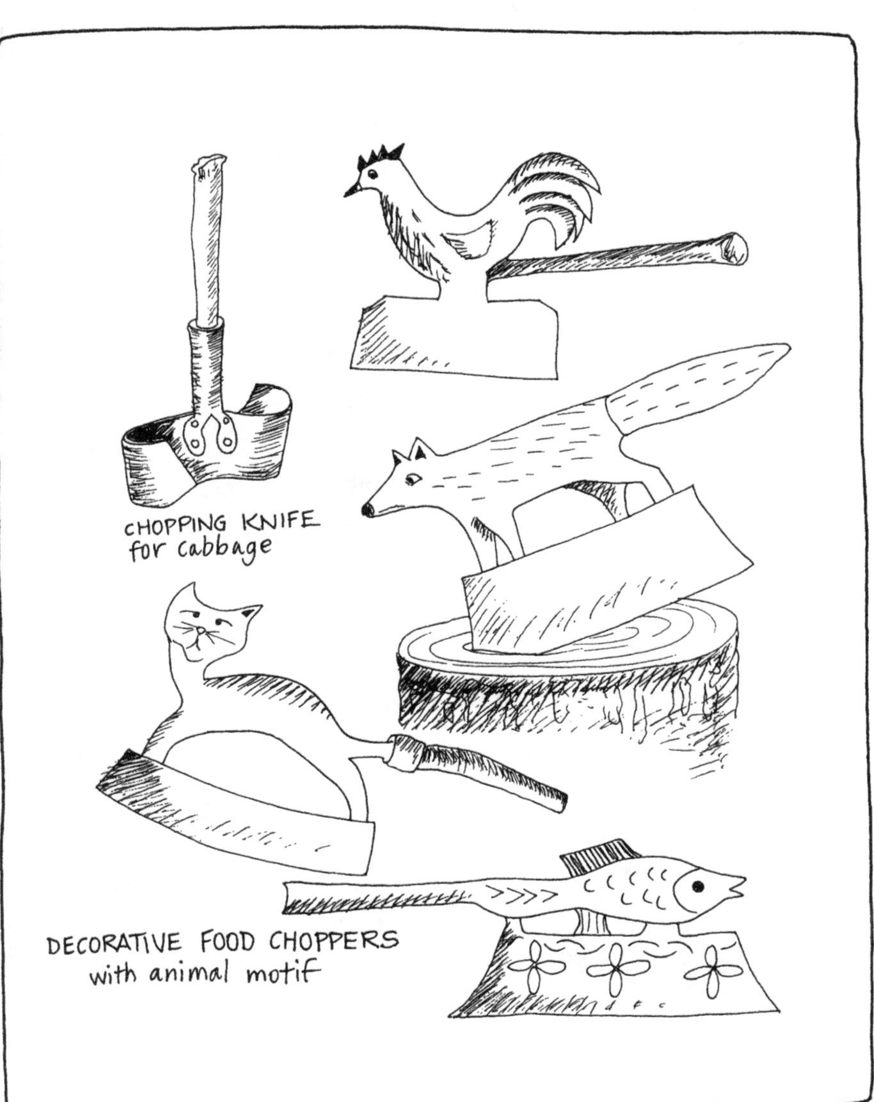
CHOPPING KNIFE
for cabbage
DECORATIVE FOOD CHOPPERS
with animal motif

HONEY PRESS

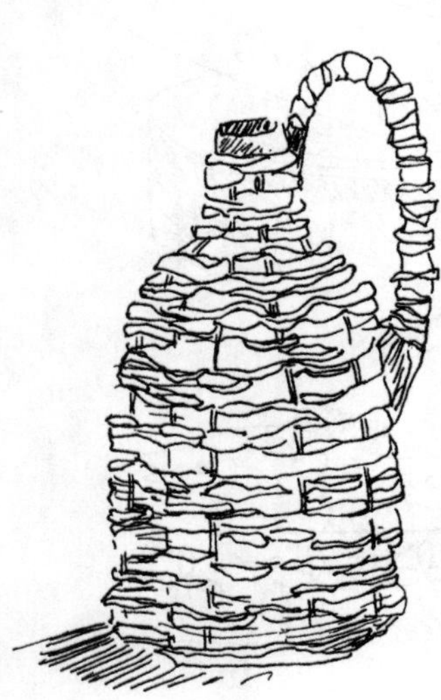

GLASS BOTTLE
enclosed in basketwork
for protection.
Used for storing honey or oil.
( Called a GĄSIOR )

*Interior of cottage. Łowicz region, 1959. Photo by B. Czarnecki. Courtesy of the National Ethnographic Museum, Warsaw.*

the 1800s spice jars appeared, labeled pepper, cinnamon, cloves, ginger, and caraway.

Frequently used kitchen utensils were also made by professional craftsmen. There were items made by the village cooper that required wooden staves made of pine, oak, or birch. The oldest utensils made of staves had a band of juniper or hazel wood to bind the staves together. In later years, the utensils had a band of iron, made by the local blacksmith, around the items. The items made by the cooper that were most needed in a country home were firkins, buckets, and kegs. The firkins, made to hold meat, bacon, sausages, or salt pork, were of varying sizes and many had tight-fitting lids held in place with a wooden rod or thin pole threaded through the two handles on opposite sides of the rim. Also available from the village cooper were casks for liquids, wooden mugs, and wooden pails as well as barrels for holding water or commodities like flour and grain. Wooden buckets for carrying water were called *konwie* while those for washing dishes and washing food were *cebratki*.

## POTTERY

Up until the 19th century, heavy earthenware crockery made of clay was used to prepare, serve, and preserve food. The crocks used to cook on an open fire were generally clay colored, without a glaze, and encased in a metal net made from itinerant tinkers to prevent cracking and withstand the heat of the fire. Many had lids and handles on the side to grasp or hang over a fire. Skillets for rendering lard were also clay fired and generally had three to four legs to place them directly over the fire. In the last part of the 19th century, open fires on the hearth gave way to cast-iron stoves. Earthenware was replaced by cast-iron pots called *grapy*. These remained in use until they were replaced by enamel pots in the period between the World Wars.

Besides making crockery to use over the fire, Polish potters made storage jars, jugs, pitchers, bowls, strainers, mugs, and milk pans. There were crocks for fermenting *barszcz* and receptacles for sweet

*Buying a crock at the market in Kazimierz, 1958. Photo by Maria Piłat. Courtesy of the National Ethnographic Museum, Warsaw.*

SALT CELLARS
PEPPER CRUSHER
PESTLE for crushing salt
•KITCHEN EQUIPMENT•
EARTHENWARE CROCK
for keeping barszcz –
Called a ŻUROCEK
DWOJAKI – Clay pots used for
taking food out to the fields.

and sour milk, as well as platters, bowls, cups, *dwojaki*, (two earthenware pots joined together), and less frequently, plates. The more affluent peasants had china crockery, plates, and cups which were carefully stored on a shelf for display. These were used on great holidays or special family occasions, such as celebration of name day, or the presence of an illustrious guest. In some houses, glass bottles, whiskey glasses, and other items made of real glass could be found. These were often bought while on pilgrimage or travels and displayed on shelves as valuable souvenirs.

## The Pantry

Many country homes also had a small pantry. The word *pantry* comes to us from the Italian *panetteria,* meaning bakery. In Poland it was called a *komora* or *alkierz*. This was a small anteroom where the all-important foodstuffs and provisions for the year were stored. Anyone visiting an old country pantry at the end of the last century would find shelves ranged along the walls along with hooks and niches for storing food. It often had a small window with a shutter or screen to let in cold air.

The importance of the pantry cannot be overstated. It was stocked against the time when the countryside was covered in drifts of snow, when roads vanished, and wolves howled at the edges of the village. A well-stocked larder was essential during these winter months when fresh food was scarce or against the time when harvests were bad and food completely unavailable. Most of the contents would have been produced at home with the exception of such items as salt, spices, tea, and sugar which were bought with a housewife's butter and egg money. The door was kept locked with the housewife carrying the key on her person.

Hooks along the walls or rafters held nets containing eggs and cloth bags containing poppy seeds, dried mushrooms, and salt. Onions and garlic were dried in the sun, plaited by their tops, and hung from a hook on a wall or pantry or rafters of the attic. Salted meats in small barrels or firkins were kept on the floor, as were crocks of fat. Rye and wheat flour as well as smaller quantities of potatoes or onions in pails or baskets were lined up on the floor. Large bottles of homemade vinegars crowded up next to sacks filled with barley and buckwheat groats. Homemade beer, wine, or liqueurs made from honey, currants, or rose hips was also stored here. Because they required a great deal of sweetening, marmalades, jams, and jellies were unknown among the villages except the most well-to-do. There were instead fruit syrups made from blueberries, blackberries, cranberries, or raspberries. These natural sweeteners were often added to hot tea. Also in the pantry were cloth bags or straw bins filled with feathers, wooden containers of beeswax, skeins of wool or linen, and candles or kerosene.

There was always a crock filled with soured dough for the next bread-baking day. Here, too, were flour and dough bins which stored the makings for the daily bread, along with peels, and in widespread use by the time between World Wars, baking pans. Milking pails were scrubbed clean, air dried, and stored in the pantry. The butter churn was stored here when not in use, as were the butter molds. If the family owned their own cabbage shredder that, too, was kept in the pantry or in the hallway. There were earthenware or wooden pots, glass jars, cloth for straining, wooden spoons in various sizes, sieves, receptacles in stoneware or terra-cotta, wooden kettles, wrought iron skillets and pots. Sometimes a bed was placed in here to accommodate a growing family or you might find a dower chest for the daughters.

Part of the pantry could also be located in the rafters or attic space. Here dried meat, salt pork, or bacon hung from nails on beams, as well as homemade linen bags filled with dried fruit and beans. If the family could afford items such as coffee, sugar, spices, and chocolate, these would also be kept under lock and key in the pantry.

❖ LUCY'S HOUSEHOLD HINTS: To keep mice and rats away from the pantry, barn or stable during the summer months, spread the fresh herb *Cynoglossum officinale** on the floor. This is a sure fire way to keep away both bothersome pests. Pull the herb directly from the earth with the roots. Dried, it looses its offensive odor and will not keep away the bothersome pests. *Hound's tongue; also called gipsy flower.

## COFFEE AND TEA

According to anecdote, it is said that when King Jan Sobieski defeated the Turkish horde threatening Europe at the gates of Vienna in 1683, among the gems, weapons, and priceless booty found in the enemy camp, were sacks and chests filled with an unfamiliar seed—coffee. A substantial amount of that cache of coffee was given to a J.F. Kulczycki, a Pole who had been of service to the king as a translator of oriental languages. With his prize Mr. Kulczycki opened the first coffee house in Vienna at Domgasse 6.

Drinking coffee as an enjoyable beverage was initially slow to catch on in Poland. At first, it was viewed as a "fatal poison from overseas." Some advocated its merits as a medicine claiming it "washes out the intestines and protects against apopleksy." But the taste for things Oriental became great in Poland after the battle of Vienna and coffee began to be served as a delicacy at court at the most important receptions and finding adherents supposedly only among the most refined connoisseurs. In 1724 the first coffee house was opened in Warsaw at the corner of Krzywego Koła and Gołębiej Street by one of the courtiers of King August II and was frequented by the German nobles at the court of the king. Cream in coffee was considered good form at the court and the custom began to spread to other parts of Poland. It became popular among the wealthy in Gdańsk. In the morning coffee was consumed with cream. If it was a fast day, a few drops of almond extract were added for flavor. After lunch, black coffee was the mode. The evening meal was followed again by coffee with cream. It became a requirement for aristocratic households, such as that of magnate Adam Kazimierz Czartoryski (1734–1823), to keep a Turk just for making coffee. Among the less fabulously wealthy it was customary to keep a servant woman whose chief task was to make the coffee.

In 1763 a second coffee house was opened in Warsaw's Old Town operated by seven sisters. By 1791, a German by the name of Kauch wrote about Warsaw: "There are two things here that are better than anywhere else: bread and coffee. The coffee is unusually clear and strong and the cream so thick you can only drink small cups." By 1822 there were some 90 coffee houses in Warsaw but some so small that they could only accommodate seven patrons. They became the favorite meeting spots of the bohemian literary and artistic types of Warsaw. By the 1830s, coffee had become fairly widespread and available even to the poor. Many of Poland's poor utilized chicory in place of real coffee. Chicory had been used as a substitute for coffee since 1769, first in Italy and then in Germany. The smooth roots of certain types of chicory were used for the manufacture of chicory coffee. The roots were dried, cut, roasted, and then ground to make an infusion that was dark and bitter. Sometimes "coffee" consisted of ground acorns, roasted barley, or wheat berries mixed with chicory.

Tea was also initially seen as a medicine rather than a drink. Herbal teas were made from rose hips, the leaves of raspberry, blackberry, blueberry, cranberry, wild grapes, dandelions, the large and small leaved linden, and the flowers of wild strawberry. Thyme and chamomile were very popular herbal teas.

## CHOCOLATE

Even more expensive than tea or coffee was chocolate. At the beginning of the 1700s it was consumed in only the most well-to-do homes since it cost three or four times as much as coffee. Documented in the writings of the *Komisja Edukacji Narodowej* (The National Education Commission) of 1776 is a notation regarding a boarding school for the poorer gentry. They allowed the students a watered-down beer for breakfast and were warned "may no one drink vodka, coffee, chocolate, tea or full strength beer–it will hurt their health."

By the end of the 19th century recipes begin to appear calling for chocolate mixed with wheat flour, milk, cinnamon, sugar, and egg yolks. The most famous chocolatier was Wedel of Warsaw. Wedel opened a confectionary store in 1851 and in 1865 his son Emil Wedel opened a chocolate factory. It is still considered Poland's finest chocolate. Forms for making chocolate rabbits were already available in the early 1900s and began to grace tables during Eastertime.

## BEER, WINE, AND VODKA

The Polish peasant pantry often held a barrel of homemade beer, wine, or vodka. During the second half of the 1600s to the end of the 1700s, the most popular drink among the masses, both in villages and cities, was beer. A brewer's guild was already established in Kraków in the 15th century and recipes for beer appear in the earliest cookbooks. There were light-colored, less expensive beers as well as dark-colored and more expensive ones. In subsequent centuries many a housewife made her own clear, light beer. Most beer had the strength of 2 or 3 percent alcohol. There were various types of beer such as that made from juniper berries and numerous ways of drinking it such as hot or cold, with spices or croutons. There was also a long tradition of drinking wine or beer as a soup or hot toddy.

A fairly common alcoholic drink was *gorzałka*, which was distilled from rye and, by the late 1800s, from potatoes. During this era Rhenish (regions around the Rhine), French, and Spanish wines were available but remained a drink for the very wealthy. The second most popular alcoholic drink was mead made from fermented honey and water. This was made in areas where there was an abundance of honey.

At the beginning of the 16th century, vodka began to appear. By the 1800s there was widespread use of vodka which was 30 percent alcohol. A mix of honey and vodka was called *krupnik*.

## SUGAR AND SWEETENERS

The first sweets known in Poland were fruits candied in honey. Sugar made from sugar cane was being imported into Poland as early as the 14th century. It was, of course, considered a rare and precious item whose cost was so prohibitive that only a handful could afford to purchase it. One kilogram (2.2 pounds) of sugar cost more than the price of two healthy oxen and remained in that price category for a very long time.

With increasing commerce and importation many other types of sweets were seen. Special sweets were constructed from sugar with a type of gum arabic that acted as an emulsifier and adhesive which allowed for shaping. The combination of sugar and emulsifiers allowed for complicated shapes such as coats of arms, monograms, and pyramids to decorate the tables of the wealthy. Also made at this time were sweet gelatins or aspics. Candied fruits were especially popular such as candied pears, oranges, lemons, and melons. Marzipan, or *marcypan*, a sweetened almond paste made of ground almonds, sugar, and egg whites, was molded into the shape of fruits or figures. Imported almonds made it an expensive sweet.

Even when sugar became more available, it continued to be very costly and was purchased only by the very wealthy. It was sold in the shape of a cone and kept under lock and key. These sugar keepers, often very ornate and made of silver with locks on them can be seen in antique shops and museums in Poland. It took a long time for sugar to reach the tables of merchant class, let alone country homes. For instance, in 1874 the household accounts of Piotr Zasęp in Kruszynie, reveal that a family of seven consumed 3 pounds of sugar, ½ pound of coffee and ¼ of a pound of chicory *in total* for that year.

The chief source of sweetening food and drinks for numerous centuries was bee honey. There are many references to the trade and consumption of honey during the Middle Ages. During this time, honey was obtained from hives found growing wild in Poland's vast forests. In later years, the raising of bees and collecting honey began to be done in a more organized manner by monasteries. Many country families prepared honey from their own bee skeps. The honey was squeezed out of the combs in a press and then poured into bottles, corked, and kept on the shelf in the pantry.

Toward the end of the 1800s, a method of obtaining sugar from the sugar beet was devised in Germany and prompted the development of the sugar beet industry. Poland was prompt to pick up on the idea and encouraged the growth of a variety of sweet specialties including the making of ice cream, waffles, caramels, and cakes. For regular home use, however, beet sugar was initially no cheaper than cane sugar and was also kept under lock and key. More commonly used was beet molasses, a dark brown syrup extracted during the process of sugar production. Beet molasses contains fewer vitamins and is less tasty than the molasses obtained from cane sugar but its use is cited in many Polish cookbooks for baking, making pancakes, and a variety of other dishes.

In some parts of Poland, the syrup from the birch tree called *oskoła* was collected much like New Englanders collect maple syrup. Syrup was also collected from maple, hornbeam, and cherry trees. Saccharin was also being used at the turn of the century as a sugar substitute.

## SALT, SPICES, AND CONDIMENTS

**By** medieval times, besides native seasonings of onion, garlic, dill, and mustard, other roots from far away places began to be added to Polish dishes. From the castle accounts of 1393–1395, it is known that Queen Jadwiga ordered large amounts of pepper, saffron, cloves, ginger, nutmeg, rice, and raisins from China. She also ordered almonds, cinnamon, and anise. Cloves were used in preparing honeyed vodkas, spice cookies, and cakes. These seasonings and flavoring were not, however, available to the common man. Homegrown condiments included garlic, dill, caraway, horseradish, wormwood, and white mustard. Wild caraway, onion, and fennel were used as toppings for bread. Salt, available by the 1500s, was poor man's chief source of seasoning. Frederick Ulrich Verdieu wrote in his diary in 1622, "No other country uses as much salt and spices as the Poles." Salt was one of those household items that had to be purchased in large chunks and was generally bought in great quantities. Initially salt came in large, dark solid pieces that had to be broken up in a mortar and pestle or grated on a grater. By 1920, white salt was available.

Vinegar, bought or homemade, was also used in great quantities in humbler homes. Vinegars were made from raspberries, currants, and the fruit of the barberry shrub. They were used for marinating herring or mushrooms, and were added as a condiment to meat aspics or homemade meats such as headcheese. Vinegar was also used for dilling pickles and sprinkled on lettuce in the summer.

By the middle of the 17th century, the use of foreign spices was on the incline and reached even the most remote villages. Pepper became very popular. Peppercorns were added to soup and crushed pepper was sprinkled over jellied pig's feet. Raisins became commonly available by 1910, often added to special holiday breads baked with fine wheat flour.

## OIL

Oils used in cooking were obtained from the seeds of wild burdock, flax, hemp, sunflower, rape, and, less frequently, poppy. The oil was used as a substitute for meat or as a fat or grease during Lent when the Polish people observed a very strict fast during the 40 days before Easter. The pressing of oil was usually done during the winter before the beginning of Lent. Any individual household could make their own oil as long as they had the appropriate equipment, often using a simple mortar and pestle. This was generally made out of a block of oak, which contained a small opening at the bottom to allow the oils to run off. This type of mortar and pestle usually had four legs to allow room at the bottom to place a collecting dish. The heated seeds were placed in a linen bag, placed into the mortar, and beaten with the pestle. When it was beaten as much as possible, it was placed into a cheese press to squeeze out the rest of the oil.

Up until the period before World War II there were numerous small oil manufacturers equipped with simple tools. The raw materials were brought in by an individual along with his family and friends to beat the seeds. These events were treated much like America's corn-husking or quilting bees. Everyone got together for a particular event to help out. It also served as a social event and entertainment—gossip was exchanged and songs were sung.

The plant *Brassica napus*, otherwise known as winter rape, is an Old World plant belonging to the mustard family. The leaves were used for cattle fodder but the seeds of the plant were squeezed to obtain rapeseed oil. The oil was extracted at a small, local manufacturing facility by first heating the seeds, then beating and finally squeezing the remainder. As payment for using his equipment, the owner would take a small amount of money and/or claim the beaten seeds. Diluted in water they served as an excellent fodder for cattle.

Sunflower oil was very popular in Poland. The oil was used for cooking during Lent when cooking with oil or fat from animals was forbidden. Medicinally it was used for rubbing on chests and backs as treatment for cough, colds, lung inflammation, and consumption. The seedcake left after the oil was expressed from the seeds was also a rich source of protein and usually feed to the livestock.

When the Polish farmer was not able to raise his own goods there were others who brought it to his door. For instance, there was the *kaszarze*, the man who sold *kasza* (buckwheat). He sold three types of buckwheat groats, buckwheat flour for making noodles, as well as flat cakes made from buckwheat called *tartuchy* door to door, and also set up his wares at local fairs and marketplaces. There were other traveling salesmen who sold rice, oil, herring, and spices. There was also a man who sold salt door to door. In some villages, traveling salesmen arrived with barrels of pickles to sell or small sacks of walnuts or dried fruit. During holy week, the village saw a deluge of traveling salesmen selling sausage, pork, beef, or lard. Sometimes homegrown potatoes or fresh eggs were bartered for saccharine or herring.

The period between the two World Wars brought changes in the availability of certain goods as well as new ideas in food preservation. Small country stores began making an appearance at the beginning of the 1900s. By this time certain foodstuffs such as macaroni, marmalade, and dried fruits were readily available at local marketplaces. Bottling became a more widespread method for the preservation of fruits and vegetables. Jars began to be manufactured which were sealed with the help of a cork and mastic. In the 1930s, canning jars were the latest innovation. Carefully processed jars of meat, fruit, and vegetables were kept in the pantry through the cool months and then transferred to the cellar when the weather became warmer. Even with the availability of bought canned goods in the 20th century, stocking the pantry continued to be a very important task for many rural Polish families.

The famous ethnographer Oscar Kolberg described a pantry from a cottage in the Poznań region:

*Onion seller. Pen and ink, 1792. Jan Piotr Norblin.*

*Tea seller. Pen and ink, 1792. Jan Piotr Norblin.*

*"The house was thatched with hay but white-washed and so clean and organized that it was a pleasure to see. From a small hallway you entered into the main room of the house. Here, one saw two beds both covered with pillows as high as a tower; this immediately shows good housekeeping and some affluence because good bed linens and pillows are not easy to come by and a good housewife would be embarrassed to "buy from the world" when she can make her own pillows from her own geese. Above the beds hang crucifixes and various pictures of the Sacred Heart, Blessed Mother and the Saints. Between the beds under the window was a large oak table and next to it a large bench also of oak. Near the wall there are a few stools made of birch. In the corner is a tile stove with a copper kettle set on top to keep water warm. Across from the stove is a cupboard with platters, plates and jugs. Next to the door is a holy water container so that all who entered here could bless themselves.*

*On one side of this spacious room there was a small alcove. Here the housewife had her pantry. There were barrels of flour and barley, poppies, butter, lard, jellies, plum jam and also large sausages and salted beef. In small drawers there were various roots and herbs of mint, chamomile, linden flower, elder flower, dried blueberries, centaury, elderberries, camphor, turpentine, vodka and even a few bottles of water filled with leeches. In this alcove there were two steps down into a cellar of two small rooms. In one, Wach (the man of the house) had beer mead and cherry liqueur. In the other room Wachowa (housewife) kept her dairy products. Cold cellars for potatoes, cabbage and other vegetables were at the other end of the house."*

## KITCHEN GARDEN

Every household had a small kitchen garden to meet the immediate needs of the family. It was a place where roses and flowers of assorted sizes and shapes mingled comfortably with herbs and vegetables and berry bushes. The housewife grew flowers to gladden her heart, brighten the outside of her home, adorn the altars at church on Sundays and holy days, and to decorate the wayside shrines that were located within the village boundaries. The unmarried girls of the house tended lilies, rosemary, and rue for bridal wreathes and bouquets, and lavender to place between the linens in her marriage chest.

Interspersed here and there among the flowers were vegetables needed on a small scale such as cucumbers, radishes, watercress, horseradish, and lettuce. Sometimes there were beets, carrots, garlic, and onions depending on the needs and tastes of the owner. Pumpkins were planted here in smaller quantities, as were currant and gooseberry bushes for making cool fruit drinks during the summer. Sunflowers, horseradish, and rhubarb grew together wherever space and sunshine allowed.

To enliven what could be monotonous daily fare, a few choice culinary herbs were planted. Every garden had parsley and tufts of feathery dill, an herb grown in cottage gardens since the Middle Ages. There was anise, sage, and fennel, which came to Poland somewhere between the 16th and 18th century, for enhancing soups and stews. There was marjoram to dry for later use when grinding sausages. Chives were also important in flavoring for eggs and soup dishes. Finely chopped and mixed with buttermilk, it became a dressing for boiled potatoes as well as an addition to homemade curd cheese. Even though it could often be found growing wild, a housewife sometimes planted herself a small patch of sorrel. Caraway was sought in the wild to enhance soups, stews, rye bread, and cheeses. The cottage garden often contained a bee skep or a few beehives for collecting honey.

# FALL

# Jesień

*Thatch-covered wagon shed in Gostwica, 1965. Photo by B. Czarnecki. Courtesy of the National Ethnographic Museum, Warsaw.*

## Putting up for Winter

One of the most important yearly tasks facing the Polish farmer in the late 19th century was growing, harvesting, and preserving enough food to feed his family through the long winter months. The onset of cool weather in Fall signaled the time to finish gathering crops and store them before the first flurries of winter. Nothing was more worrisome to the Polish farmer than the dreaded possibility of hunger due to lack of provisions. There were too many memories of times of hunger and starvation to take the matter lightly.

In 1837, Jadwiga Zamoyska wrote, "This year there is a terrible famine in Galicia (Austrian occupied Poland). The people are tearing the straw off the roofs in order to cook it and eat it." Ten years later Franciszek Ksawery Prek also documented another famine: "at this time there is such a great famine that it is hard to feed the beggars that came to the door. In the Tarnów district, there was a tenant that died of hunger and left a wife and five children to go begging." Goszcynski wrote, "Yesterday I received letters from Galicia of the unprecedented destitution. There is hunger beyond remembering, people dying alongside the road. In the Congress Kingdom of Poland every one in five individuals are dying of hunger."

Unlike today where foodstuffs are readily available for purchase all year long, most Polish families were entirely self-sufficient. There were some items of necessity such as salt, kerosene, and matches that were store bought. Everything else came from the forests and fields that the farmer and his family grew, picked, and preserved by drying, pickling, bottling, and storing in pantries and root cellars.

Preparation for winter was a yearlong endeavor beginning in early summer when the woods and fields began to yield their fruits. Children of all ages were sent out to gather the raspberries, elderberries, black currents, blackberries, blueberries, apples, and pears that grew wild in the woods and fields. All were candidates for drying and preserving. If all the moisture was removed from the fruit it could last all winter. There were two basic methods for drying fruit: air drying and oven drying. Fruits such as apples and pears were sliced and threaded on long loops of string and hung against the side of the stove, the sunny side of the house, or spread in a single layer on boards in the sun, turned frequently and brought in at sunset, taking care not to expose the fruit to dampness to avoid mold setting in. For oven drying, the fruit was spread in thin layers or on the thorns of a blackthorn branch and placed in the oven still warm from the day's baking. When sufficiently dried, they were packed in cloth bags or baskets in the attic. When the housewife wanted fruit for a compote, she reconstituted the fruit by cooking it in liquid. As the summer season continued, sweet and sour cherries, apples, peaches, pears, and plums were also candidates for drying and preserving, especially in homes that lacked a root cellar. Fruits were also turned into jams much like today's apple butter. Big copper pots were used over open fires out of doors to turn fruit into fruit butters, thick jams, and preserves. Cranberries, culled in November and even later, were used in making marmalades and syrups and in some parts of Poland used in the preparation of fresh cabbage.

The oven was used for quickly drying herbs, preserving their flavor and aroma. Children pasturing the cows in fields during the summer months were told to be on the lookout for herbs which grew in the wild such as garlic, caraway, and fennel. Herbs such as chives, dill, or parsley, grown in the kitchen garden, were collected and carefully dried in the oven. When dry, they were crushed and placed into cloth bags or bottles with corks.

Honey for sweetening hot tea and cookies was also collected in the summer months of July and August and sometimes even into September and stored in receptacles called *kadłubach* which were hollowed out trunks of small trees such as the linden tree.

Fall was also a time when Polish housewives made their own vinegars. The earliest existing cooking recipes in Polish, written in the 16th century, concerned themselves with making vinegar and had many uses in a country kitchen. It was made from fermenting sliced apples, including the peel and seeds, and water. The mixture was then strained and crushed herbs were added. It was sealed in bottles, and stored in a cool pantry or larder. It was sprinkled on greens for a salad or made into a brine for dill pickles in the summer. It was also used to marinate fish, especially herring, or sprinkled on meats such as headcheese or meat aspics for added flavoring.

Poppy seeds were another important harvest. Large patches of poppies were grown for sale and home consumption, especially for dishes at Christmastime.

## Granaries and Root Cellars

Homegrown grain provided food for the Polish peasant and his family for centuries. This included barley, buckwheat groats, millet, oats, rye, and wheat. All of the grains were cooked and eaten as porridge. They were also ground into flour to make noodles or pancakes or a variety of different breads. Collecting and preserving grains over the winter was the single most important endeavor of the entire year.

There were different methods for storing the grains depending on the various regions of Poland. The grains were stored whole as kernels and ground as needed on a weekly basis or ground into flour all at once, and were stored in tall, straw-plaited containers resembling barrels or in hollowed-out logs. The straw-plaited containers were woven so tightly that they could hold ground flour without it seeping out. To protect against dampness the containers were placed on a wooden base or foundation.

Grains and flour were also stored in large bins or chests that were partitioned into different sections. Their sizes varied but often reached proportions of 5 to 6 feet long, 2 feet wide, and 2 feet high. They were made of pine and had as many as four and five compartments. Near the chests were large paddles made of poplar which were used to occasionally stir the flour or grains to prevent it from packing down and spoiling.

Grains and flour were also stored in large square or rectangular free-standing granaries located close to the house or outbuildings. Made of pine logs joined together in a dovetail at the corners they

• VESSELS FOR HOLDING GRAIN •

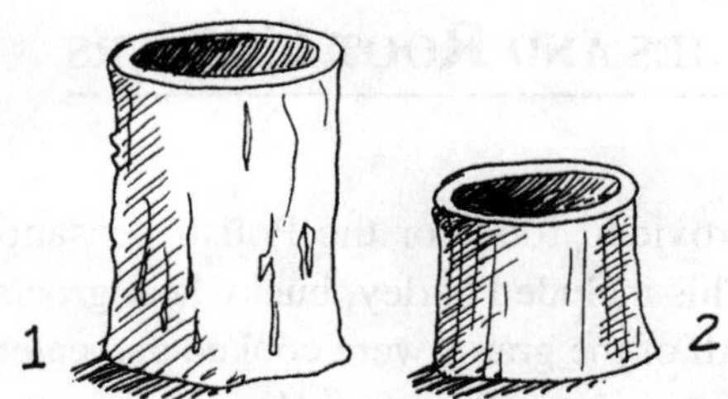


1+2 • HOLLOWED OUT PINE OR LINDEN LOGS

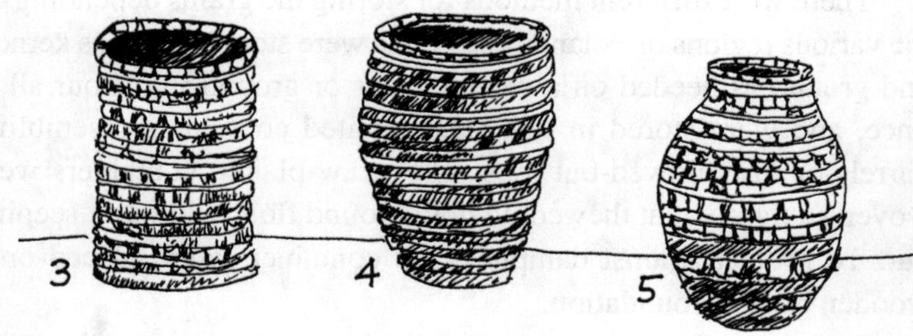


3,4+5 • WOVEN FROM STRAW OR WILLOW

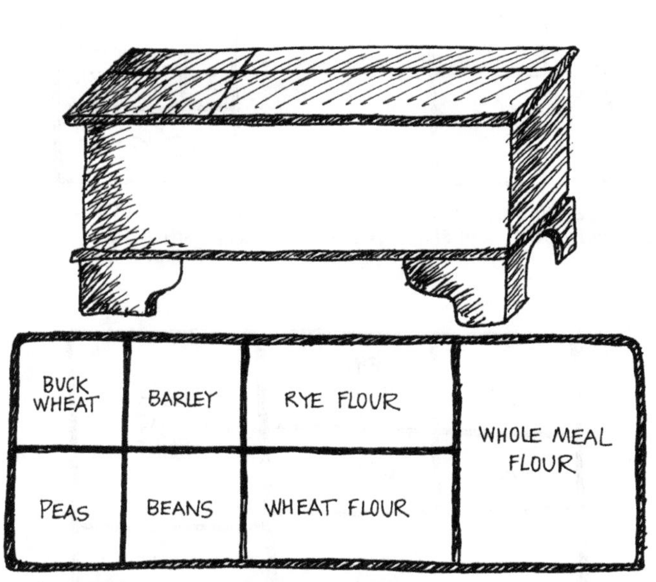


• WOODEN CHEST PARTITIONED INTO SECTIONS •

BARN WITH CELLAR AND GRANARY

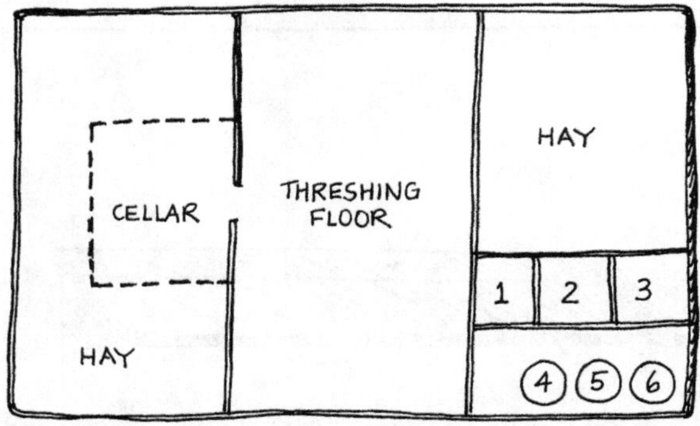


1• RYE 2• WHEAT 3• BARLEY 4• BARREL WITH SAUERKRAUT
5• STRAW BARREL WITH PEAS 6• STRAW BARREL WITH APPLES BURIED IN OAT HUSKS

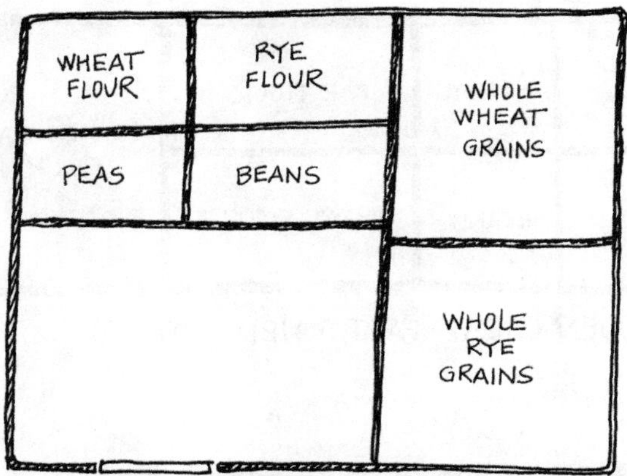


FREE STANDING GRANARY
PARTIONED INTO SECTIONS

rested on solid foundations or were supported at the corners on stone or blocks. The buildings ranged in size from 12 × 12 feet to 18 × 18 feet. They generally had gable roofs which created lofts where more items, such as peas gathered with their stalks and stems, were stored to dry out. It, too, was partitioned off into sections to hold various grains.

Another place to store flour and grains was a granary located in an existing barn. The granary portion was separated from the rest of the barn by stout, tight-fitting doors, walls, ceilings, and floors to prevent mice and other undesirables from finding their way in. Inside, the room was separated by partitions where the grain and flour were stored. There was also room for wooden barrels or vats of sauerkraut, pickled mushrooms, apples, cucumbers, and beets as well as straw-plaited containers for apples buried in oat husks.

Late fall was the time to pick and store the last of the vegetables. The Polish peasant ate a steady diet of vegetables that were known since the Middle Ages. These included carrots, parsnips, turnips, and rutabaga. Parsnips were at one time a large part of the Polish diet. The preferred method of keeping parsnips was to slice them into strips and dry them in the bread oven until hard. They were stored away in linen bags and cooked during the cold winter months. Turnips and rutabaga were also dried in the sun or in a heated bread oven or placed on straw in root cellars, or hung from the rafters in attics. Rutabaga was also stored fresh like potatoes. Carrots ruled undisputed for centuries in the Polish country kitchen. All the dried vegetables were later cooked as soups or stews. Parsnips were paired with potatoes and cabbage. The Polish proverb *Dobre kluski z makiem, jesczce lepsze z pasternakiem* (Noodles with poppy seeds are good but better with parsnips), indicates another way that parsnips were prepared.

In the winter months the dried slices of carrots were cooked with potatoes along with a piece of smoked meat if it was available. During the summer months, small chunks of carrots were cooked and paired with fresh peas. Rutabagas were cooked most often with potatoes and a lamb or pork bone. In the absence of any kind of meat, the potatoes and rutabagas were cooked until soft, and served with milk.

Onions were brought to Poland by the Cistercian and Benedictine monks and initially grown in monastery gardens before becoming widespread. Peas were a major staple from ancient times.

In some homes they gathered as much as eight or more bushels. They were added to cooked sauerkraut or ground down and made into a thick soup, which we know as split pea. In smaller quantities but equally important were beans. The broad bean *(Vinca fabia)*, sometimes called the fava bean, was also well known in Poland as *bób* and eaten fresh or dried for later use. This bean is believed to be native to North Africa and southwest Asia and is considered one of man's oldest cultivated crops. It is the bean of history, esteemed as food for man and beast, and became very popular as a vegetable in Europe.

In the 16th century, Queen Bona Sforza, an Italian princess who became the second wife of Polish King Zygmunt I, introduced a variety of foods to Polish cuisine. To this day, bouquet garni, called *włoszczyzna* in Poland, meaning "Italian greens," is added to broth and soups and is attributed to Queen Bona. More importantly, Bona enriched Polish gardens by introducing celery, asparagus, lettuce, and artichokes. Later the gardens boasted radishes and to a lesser degree rhubarb and occasionally, the tomato. These, however, were considered luxury items appearing mostly at the tables of the rich. Many country girls gave up their posts among the wealthy because they couldn't get used to eating tomato soup. The tomato began to make an appearance in the cottage garden in the 1890s and became more common during the period between the two World Wars. It then zoomed into massive popularity. Planting could be staggered throughout the growing season and made fresh tomatoes available until late fall. The proverb says "*Kto jada dużo pomidorów, ten nie potrzebuje doktorów*" (He who eats lots of tomatoes, has no need for doctors). For the most part, however, the Polish peasant continued a steady diet of the more commonly known vegetables, including cabbage, potatoes, carrots, turnips, onion, parsnips, rutabaga, and beets.

Old inventories of crop plantings between the 16th and 18th centuries in Great Poland reflect the order of importance of particular vegetables in the Polish diet. First on the list was cabbage, followed by carrots, then parsnips, kale, onions, beets, turnips, rutabaga, cucumbers, and pumpkins. Kale and rutabaga were grown more in Great Poland than any other region. Kale was at one time so popular in Great Poland that spinach (*szpinak*) was also called *jarmuż*, the Polish word for kale. Pumpkins, called *banie*, were also grown and eaten especially in the Kurpie and Pomorze regions where they were cooked in water until soft and pressed through a sieve. Milk was added later and it was eaten with noodles or potato dumplings. The people of the White Kurpie region enjoyed a pumpkin soup filled with dumplings called *prażucha*. The dumplings were made with wheat flour, cooked in water, and then fried with onions and melted pork fat. Sometimes the pumpkin soup was poured over cooked millet. Roasted pumpkin seeds were also popular in the Kurpie region. The seeds were roasted in the oven while bread was baking. In the 18$^{th}$ century, potatoes began to be grown and supplanted many of the older vegetables especially parsnips, turnips, and rutabagas.

There were a variety of methods for keeping and storing vegetables over the winter. One of these methods was placing the vegetables in a cool dry place called a root cellar. Oftentimes, there was a root cellar beneath the floors of house or barn. The cellar did not run the full length of the barn or house but only covered a portion of it. The walls were made of wood, fieldstone, and less often with bricks and cement. The area was generally large enough to house a hundred bushels of potatoes.

There were also free-standing cellars dug down into the earth away from the house and barn. These cellars consisted of a few steps leading down to a door and a small entryway, followed by another door that accessed the cellar. The walls were of stone that reached above ground level and had a thatched or wooden roof and in later years a domed concrete roof. There were small openings for ventilation and special openings at ground level which allowed for dropping in the potatoes from the outside. A more primitive type of root cellar was an excavation made into the side of a hill. Inside, a stout frame of timber and planks or logs was erected. Over the frame a strong roof was constructed. Then the earth that had been excavated was thrown over the structure. Vegetables were buried in straw. Apples were stored in sawdust or carefully wrapped in straw or oat husks. The horseradish root which became popular in Poland in the 18$^{th}$ century was often left in the ground until first freeze. It was then dug up and stored in damp sand in the root cellar. It was used as an important condiment for foods such as pork, eggs, and beets. It is high in vitamins and aids the digestion of beef and pork.

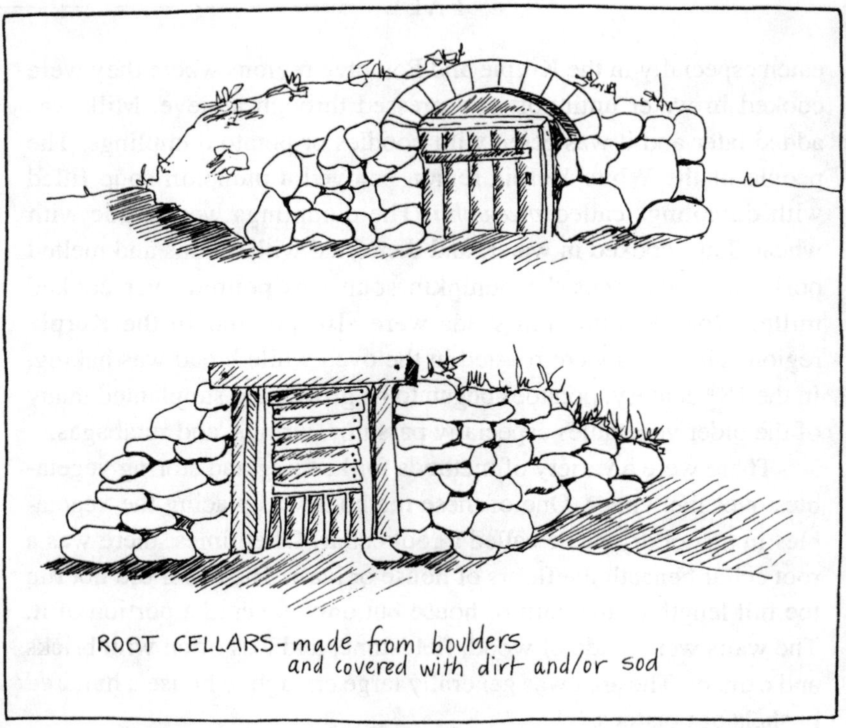

ROOT CELLARS- made from boulders
and covered with dirt and/or sod

*Stone root cellar, 1965. Photo by B. Czarnecki. Courtesy of the National Ethnographic Museum, Warsaw.*

## VEGETABLE SOUPS *(Zupy)*

Soups were made from turnips, parsnips, carrots, rutabaga, beans, peas, and cabbage. The turnips were cut into chunks and cooked with some meat bones and a few potatoes. Parsnips were also paired with potatoes, sweet cabbage, or cooked noodles. Rutabaga was cooked most often with potatoes on some lamb shank or pork bone if there was one to be had. Sometimes if there was only a few vegetables to throw together, everything was cooked to softness, pressed through a sieve, and milk or cream added to create a thicker, more filling meal.

Writing in the late 1800s, Łukasz Gołębiowski documents a variety of soups including *miszkulancya*. Literally translated it means "hotchpotch" or the more familiar word hodgepodge, meaning a medley or jumbled mixture. *Miszkulancya* was a sweet soup made in convents and monasteries from various vegetables in a chicken or wild duck stock that was seasoned with cream.

A pea soup called *grochówka* was made with smoked pork and eaten with croutons.

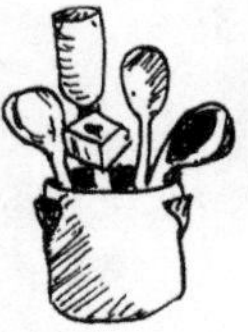

## Pea Soup

***(Grochówka)***

***Pea soup ranks as one of the oldest and most popular of Polish soups. Old Polish cookbooks always like to include potatoes as additional filler and use pepper and marjoram as flavorings.***

2 cups yellow or green dry split peas
3 quarts water
1 ham hock or meaty ham bone
1 small onion, chopped fine
1 teaspoon whole peppercorns
½ teaspoon dried marjoram
1 large carrot, diced or cut into medallions
2 large potatoes, diced

1. Rinse split peas in water and drain. Pick out any discolored pieces.
2. Place peas, ham bone or ham hock and water in a large kettle. Add onion, peppercorns, and marjoram. Cover and simmer for 1½ to 2 hours until peas completely soften and lose their shape and ham hock is tender.
3. Add carrots and potatoes and cook until tender. Served hot with rye bread and butter, this soup is a meal unto itself.

MAKES 3 QUARTS

# THE ALL-IMPORTANT POTATO

Potatoes made an appearance in Poland for the first time during the reign of King Jan Sobieski III (1674–1696). Jan III sent them from Vienna, where he had won a smashing victory over the Turks, to his gardener and told them to plant them at his palace in Warsaw. No one had much interest in them as a foodstuff but they were grown in the flowerbeds for the court to enjoy the blossoms. According to legend, the king, imitating a French method, instructed his chef to cook a few of the tubers and to serve it to a few handpicked guests. The potatoes were not greeted with much enthusiasm. In spite of this, the son-in-law of the king's gardener was determined to plant a larger crop on his own plot of ground. He then took them to the marketplace where the lesser nobility found out that the queer looking vegetable was being eaten at the king's court. The enterprising gardener demanded an exorbitant fee for them, which caused the wealthy Warsaw merchants to want them even more. Slowly, the *ziemniaki* (potatoes) began to appear on the tables of the middle class. The price kept dropping since they grew so well in the Polish climate and soil. Over time they managed to arrive at the home and fields of the Polish peasant. At first the clergy fought against them, asserting that they were unhealthy. The church had definite apprehensions especially in regards to potato flour which shortly began to be made in large quantities. They feared that the communion host, made of a mix of wheat and potato flour, would not be suitable for liturgical purposes. The Vatican calmed the Polish priests on that matter.

The potato began to replace parsnips, turnips, and rutabaga which had, up until the appearance of the potato, served as the primary foodstuff for the peasants. It also replaced eating the tuber of the Jerusalem artichoke which had been common in Poland. Towards the end of the reign of August the III (1733–1763), all of Poland and Lithuania were eating potatoes every day and they became the salvation of the poorest peasant, oftentimes the single most important item keeping them from starvation. Growing potatoes in large quantities began first in the Prussian sector of Poland such as Pomorze (Pomerania) and in Śląsk (Silesia) and then spread to other regions. By 1810, a single individual in Warsaw was eating approximately ninety pounds of potatoes a year; by 1820, 200 pounds and by the middle of the 18th century there were more potatoes grown per pound than grain.

The potatoes were dug in late fall to be carefully stored away as a main staple throughout the winter. One of the main highlights of concluding a day of digging potatoes was to roast them over an open fire. The women brought a pitcher of beet soup or sorrel soup to pour over the potatoes or they were simply eaten plain.

Potatoes were boiled, baked, made into pancakes, noodles, or filler for pierogi, were used in soups and added to bread as well. One type of potato noodle was called *rejbaki* in some regions and *pyzy, pezy,* or *pezaki* in other areas. The potatoes were grated, placed in cloth bag in order to squeeze out any water, mixed with flour and shaped into ovals the size of a palm, and dropped into boiling water. Some regions poked a hole through the middle to help them cook through the center. *Gały* was the name of a dish made in spring from frozen potatoes which were grated, added to flour to make dumplings and cooked in water or milk. *Bieda* was the name given to a simple dish of old, wrinkled potatoes cooked with parsley and pepper until tender.

In its early days, potato soup was simply boiled mashed potatoes with a little bit of bacon fat mixed in for flavoring and liquefied with the addition of milk, cream, or buttermilk. Later on the potatoes were cooked in the broth of smoked sausage or other meats. Celery, parsley, and carrots were gradually added. Potato soup was often the main meal of the day and in order to be filling had to be so thick that a spoon could stand in it.

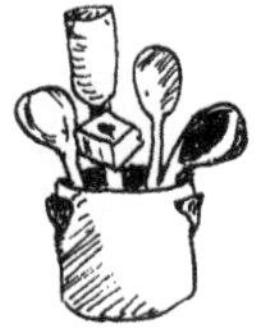

# Potato Soup

***(Zupa Kartoflana)***

*Regardless of what some of today's modern cookbooks say, soup without some kind of stock made from vegetables, chicken, or beef bones lacks flavor and substance. Don't throw away the backs, necks, wings, or gizzards of chicken or turkey. Use them to make this great potato soup.*

2 to 3 quarts water
½ pound chicken necks and backs
1 small onion, chopped
1 large celery stalk, chopped
4 to 5 medium size raw potatoes
1 tablespoon dried parsley
1 large carrot, diced
½ teaspoon salt
¼ teaspoon pepper
1 cup milk, cream, or half and half

1. Place chicken backs and necks in water in a medium-size stockpot. Add onion and celery. Bring to a boil and simmer uncovered for 30 to 45 minutes.
2. In the meantime, peel potatoes and cut into cubes. Keep in cold water until ready to use or they will discolor.
3. Remove chicken necks and backs from pot with slotted spoon. If there's any meat on the bones, pick clean and add meat back to stock. If not, simply discard.
4. Add parsley, carrot, and cubed potatoes to pot and cook an additional 10 minutes or until the potatoes become soft and mushy. Remove some of cooked potatoes from the pot into a bowl, mash well with a fork and return to the pot. Add salt and pepper.
5. Add milk or cream if you like your potato soup creamy.

SERVES 4 TO 6

# Potato Dumplings

***(Kopytka)***

*This is a dish my mother made frequently out of leftover boiled potatoes and is one of my all-time favorite comfort foods. Run the leftover boiled potatoes through a food mill or ricer. Mashed potatoes will do nicely also. The key to light dumplings is a higher proportion of potatoes to flour.*

2 quarts water
2 teaspoons salt
1 cup flour
3 cups mashed or riced potatoes
1 egg, beaten

1. Place the 2 quarts of water in a large cooking pot with 1 teaspoon salt and bring to a boil.
2. While water is coming to a boil, place the flour in a mound on a large dough board, kitchen table or countertop. Sprinkle the salt on the flour. Add the mashed potatoes on top of the flour. Make a well in the center and add the beaten egg. Work the mixture slowly and lightly with your hands until everything comes together. Knead lightly. The dough should be soft and light. Separate the dough in half and roll into a long roll on floured board in the shape of a sausage. Cut off pieces at an angle, ¼ inch thick, with a sharp knife.
3. Gently drop the dumplings in the boiling water two or three at a time until all have been placed in the pot. Stir very gently and within a few minutes they will float to the top. Boil very gently another minute. Carefully remove the dumplings in small batches from the pot with a slotted spoon into a colander and allow to drain briefly. Place on a well-buttered platter. Do not allow the dumplings to overlap one another as they will stick. Remove the rest of the dumplings in like manner. Serve while hot. In Poland the *kopytka* are drizzled with bacon drippings and bits of bacon. They are also delicious with any type of leftover gravy and a vegetable on the side for a meatless dinner.

SERVES 3 TO 4

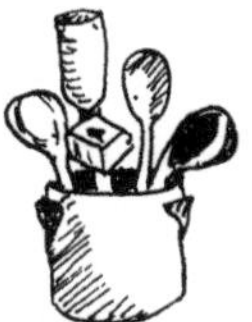

# Potato Pancakes with Chives

***(Placki Kartoflane)***

*Old Polish cookbooks claim that potato pancakes are best fried in a liquid oil rather than a solid shortening that has been melted.*

7 medium-size potatoes, peeled
1 small onion
3 large eggs
⅓ cup all-purpose flour
1 teaspoon salt
½ teaspoon ground pepper
Oil for frying
½ cup sour cream or sugar (optional)

1. Preheat oven to 375°F. Into a large mixing bowl half filled with cold water, coarsely grate the peeled potatoes. Drain the shredded potatoes through a clean dishtowel placed into a colander. Wrap the potatoes in the towel and squeeze the towel to remove as much water as possible.
2. Grate onions into another bowl. Beat in the eggs. Add the potato mixture, flour, salt, and pepper and mix thoroughly.
3. In large cast-iron or nonstick frying pan, heat 4 tablespoons of vegetable oil over medium heat. Add a scant ¼ cup of potato mixture to pan and flatten to a round pancake. Make additional pancakes as will fit in frying pan. Fry pancakes until golden brown for about 4 minutes. Turn over to other side and cook an additional 3 to 5 minutes longer.
4. Transfer cooked pancakes to baking sheet and place in oven to keep warm. Make rest of pancakes adding oil to pan as needed. Transfer to baking sheet.
5. Bake pancakes an additional 10 minutes or until thoroughly cooked through. Serve while hot topping with sour cream or sugar.

MAKES 12 PANCAKES

## MUSHROOMS

Fall was also a time to harvest from the forest. Children were sent to the woods with burlap sacks to gather hickory nuts and walnuts in their green husks. The fruits of oak and beech were dried and grated and used as additives to coffee made of grain. One of the most important yields of the forest, however, were mushrooms.

Poland has made widespread use of mushrooms for centuries. Not only did mushrooms fill a very real need within the home as a food but they were also a method of earning extra cash by selling them at the market. While some mushrooms could be located in fields and pastures, the forest mushroom was the most desired and more highly valued.

Entire families took to the forests to search for mushrooms. Mushroom hunting was both a necessity and favorite pastime. Many individuals believed that each person had a certain amount of mushrooms awaiting him or her in the woods and regardless of how long the search, they would find only those that were meant to belong to them. It was also believed that the mushrooms were more plentiful during a full moon and that mushrooms were best when picked after the Feast of St. Peter (June 29).

Mushrooms were used at home in a variety of ways. They were cooked loosely in soup; mixed with buckwheat groats, noodles, or potatoes; used as filling for dumplings; and marinated for use as hors d'oeuvres. Mushrooms are known by a variety of different names in Poland. These include:

*Armillaria mellea* (honey mushroom)—*opieńki*
*Boletus badius*—*chojnówka, jagodziarz*
*Boletus borvinus*—*sitarz, sitka*
*Boletus cyanescens*—*siniak, grzyb piaskowy*
*Boletus edulis* (cèpes, porcini)—*prawdziwki*

*Boletus luteus—maślak*
*Boletus rufus—kozak czerwony*
*Boletus scaber—kozak biały*
*Boletus subtamatosus—zajączki*
*Boletus variegatus—bagniak, maruniak, smużok*
*Boletus xerocomus chrysteron—czerwona noga, podgrzybiczka*
*Cantharellus cibarius* (chanterelle)—*kurka*
*Cratervellus cornucopiode—skórak, cholewka, lejkowiec gładki*
*Helvella esculenta—babie uszy*
*Hydnum imbricatum—sarna, koziołek*
*Lactarius deliciosus—rydz*
*Lactemius vellereus—chrząszcz, mleczarz, biel, gorzkówka*
*Leccinum scabrum—breziak, babka, koźlak*
*Marasmius oreades—podróżka, tańcownica, gromadka, panienka, szlachcianka*
*Paxillus atromentosus—aksamitek*
*Paxillus involutus—olszówka, świnka, krowia warga*
*Pholiota rozites caperata—turek, czubka*
*Psalliota campestris—pieczarki*
*Russula alutacea—gołąbek czerwony, gołąbek cukrowy*
*Russula virescens—gołąbek zielony, zielonka, cyganka*
*Sparassis crispa—siedź, sieduń, orysz, kwoka, kozia broda*
*Tricholoma vaccinum—krowie gęby*
*Tricholoma equestre—gąski, gąska zielona, gąska żółta, prośnianka*
*Tricholoma portentosum—gąska siwa, siwka*

At a time when storing food for the winter was limited to a few methods, drying was the most important method for preserving mushrooms. The mushrooms that lent themselves well to drying were *Armillaria mellea*, *Boletus luteus,* and *Boletus edulis*. The latter mushroom, *Boletus edulis*, is considered one of the finest mushrooms in the world. Its nickname, *prawdziwek*, translates into "the true ones" and it is known as the king of mushrooms.

The mushrooms were pierced on the thorns of the blackthorn branch and laid out on straw in the bread oven or threaded on a string in the shape of a wreath and hung on the sunny side of the house.

Sometimes the stem was dried separately as was the cap. The stem was used for home consumption and the latter for sale or barter for other goods. Other mushrooms that were popular for drying were *Leccinum scabrum* and *Boletus borvinus*. *Lactarius deliciosus* and *Russula virescens* were dried and used in making dressing for stuffing wild game that was to cook over an open fire.

With the increasing availability of salt in the 16th century, mushrooms could be preserved by pickling. As reserves for winter, they were pickled in small wooden barrels, buckets, or stone crocks. Mushrooms used for marinating and pickling were *Lactarius deliciosus*, *Russula virescens*, *Tricholoma equestre*, and *Pholiota rozites*. The mushrooms were marinated in onions, bay leaves, and allspice and some vinegar and served with either hot or cold potato dishes.

In this country, *Boletus edulis* is known by a variety of names including king bolete, cèpe, porcini, and Steinplize. The most commonly known and readily available type of mushroom is the white button mushroom found in supermarket produce sections. Dried boletes come in two ways: dried cèpes or porcini. These are available in larger supermarkets. If you cannot find them at your local store there is a source at the back of the book.

# Mushroom Soup

*(Zupa Grzybowa)*

*I make this mushroom soup for Christmas. I use a combination of fresh mushrooms and dried mushrooms from Poland. I don't have access to mushrooms the way my ancestors did and making a rich flavorful soup from just dried mushrooms gets expensive. This works out well.*

12 to 16 ounces fresh baby bella mushrooms
¼ ounce dried cèpe or porcini mushrooms
2 quarts water
⅓ cup butter
½ cup finely chopped onion
½ cup finely chopped celery
3 tablespoons flour
4 cups homemade or canned vegetable stock
¾ cup small-size homemade or store-bought macaroni

1. Clean fresh mushrooms of dirt by running under cold water and wiping with paper towels. Slice the fresh mushrooms in half or thinner slices, depending on preference. Place both fresh and dried mushrooms in a medium-size saucepan with 2 quarts of water. Bring to a boil, reduce heat, and simmer uncovered for about 20 minutes.
2. In the meantime, melt butter in frying pan and add chopped onion and celery. Sauté until soft, about 10 to 15 minutes. Sprinkle the flour over the onion and celery and mix together until absorbed. Add 1 cup of mushroom liquid to the frying pan, bring to a boil and then simmer another 10 minutes. Strain the contents of the frying pan into the pot with the mushroom liquid. Purée the solids through a food mill or press through a fine mesh strainer and add puréed material to the pot containing mushroom liquid. Add the vegetable stock.
3. Bring to a boil. It will thicken slightly due to the flour. Add macaroni. Bring back to a boil and simmer gently for 5 minutes. Like most soups this will improve in flavor as it stands overnight. If it becomes too thick, add small increments of water until it thins to desired consistency.

SERVES 4 TO 6

# Pickled Mushrooms

***(Grzybki Marynowane)***

***Serve these mushrooms along with pickles, herring, hard-boiled eggs and pickled beets for a tempting appetizer platter.***

12 to 16 ounces fresh porcini mushrooms
4 cups water
1 small onion, very thinly sliced
¼ cup white vinegar
¾ teaspoon salt
1 bay leaf
¼ teaspoon black pepper

1. Clean mushrooms of dirt by running under cold water and wiping with paper towel. Place mushrooms in a medium-size saucepan with the water. Bring to a boil, reduce heat, and simmer uncovered for about 15 minutes. Drain, reserving liquid. Layer mushrooms and onions in a quart jar or container.
2. In same pan, place reserved mushroom liquid, vinegar, salt, bay leaf, and pepper. Bring to a boil, reduce heat, and simmer uncovered for 2 to 3 minutes. Pour hot liquid over mushroom and onions. Allow to cool. Cover and chill for 24 hours or longer for flavors to blend together.

MAKES 2 TO 3 CUPS

# Marinated Mushrooms

**(*Grzybki Marynowane*)**

***I use the little white button or baby mushrooms if they are available. Offer these along with cold cuts, herring, hard-boiled eggs, pickles, and olives for a cold appetizer platter.***

12 to 16 ounces fresh white or porcini mushrooms
¼ cup vegetable or olive oil
2 tablespoons white vinegar
2 tablespoons lemon juice
1 teaspoon salt
½ teaspoon basil leaves
¼ teaspoon dry mustard
¼ teaspoon pepper
1 clove garlic, crushed
½ tablespoon dried parsley

1. Clean mushrooms of dirt by running under cold water and wiping with paper towels. Cook mushrooms in 2 cups water for 10 minutes and drain, saving mushroom liquid to freeze and add to some other dish such as soup or *kasza*.
2. Mix all other ingredients together. Pour over warm mushrooms. Cover and refrigerate overnight or for at least 2 hours for flavors to blend together.
3. Next day bring to room temperature. Drain mushrooms and serve.

MAKES 2 TO 3 CUPS

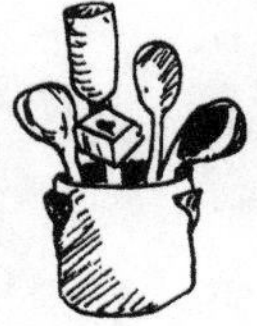

# Mushroom Gravy

***(Sos Grzybowy)***

1 pound fresh mushrooms
2 cups water
1 cube chicken, beef, or vegetable bouillon
2 tablespoons flour
3 tablespoons butter

1. Clean mushrooms of dirt by running under cold water and wiping with paper towels. Slice. Place water with bouillon cube and sliced mushrooms in a medium-size saucepan and bring to a boil. Reduce heat continue simmering over low heat for 5 to 10 minutes.
2. While mushrooms are cooking, place flour directly on large frying pan and stir flour constantly over medium heat with wooden spoon. Flour will begin to brown and give the gravy a nice color. When flour has browned, add butter and stir together making a roux.
3. Slowly pour the mushrooms and liquid into the frying pan, stirring constantly until the mixture thickens. If too thin, continue cooking until water reduces and mixture thickens. Serve over *kasza*, rice, or preferred dish.

MAKES 1 TO 2 CUPS

## OINK! OINK!

*Bez kiełbasy nie ma świąt.*
Without sausage, there is no holiday.

*Kto zabije wieprza na Św. Katarzynę*
*Najtwardszą ma słoninę.*
Whoever slaughters on Feast of St. Catherine
Has the hardest pork fat.

Within the course of day-to-day eating, the Polish peasant saw very little meat or poultry. Chickens were rarely killed since their eggs were needed to sell at the market in order to buy such items as kerosene, salt, pepper, and matches. In some regions, lamb was available but eaten only when the animal had met with an accidental death. Sheep were raised to be sold for cash. An individual could fish, trap, or shoot wild game but most of the time pork was the meat that was most readily available since it could be homegrown. The winter larder depended on it and the autumn pig killing was an occasion for seriousness as well as celebration.

In peasant households, hogs were slaughtered once or twice a year at the conclusion of the harvest in the fall and in spring before Easter. Exceptions to this were special family occasions such as a wedding or a christening. In every shed or hallway there was a large hook which was used to hang a hog head down so that the blood could be collected and then properly cleaned and prepared. The blood was saved for making a variety of dishes including soups and sausages. To remove the hair, the hog was scalded by plunging it into a barrel of boiling water and scraping it clean with a sharp knife. Meat designated for hams was salted down for 2 weeks, sometimes a month. After salting, the meat was hung and smoked. The rest of the meat was salted and marinated in wooden tubs using saltpeter and coriander for 6 weeks to 2 months.

Because peasants could rarely afford meat, they made sure they used every part of the pig when they had one. Butter was rarely used in cooking since it could be sold to buy other items, so the pork fat from the pig was very important. It was salted down into salt pork and stored in barrels or crocks, or it was rendered into lard. Rendering consisted of cooking the fat until it had melted and only the residual tissues called cracklings, or *skwarki*, remained. The browned cracklings were often spread on bread and salted a little and were considered a real treat. Or, they were saved for later use as an additive to other dishes such as when frying potatoes or for cooking with cabbage or sauerkraut. The lard was shaped into loaves and sewn in the bladders or stomachs of animals.

The feet of the pig were boiled and then made into an aspic called *zimne nogi* (cold feet). The scalded and cleaned feet were cooked with allspice, bay leaves, carrots, and onions until the meat fell off the bone. The meat was chopped, placed in a bowl or pan along with the broth and vegetables, and chilled. Cut into slices, sprinkled with freshly ground pepper and a dash of vinegar, and served up with rye bread, the dish was (and still is) considered a real treat and saved for special occasions. The stomach of calves, sheep, and pigs, besides being used to store lard, was also cooked and prepared in a dish called *flaczki,* or tripe. The stomach was very carefully scrubbed and cooked. After cooking it was cut into smaller pieces and cooked again with the addition of salt, allspice, carrots, and pepper. This was served as a soup or poured over potatoes. Sometimes the tripe was fried in pork fat and served for breakfast.

One type of soup was called *czarnina*, *czernina*, *czerlina,* or *szary barszcz*. These names, derived from the word meaning dark or black, are often interchangeable for a soup that was made with the addition of animal blood. The blood of ducks and geese was collected for this soup as well as that of rabbits and pigs. In Podlasie, beef blood was used. In northern parts of Podlasie another term for soup made from blood was *jucha*, or *juszka*. In Śląsk (Silesia), where the blood of ducks and geese was more common, it was called *czarna polewka*. At the time of slaughtering, the fresh blood was mixed with salt or vinegar to keep it from clotting. This gave rise to another name—*kwaśna* (sour), since it was soured using vinegar. The soup was prepared from a stock made with the bones or pieces of duck or goose such as the neck, back, and gizzards. The blood was added to the stock with the addition of prunes or raisins. Sometimes cherries, pears, and occasionally apples were added. Spices and seasonings included marjoram, pepper, allspice, ginger, cinnamon, and honey. The soup was poured over noodles or hot potatoes. It's becoming harder and harder to find the duck blood for soup these days unless you're shopping at a Polish market.

*Kiszka*, sometimes called *kaszanka*, was another food prepared with the blood of certain animals. This is not a foodstuff indigenous only to Poland. *Kiszka*, otherwise known as black pudding, blood pudding, or blood sausage, is one of man's oldest meat preparations and is known in the British Isles and throughout Europe. *Kiszka* in Poland was known in as many different ways as there were cooks and butchers. There was *kiszka* made with grated potatoes mixed with animal blood, melted pork fat and cracklings and wheat or buckwheat flour. The mixture was stuffed into cleaned pork intestines or casings that had been cleaned and salted and then carefully cooked. *Kiszka* was also made from millet and barley and had to be prepared very carefully since both millet and barley swells on cooking and could cause the casing to burst. The most well known *kiszka* was made with barley and buckwheat groats or buckwheat groats alone with the addition of blood, bits of liver, pork fat, and cracklings. After cooking, it could be eaten hot or cold.

Headcheese, called *salceson* in Polish, was made from the meat and skin of a pig's head and any other leftovers such as the heart, lungs, ears, feet, or tongue. The mixture was stuffed into the pig stomach or bladder and boiled. After cooling it was squeezed into a cheese press.

# Duck Blood Soup

***(Czarnina, Czernina)***

***Ever since the day my mother sent me out to the barn with a bowl of vinegar to catch the blood as my father sliced open the neck of a goose, I lost my appetite for this dish. Our beautiful white goose! Believe you me, my mother was not impressed with my sentimentality when I refused to eat it. However, if it makes your salivary glands go into overtime, I wish you*** **smacznego** ***(good appetite).***

1 pound pork bones or duck or goose pieces (back, neck, wings, gizzards)
2 quarts plus 1 tablespoon water
1 or 2 dried mushrooms
1 large stalk celery, chopped
1 small onion
2 bay leaves
1 teaspoon dried marjoram
1 teaspoon whole peppercorns or whole allspice
1 cup raisins or dried prunes
1 tablespoon flour
1 cup duck or goose blood premixed with vinegar
1 tablespoon sugar and/or vinegar (optional)
Cooked noodles

1. Rinse off bones or poultry pieces and place in 2 quarts water. Bring to a boil. Skim off any foam that forms with slotted spoon. Add mushrooms, celery, onion, bay leaves, marjoram, and peppercorns or allspice. Allow to simmer for 1 to 1½ hours. Remove bones, cooked celery, bay leaves, and peppercorns with slotted spoon. Pick meat off bones and return to pot.
2. Add raisins or prunes and simmer for 5 to 10 minutes until soft. Mix the flour and the 1 tablespoon of water and add to the pot. Add the blood. Bring soup just to a light simmer. Do not boil after putting in the blood. The soup should be on the sweet and sour side. Add a tablespoon of sugar or vinegar to suit personal taste. Pour over cooked noodles.

SERVES 4 TO 6

# Jellied Pigs' Feet

*(Nóżki w Galarecie)*

*My mother always poured the stock into clear Pyrex loaf pans. For serving, she inverted the pan onto an oval serving platter and cut it like bread slices. My father loved his pigs' feet with plenty of vinegar.*

4 pigs' feet, cut in halves
2 pork shanks
2 quarts cold water
1 onion, cut in quarters
2 whole medium-size carrots
1 stalk celery
1 sprig parsley
1 clove garlic
5 whole peppercorns
2 bay leaves
2 teaspoons salt
⅓ to ½ cup white vinegar

1. Have the butcher split the pigs' feet. Rinse well. Place pigs' feet and pork shanks in the water along with the onion, carrot, celery, parsley, garlic, peppercorns, bay leaves, and salt. Bring to a boil. Skim off any foam with skimmer and simmer for 2 to 3 hours or until meat is tender and begins to fall off the bones.
2. Remove meat, vegetables, and spices from pot with slotted spoon or skimmer and allow to cool. Discard the onions, celery, and spices. Discard the skin from the feet and bone from the pork shank. Pick off the meat, dice, and set aside. Dice carrot. Place meat and carrots into bottom of a bowl, a 9 × 13-inch glass cake pan or 8 × 11-inch glass loaf pan. Pour in stock. Place in refrigerator to jell.
3. To serve, scoop with spoon if jelled in a bowl, cut into squares if in a 9 × 13 pan or slice like for bread if in a loaf pan. Have vinegar on table to sprinkle over the jellied pigs' feet.

SERVES 6

## MAKING SAUSAGE

After cutting off the pork fat, the meat destined to become sausage was chopped and mixed with salt, pepper, garlic, allspice, and marjoram and stuffed into casings made from cleaned intestines. To keep the length of the intestine open so that the ground meat could pass into it, a small metal tube was used. In the absence of that, the horn of an ox was a good substitute. Some sausage was eaten fresh while some was designated for consumption later on. This meat was smoked. If a house had a chimney the sausages were hung directly in the chimney to smoke or in the attic next to the chimney in the bags that they had purchased salt in. If the house was chimneyless with just a hole in the roof for the smoke to escape, the meat was hung in the rafters. Sometimes, the more well-to-do had a separate smoke house or system for drying sausages.

The word *kiełbasa* is a generic term referring to sausage. If it is freshly made and unsmoked it is called *świeża kiełbasa.* If it's smoked, it's referred to as *wędzona kiełbasa.* Smoked sausage is at the heart of a Polish kitchen and has been a perennial favorite for centuries. During the reign of King August III Sasa (1733–1763) when much attention was being paid to food, a good chef would know how to prepare *kiełbasa* twelve different ways and a chef cooking for a noble family would know at least twenty-four different ways. The chef for August III, a man named Wereszczak, became associated with "kiełbasa a lá Wereszczak." The sausage was cut into coins and topped with a sharp, tangy sauce. It was eaten with a spoon and subsequently gave rise to the proverb:

*Za Króla Sasa, łyżka kiełbasy.*
Under King Sas, a spoon of kiełbasa.

Kiełbasa stuffed into a large intestine was called *dorotka*. Jakub Kazimierz Haur (1632–1709) who wrote books on farming and agriculture in the 17th century wrote:

*Jak wieprza zabijesz, będziesz miał:*
*Kiełbasy, kiszki, maćki, dorotki.*

When you kill your pig you will have
Sausage, kiszka, macki and dorotki

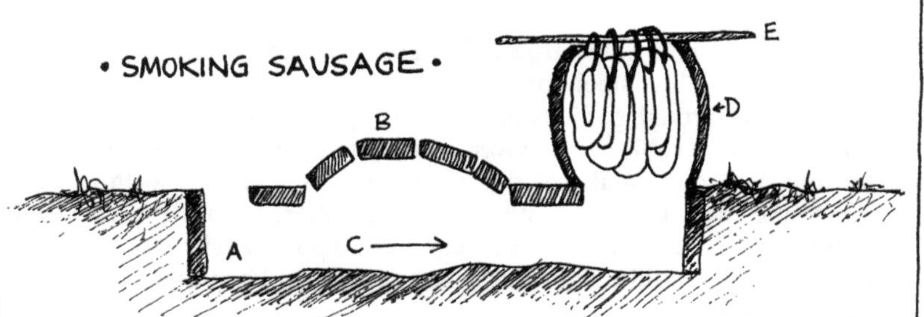


CROSS SECTION OF A HOME SMOKER IN ŁOWICZ REGION DURING THE PERIOD BETWEEN THE WORLD WARS.
A• FIRE B• CLAY DOME C• SMOKE RUN D• SIDES OF BARREL
E• STICK WITH HANGING SAUSAGES

# Fresh Sausage

***(Świeża kiełbasa)***

*One of the key herbs added to fresh homemade sausage in old Poland was marjoram. Often called* majeranek *or* majeronka, *it aided in the digestion of pork.*

11 pounds pork shoulder
6 to 8 cloves garlic
5 tablespoons salt
2 tablespoons ground pepper
2 teaspoons marjoram
2½ cups warm water
1 container pork casings

1. Cut pork shoulder into large cubes and place into very large bowl, or enamel or stainless steel pot.
2. Crush garlic through garlic press and add to pork. Add the salt, pepper, marjoram, and water. Mix well, cover, and let stand overnight in refrigerator.
3. On the next day, soak casings in warm water and rinse thoroughly. Assemble meat grinder using the coarse cutter. Coarsely ground meat will have a loose texture while finely ground pork will be more dense and compact. Also cold meat grinds more easily so keep meat refrigerated until ready to grind.
4. Attach the funnel-shaped stuffing attachment to the front of grinder. Slip on a length of casing carefully without tearing. Place meat into hopper and begin grinding, carefully controlling the thickness of the meat as it slips into the casing. The casings will stretch a fair amount but too much will cause them to split. Remember, too, that the final product will be thinner after cooking so you have to use a little judgment on how thick to stuff the casing. Keep grinding until length of casing is used up. Tie off both ends with piece of cotton string. Apply another length of casing if there is still meat left to grind. You should have nice long coils of fresh, homemade Polish sausage.
5. Carefully transfer to large stainless steel or enamel pot. Fill with water. Cook on top of stove for at least 45 to 60 minutes. Remove carefully from pot and allow to cool on platter. Save the liquid from cooking the sausage to make red *barszcz*.

SERVES 10 TO 12

# CABBAGE

No one knows for sure when cabbage was first grown and eaten in Poland. Some believe that it was the Romans who first brought cabbage to Europe and that as trade and travel increased in Europe somewhere between the 10th and 11th centuries, it made its way to Poland. We do know cabbage was being grown in the gardens of Poland in the Middle Ages along with poppy and vegetables such as peas, onions, and turnips. From the housekeeping accounts of Queen Jadwiga for October 27, 1393, three *kopy*, that is 180 heads of white cabbage, were delivered to the castle. In later years, the writer and chronicler Mikołaj Rej (1505–1569), the first poet to describe Polish life in the Polish language, mentions the preparation of cabbage in his writings. Polish ethnographers indicate that the same type of red and white cabbage was being produced in the 19th century that was mentioned in Krzystof Kluk's *Dykcyonarz Roślinny* (Dictionary of Plants) of 1786.

The importance of cabbage in the life of Polish peasants is highlighted by the fact that a vegetable garden was at one time called a *kapustnik* (cabbage patch). Cabbage, along with potatoes, was the mainstay of most Polish country kitchens. It was eaten all year long. During the summer months when it was available right from the garden, it was eaten fresh in infinite variations. When it was eaten raw, such as in coleslaw, it was called *surówka*. Fresh cabbage cooked with milk or water was called *pazibroda* or *farnuska*. The terms *kapuśniak* or *kapuśnica* meant soup made from sauerkraut. The sauerkraut was cooked in water along with some kind of pickled or brined meat with the addition of marjoram, caraway seeds, and onions. Potatoes were added to the soup for further substance. In the absence of some brined meat, pork was a suitable substitute. *Kapuśniak* also refers to a soup made with fresh cabbage and sour apples or plums. Another approach was to pour whey or fermented red beet juice over the cabbage.

Red cabbage was called *modra*, *czarna,* or *brunatna*. It was generally pickled and cooked with a variety of additions. White or red, eaten plain or with potatoes, it was the daily fare of the peasant. *Gołąbki*, or "pigs in the blanket," was a dish made of grain or rice and, if one had it, meat, wrapped in cabbage leaf. There were also pigs in the blanket made from the leaves of red beets. In earlier times, when cabbage heads were being fermented whole instead of shredded the way we know it now, the whole fermented leaves were used to make *gołąbki*. In the Lublin region, *gołąbki* were cabbage leaves stuffed with buckwheat or millet and in the Rzeszów and Kielce region, stuffed with barley. Meatless *gołąbki* made from buckwheat groats and mushrooms was a very ancient, traditional dish served for *wigilia*, the Christmas Eve supper.

# Stuffed Cabbage "Pigs in the Blanket"

***(Gołąbki)***

*Some people like more meat than this recipe calls for in which case you can make some adjustment. I like the taste of the rice and cabbage so I minimize the meat. Costs less, too! I make these a day ahead of when I want to serve them. This recipe has one time saving step for today's busy homemaker—freezing the head of cabbage instead of the traditional method of parboiling on the stove.*

1 medium to large head cabbage

FILLING
2 cups uncooked medium-grain white rice
4 cups water
3 teaspoons salt
1 small onion, chopped
1 to 2 tablespoons bacon fat, butter, or oil
1 pound raw lean ground beef or pork/beef/veal mixture
1 teaspoon pepper

SAUCE
Two 8-ounce cans tomato sauce
2 tablespoons brown sugar

1. Trim and/or remove any dirty or blackened leaves on the outside of the head of cabbage. With a sharp knife, cut out the core of the cabbage very well. Wrap in heavy-duty plastic bag and place in freezer for at least 24 hours but can be longer.
2. Thaw the frozen head of cabbage overnight. Separate the cabbage leaves and remove the tough leaf stems. Some of the inner leaves may be too small to use for wrapping. Place these at the bottom of a heavy duty cooking pot that can be used on the stovetop and then placed in the oven.
3. Cook the 2 cups of rice in the water with a teaspoon of salt. Cover and cook over low heat until done. Transfer the rice to a large mixing bowl and allow to cool.

4. Cook the chopped onion in a small frying pan with the bacon fat until golden brown. Add the onions and the fat to the rice. Add the ground meat, pepper, and the remaining 2 teaspoons of salt. Mix together very well.
5. Take a cabbage leaf and place 2 to 3 tablespoons of rice and meat mixture inside the cabbage leaf near the stem in a round mound. This is an estimate since the size of leaves varies. More may be necessary if the leaf is very big.
6. Roll the stem end over the mixture. Then bring both sides of cabbage leaf, one at a time, over to the center as if making an envelope. Roll the entire mound tightly towards the end.
7. Place the stuffed cabbage roll into the pot so that what would be the loose end or flap is facing down.
8. Repeat process until all cabbage leaves are used up, making sure to fit the stuffed rolls tightly up against each other in the pot to prevent them from floating while cooking and baking.
9. Place pot with the stuffed cabbage leaves on stove. Add water until the cabbage rolls are completely covered and then add another inch of water. Bring to a boil and simmer gently for 30 minutes with the cover half on and half off.
10. Preheat oven to 350ºF. Mix the tomato sauce and brown sugar. Pour over the stuffed cabbage rolls. Place the pot in oven and bake for an hour. This dish always tastes better the next day. The entire pot can be reheated or a few cabbage rolls can be heated up in the microwave.

YIELD 12 TO 24 CABBAGE ROLLS, DEPENDING ON SIZE OF CABBAGE HEAD.

## • STEPS FOR MAKING STUFFED CABBAGE •

1• Using a paring knife, trim heavy leafy stems.

2• Place 2-3 Tbsp. filling on cabbage leaf near base. Fold bottom of leaf over filling.

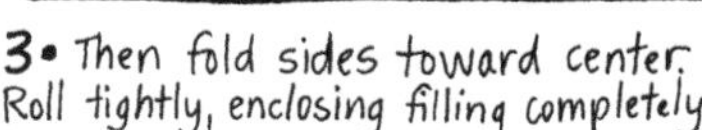

3• Then fold sides toward center. Roll tightly, enclosing filling completely.

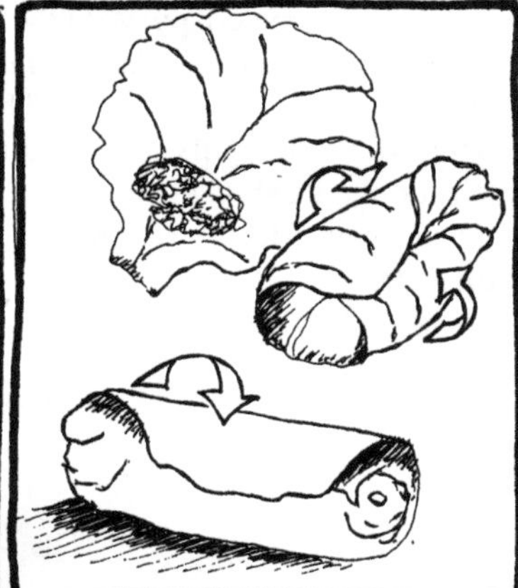

4• Place seam end face down in pot to prevent unraveling during cooking.

# Sweet Cabbage

***(Słodka Kapusta)***

3 quarts plus ½ cup water
1 small head cabbage (about 2 pounds)
3 to 4 strips bacon, diced
1 medium-size onion, chopped
2 tablespoons flour
¼ cup brown sugar
One 8-ounce can tomato sauce
¼ teaspoon pepper

1. Place 3 quarts water in large kettle on stove over high heat. Cut cabbage head in half. Cut out core and shred cabbage fine with knife or slicer. Place all cabbage in kettle with water and bring to a light boil. Continue cooking until soft and tender, 10 to 15 minutes.
2. In the meantime, place diced bacon in frying pan and fry. When juices begin to release, add onions and fry until onions are soft and golden and bacon has become crispy. Add the flour and stir together with bacon fat and onions until mixed. Add sugar and ½ cup water and mix together. The sauce will become thick. Then add the tomato sauce, salt, and pepper. Mix thoroughly and bring to a light boil for 1 minute.
3. Drain cooked cabbage in colander. Return to pot and add contents of frying pan. Mix thoroughly. If the mixture thickens too much, add extra water.

SERVES 4 TO 6

# Red Cabbage Slaw

***(Surówka z czerwonej kapusty)***

*This economical and tasty dish is offered everywhere in Poland as a summer vegetable side dish accompanying any meat. For best results, prepare day ahead for flavors to blend and cabbage to wilt.*

½ small head red cabbage
½ cup brown sugar
½ cup water
½ cup red wine vinegar
2 tablespoons vegetable oil
½ teaspoon salt
1 clove garlic, crushed

1. Finely shred the red cabbage and place in bowl.
2. Whisk together remaining ingredients and pour over shredded cabbage. Mix together very well.

SERVES 3 TO 4

# Braised Red Cabbage

*(Czerwona kapusta zasmażana)*

½ cup chopped onion
2 tablespoons olive oil
6 cups finely shredded red cabbage (about 1 small head)
1 cup water
4 tablespoons wine vinegar
4 tablespoons brown sugar
½ teaspoon pepper
1 teaspoon salt

1. In large saucepan or frying pan fry onion in oil until soft. Add shredded cabbage and mix.
2. Mix the water, vinegar, and brown sugar together. Add to the cabbage. Add pepper and salt. Sauté mixture until tender, 15 to 20 minutes. Refrigerate overnight to improve flavors.

SERVES 6

## SAUERKRAUT

*Lepsza swoja kapusta niżeli cudza gęś tłusta.*
Better one's own sauerkraut than someone's fat goose.

*Gdzie jest barszcz i kapusta, tam chata tłusta.*
Where there is beet soup and sauerkraut, there is plenty.

*Kapusty nigdy nie przekrasisz.*
You can never put too much fat in sauerkraut.

The single most important feature of cabbage that contributed toward making it a basic staple for all of Poland was that it could be fermented and kept for long periods of time, thereby providing meals for most of the year.

In ancient Slavic, the word *kapusta* meant a dish made from sour or sweet greens. Among Polish Americans the word has almost become synonymous with the fermented cabbage known as sauerkraut and can sometimes cause confusion when ordering food in Poland. *Kapusta* means a sweet or sour dish made from cabbage. A cabbage dish made from fresh cabbage would be called *słodka kapusta* (sweet cabbage) while a dish made from sauerkraut would be *kwaśna kapusta* (sour or fermented cabbage).

Every Polish family prepared for the winter by putting up numerous barrels of sauerkraut. A family could prepare as many as 180 to 300 heads of cabbage for the winter depending on the size of the cabbage heads. Its importance in daily fare is seen in its proverbs. For instance, *Gospodarz bez kapusty miewa brzuch pusty* (A farmer without cabbage has an empty stomach) and *Póki kapusta w kłodzie bieda nie dobodzie* (While there is cabbage in the barrel, want will not press).

One of the earliest forms of preserving cabbage over the winter in the form of sauerkraut was done by fermenting entire cabbage heads. Polish ethnographers have documented this very old and interesting method of storing sauerkraut called *skałbuny*. The term refers to early, deep medieval caves in which early Slavs hid their grain. In the 16th and 17th centuries, barrels of cabbage were kept in special clay pits that were also called *skałbuny*. Entire heads of cabbage were tightly packed into barrels with bare feet and prepared for the fermentation process. The cabbage was then securely covered with boards made of oak over the top of the barrel. The barrels designated for burying in the earth were carefully covered with cloth and covered with clay so as to make as tight and waterproof as possible and lowered into the *skałbuny*. These special pits were generally dug in areas where the earth consisted of heavy clay. The pits were wide, most often round and gradually became narrower towards the bottom and ranged from 1½ to 2 yards deep. The interior of the pit was lined with straw and the barrels secured within the pit. The pit was then covered with boards, followed by a coating of more straw or leaves, and then topped with earth.

These pits were carefully hidden from the prying eyes of neighbors and sometimes even from some members of the family. All activities involved with this type of krautmaking took place under cover of the night and were hidden in areas that saw little traffic. This sauerkraut was designated to be saved until spring when foodstuffs were often scarce. It also became a main food source against starvation during times of war or famine. In the 1920s two such sauerkraut pits were uncovered near Radom and were believed to have originated in the first half of the 19th century.

It wasn't until much later in culinary development that cabbage was shredded by hand using a chopper called a *siekacz* or a *hebel do kapusty,* a plane iron. In the second half of the 19th century a cabbage slicer/shredder became popular to help in the preparation of sauerkraut. Those who could afford it bought their own or borrowed from their neighbor. If neither of these were available, there were peddlers who went from house to house who would shred the cabbage for a fee. An article in the *Kurier Warszawski* (The Warsaw Courier) in 1849 wrote: "Every year at this time we see individuals roaming the streets with cabbage shredders on their backs and carrying a pounder. It wasn't so long ago during the time of our grandmothers that all that was needed was a good knife and a pair of strong legs. There are still those who give first place to sauerkraut prepared with feet." Who can forget the scene from *Chłopi*, based on Władysław Reymont's Nobel prize-winning book by the same title, where Boryna keeps gawking

ITINERANT CABBAGE SHREDDER - Warsaw 1865

at Jagna's legs when she raises her skirt to stomp on the cabbage with her bare feet?

The saying, *Zwykle w listopadzie kapusta się kładzie* (Generally one makes sauerkraut in November), testifies to the time of year when families took on the task of making their supply of sauerkraut. Very often families or neighbors got together to help each other with the task much in the same vein as an early American barn raising or corn husking. The men picked through the cabbage and separated the outer leaves. The women cut the cabbage into thin strips by hand. In the middle of the room stood a clean wash tub into which the cabbage was placed as it was shredded. The barrel, cleaned and scalded, was rubbed with onion and the bottom lined with cabbage leaves. Some regions of Poland placed the leaves of the cherry tree at the bottom as well. In the White Kurpie region, a barrel of beaten cabbage was called a *kłodka*, the barrel being made from one log or block of wood. The housewife took the shredded cabbage and placed it in the barrel, adding salt and dill. In some regions, the cabbage was fermented with the help of sour apples or beets. Some families liked their sauerkraut fermented with caraway seeds, dill, carrots, bay leaves, peppercorns, or allspice.

The men took turns beating the cabbage with a large oak pestle called an *ubijak*, packing it tightly together until the juices ran. The cabbage was also packed down by stomping on it with feet. When the barrel was full, the sauerkraut was kept submerged in its own juices with the help of a clean wooden board topped off by a clean, heavy stone which was saved and used from year to year for the same purpose. It was then placed somewhere warm where it could begin fermenting. When this major task was completed, the housewife celebrated by offering those who came to help a small repast consisting of bread, butter, or cheese. Perhaps she had prepared doughnuts ahead of time or made a pot of beet soup and poured it over hot, boiled potatoes. The work was tiring and time consuming and those who participated ate the food with gusto.

After the cabbage was done fermenting, it was placed in a cold storage area to keep from spoiling. When preparing to cook, the housewife would pull out as much as she needed from the barrel. The sauerkraut was prepared with pork fat, bacon, or spareribs if it was

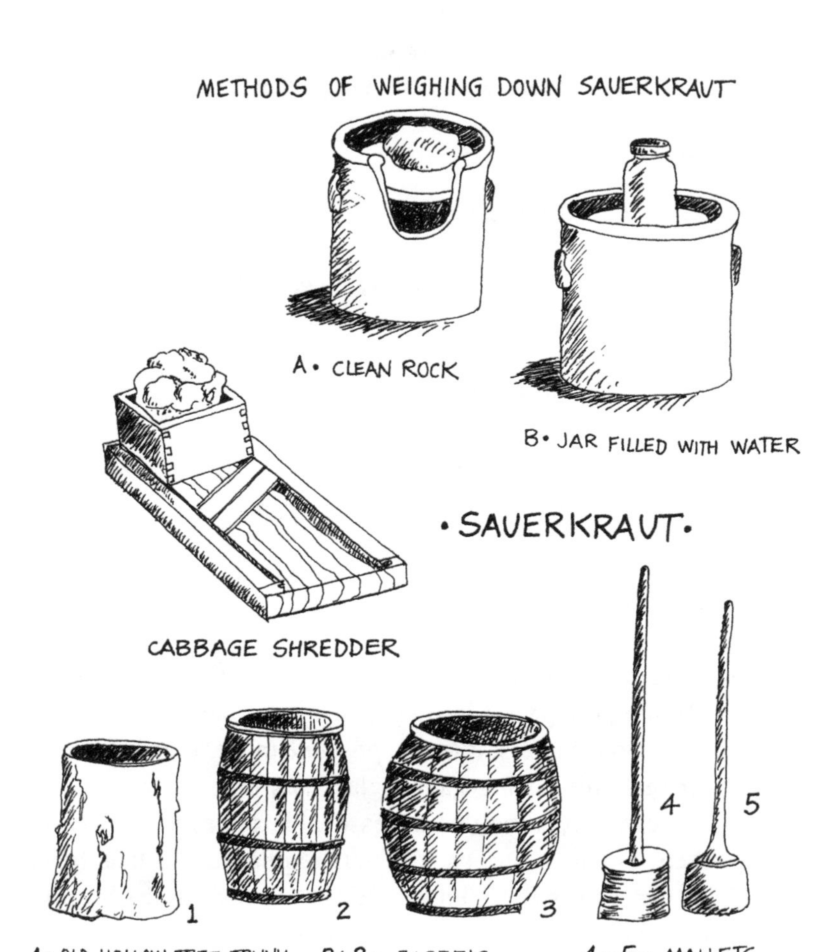
METHODS OF WEIGHING DOWN SAUERKRAUT
A• CLEAN ROCK
B• JAR FILLED WITH WATER
CABBAGE SHREDDER
•SAUERKRAUT•
1
2
3
4
5
1• OLD HOLLOW TREE TRUNK for storing sauerkraut.
2+3• BARRELS made with staves
4+5• MALLETS for tamping (pounding in sauerkraut)

available. All too often it was eaten plain as the folk song from Nowy Sącz testifies:

*Jadłoby się kapustecke, oj jadło*
*Żeby jej tak dać spyrecki i sadło.*
We would eat sauerkraut, oh yes we would
If only it had some cracklings and lard.

Another proverb states:

*Kapusta kwaśna*
*ale nie krasna*
*Trzeba do niej wieprzego sadła*
*Toby się zjadła.*

The sauerkraut is sour
But not tasty
It needs some pork fat
For it to be eaten.

### *Making Your Own Sauerkraut*

Making your own sauerkraut is not difficult—it is only time consuming. While Polish families in the past put up great vats of sauerkraut in enormous barrels, it is also possible to make your own kraut in smaller quantities using gallon glass jars or one- or two-gallon crocks that can still be bought at reasonable prices at garage sales, flea markets, or antique shops. The only requirement is that they not leak. This can be easily tested by filling the crock to the brim with water and watching for seepage. The large old-fashioned shredders can still be found as well as a variety of smaller ones, and are very helpful if you want to make larger batches of kraut. If you simply want to make a gallon of kraut, a knife works fine.

The following recipe is for a larger batch. Cut the recipe down if you would like a smaller batch. What's important in kraut making is not the exactness of the measured ingredients but following through with the process.

## Sauerkraut

***(Kiszona kapusta)***

*To keep our sauerkraut cold, my father placed it in our unheated barn not too far from the coal bin. When my mother needed sauerkraut she would go out to the barn with a large enamel bowl and a hatchet to chop away at the frozen kraut.*

40 to 50 pounds cabbage
1 to 2 cups canning or kosher salt
2 to 3 tablespoons caraway seeds (optional)
10 to 12 bay leaves (optional)
½ cup peppercorns (optional)
10-gallon crock or two 5-gallon crocks

1. Remove any dirty outer leaves of the cabbage and set them aside. Cut all the clean cabbage heads into quarters and cut out core at the top. Using a shredder (or sharp knife) cut all your cabbage into shreds about the thickness of a dime.
2. In a clean container (anything except aluminum) that will hold the shredded cabbage, mix with the salt. Let the salted cabbage stand until it wilts slightly. This will make it easier later to pack the cabbage. In the meantime wash the dirty outer leaves by rinsing under water until clean. Place a few of these leaves at the bottom of the crock or jars. If you have extra, stack them one on top of the other and also shred fine. Add to the salt and cabbage mixture. None of the cabbage leaves should be wasted unless yellowed or decayed.
3. Place some of the wilted cabbage on the bottom of the crock or jar on top of the cabbage leaves. Using a pounder, large wooden spoon, or your hands (my preferred method), press the wilted cabbage down firmly until juice comes to the surface.
4. Repeat the process of ***firmly*** packing the cabbage into the crock or jar until it is filled to within 6 inches of the top. There must be at least 2 to 3 inches of salted water covering the cabbage when you are finished packing the cabbage into the crock. This leaves 2 to 3 inches for the bubbling fermentation process that will occur or it will overflow down the sides of your container and only make a sloppy mess and unnecessary work.

5. Cover the cabbage with a clean, white cloth. Place the cloth directly on the cabbage. Cover the cloth with a plate large enough that when placed upside down it fits securely over the cabbage almost to the sides of your container. Another option is to place strips of seasoned oak or some other hardwood closely together so that they fit just inside the crock. On top of this place a heavy weight such as a large, clean rock or a quart jar filled with water. The cloth, the plate, and the rock should all be submerged in the salted water. This can all be covered with another clean cloth.
6. Place your jar or crock in a warm place. Room temperature of 68° or 72°F is best for fermenting the cabbage and generally a kitchen is a good place both for warmth and for keeping an eye on the fermentation process.
7. Formation of gas bubbles indicates that fermentation is taking place. Fermentation takes 2 to 3 weeks, or longer for larger batches. Two or three days after fermentation has started, remove the weight, the plate, and the cloth. Wipe any scum off the inside of the jar or crock. Wash and scald the plate or hardwood strips and pat dry. Replace the cloth with a clean one, top again with the weight and cover. If at any time during the fermenting process, the sauerkraut is no longer covered in brine, you will have to add a salt solution. Do this by bringing 1 to 2 cups of water containing 1 or 2 teaspoons of uniodized or kosher salt to a boil. ***Allow to cool completely*** before adding to your jar or crock.
8. When the bubbling stops, the sauerkraut is ready. At this point it must either (1) be stored in its container in a continually cold place, or (2) be put up in jars or frozen in plastic bags in a freezer. A gallon jar can be kept in a refrigerator indefinitely and the sauerkraut used as needed. Unless you have an outbuilding and the weather remains consistently cold, larger amounts need to be put up.
9. To can sauerkraut: Pack the sauerkraut into clean jars. Cover with brine from the crock to neck of jar. If you run out of brine, make your own solution of water and salt following directions in step 7. Complete the sealing process following general canning procedures. Process quarts in boiling bath water for 15 minutes.
10. Freezing is a simpler method. Just pack into quart-size freezer bags, freeze, and defrost as needed.

MAKES 10 GALLONS

# Sauerkraut Soup

***(Kapuśniak)***

Kapuśniak *comes in many variations. It could be made from shredded sweet cabbage, sauerkraut, or its juice along with some kind of pork, bacon, or sausage. Poured over plain boiled potatoes in a large soup bowl, it makes a complete meal.*

½ pound fresh or smoked Polish sausage or combination of both
2 quarts water
1 pound sauerkraut
1 pound fresh mushrooms or 1 ounce dried mushrooms
2 tablespoons bacon fat or vegetable oil
1 large onion, chopped
1 tablespoon flour
1 teaspoon caraway seeds (optional)

1. Cook sausage in the water for 45 to 60 minutes. In the meantime, rinse sauerkraut in cold water at least once, twice if a milder, less tart taste is preferred. Squeeze out excess water from the sauerkraut with hands, reserving the liquid. Chop the sauerkraut into smaller pieces.
2. If using fresh mushrooms, slice the caps and stems. If using dried mushrooms, place in 1 cup water and bring to a boil. Let simmer for 1 to 2 minutes. Remove from heat and allow to stand until cool. Remove mushrooms from water, reserving the water, and slice.
3. Place bacon fat or oil in large frying pan and brown onions. Sprinkle the flour over the onions and stir into a light paste.
4. Remove the cooked sausage from the pot. Add the sauerkraut, sliced mushrooms and the mushroom water if using dried mushrooms, and the paste from the frying pan. Cook for at least one hour until the sauerkraut is soft. Taste periodically as sauerkraut is cooking. If too mild, add some of the reserved sauerkraut juice. If too tart, add additional water. Add the caraway seeds, if desired. Slice the sausage into coins and add to the sauerkraut just before serving to heat through.

SERVES 6

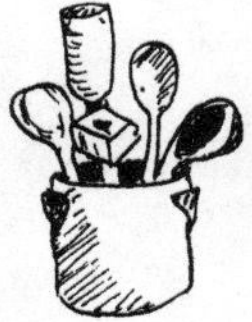

# Sauerkraut with Mushrooms

***(Kapusta z Grzybami)***

1 ounce dried mushrooms *or* ½ pound fresh
3 cups water
One 2-pound bag sauerkraut, rinsed to taste
1 bay leaf
1 large onion, chopped fine
3 tablespoons butter or bacon drippings
2 tablespoons flour
¼ to ½ cup sour cream
1 tablespoon caraway seeds (optional)

1. If using dried mushrooms, place in small saucepan and boil in 1 cup of water for 15 minutes. Remove mushrooms from the water with slotted spoon and chop coarsely. Set aside. Drain the water out carefully into a separate small bowl, discarding any particles or soil left at the bottom of the saucepan. If using fresh mushrooms, rinse carefully and slice lengthwise.
2. Place the rinsed sauerkraut in 2 cups water with caraway seeds and bay leaf for about 15 to 20 minutes until soft.
3. Preheat oven to 350°F. While sauerkraut is cooking, brown onions in the butter or bacon drippings in frying pan until golden. At this point add the mushrooms and continue to sauté slowly.
4. In the meantime, drain the cooked sauerkraut as you would potatoes, using the lid of the pot. If you have used dried mushrooms, add the saved mushroom water to the sauerkraut and place on stove again over low heat. If using fresh mushrooms, add 1 cup fresh water to the cooked sauerkraut instead and return to stove over low heat.
5. Mix the flour with the sour cream and add to the onions and mushrooms in the frying pan. Cook over low heat until slightly thickened. Add to sauerkraut mixture.
6. Turn sauerkraut mixture into greased casserole and bake for 1 hour.

SERVES 4 TO 6

# Easy Sauerkraut in Crock-Pot

*I get up half an hour early and throw this together before I go to work. When I come home, the kitchen smells delicious and all I have to do is peel some potatoes.*

One 2-pound bag, can, or jar sauerkraut
1 medium onion, chopped
1 to 2 tablespoons butter, oil, or bacon drippings
1 pound pork chops or spareribs
One 10½-ounce can cream of mushroom soup
½ pound fresh mushrooms, sliced (optional)
½ cup barley, uncooked (optional)
½ cup green or yellow split peas, uncooked (optional)

1. Empty sauerkraut into colander and rinse under running water. If you enjoy very tart kraut this step can be omitted. If a milder taste is preferred, rinse once or twice, and squeeze out water with hands.
2. Fry onion in large frying pan with butter, oil, or bacon drippings.
3. When onions are lightly browned, add sauerkraut to frying pan and mix with the onions.
4. If you would like to serve pork chops or spare ribs and make it a meal in one pot, brown the meat lightly in the frying pan with the onions for a few minutes on both sides and place in the bottom of the Crock-Pot. Replace frying pan back on stove, add the sauerkraut and continue with Step 5.
5. Add mushroom soup and 1 can of water to the sauerkraut mixture and mix thoroughly. If you wish, you can add mushrooms, barley or green or yellow split peas at this stage.
6. Place entire mixture in Crock-Pot and allow to cook on low setting for 8 to 10 hours. If it begins to look a little dry as it cooks, add a little water to keep moist.
7. Serve with plain boiled potatoes or noodles.

SERVES 4 TO 6

## BIGOS

The word *bigos* can mean a soup made from grated wild pears or it can refer to a hearty cabbage stew. According to Polish ethnographers, the word *bigos* comes from the German *beiguss*, meaning sauce or from *bleiguss*, chunks of fat. Mikołaj Rej, that great chronicler of Polish life during the 16th century, mentions *kapusta* in his works but not *bigos* which leads Polish historians and ethnographers to feel that the word was not known during that time.

At its heart, *bigos* is a hearty stew made with sauerkraut, meat, mushrooms, and spices. It has come to be considered Poland's national dish much like corned beef and cabbage has come to be associated with the Irish and beef stew with New Englanders. Its importance in Polish fare has withstood the test of time and is heavily documented in Polish literature.

Wincenty Pol wrote:

*Miodek to napitek!*
*Bigos to potrawa!*
*Kulig to zabawa!*

Honeyed vodka is a drink!
Bigos is a dish!
Kulig is an entertainment!

Stanisław Jachowicz wrote:

*Bigos i kiełbasy*
*Odnawiają one w pamięci owe świetne czasy.*

Bigos and sausage
Renew one's memories of great times.

It is Poland's most famous poet Adam Mickiewicz, however, who forever immortalized *bigos* in his epic poem *Pan Tadeusz*:

*W kociołkach bigos grzano—w słowach wydać trudno*
*Bigosu smak przedziwny, kolor i woń cudną*
*Słów tylko brzęk usłyszy i rymów porządek*
*Ale treści ich miejski nie pojmie żołądek.*

The bigos is being cooked. No words can tell
The wonder of its colour, taste and smell.
Mere words or rhymes are jingling sounds, whose senses
No city stomach really comprehends.
(Translation by Kenneth R. McKenzie)

In this particular section of his long epic poem, Mickiewicz was describing the making of *bigos* over an open fire while out hunting in the forest. Hunting was a much loved sport among the Polish aristocracy complete with the fanfare of the hunt horn, formal dress, and warmed wine served in stirrup cups. No hunt was complete without the traditional hunter's stew called *bigos myśliwski* which was made with sauerkraut with a variety of meats from the forest with the addition of spices and mushrooms cooked over a slow open fire. There was even a special copper pot called a *bigośnica* for either cooking or reheating *bigos*. In 1882, Zygmunt Gloger, famous for his four-volume *Encyklopedia Staropolska*, wrote that when he and author Henryk Sienkiewicz went traveling to the Puszcza Białowieska on horseback, they took *bigos* for the trip.

*Bigos* was not limited to cooking over an open fire out in the woods or for taking on the road where it could be reheated when reaching one's destination. It was often made at home for the family or in preparation for guests coming to celebrate a special event. The preparation of *bigos* for social get-togethers supposedly accounts for its other name of *bigos hultański*. It was offered to guests who had *hulali* that is, been making merry and carrying on the night before. Carnival time just before Lent was a time of great revelry and feasting with much socializing and visiting one another's homes. Among the gentry, *bigos* was always a popular dish served to the sleighloads of revelers who visited each other's homes to test the kitchen and cellar during a *kulig*. It could be prepared ahead of time and stored in a cold cellar in anticipation of guests. Some Polish historians claim that *bigos* was offered as the first dish, even before the soup course, to start a dinner. Preparing a decent kettle of *bigos* was the pride of every housewife, each having her particular secret or special recipe for it.

Making *bigos* can generate a lot of controversy and discussion as some claim it should be made from a mix of sauerkraut and fresh cabbage. Others say it can be made from fresh cabbage alone. People like my mother claimed it could be made either with fresh cabbage or with sauerkraut, depending on availability. The greatest number of proponents claim it should be made from only from sauerkraut. In describing the process of making *bigos* in *Pan Tadeusz*, Mickiewicz states "bierze się siekaną, kwaszoną kapustę" (you take chopped sauerkraut).

Almost any meat can be added to the sauerkraut to make *bigos*: pork, pork fat, bacon, beef, veal, poultry, smoked or fresh sausage, or wild game. Herbs and spices such as allspice, marjoram, bay leaves, peppercorns, as well as pitted prunes and dried or fresh mushrooms were added to the sauerkraut and meat mixture. Some liked their *bigos* with a cup of red wine added at the end for extra flavoring. Others felt this did nothing at all.

In the recipe for *bigos* in *Uniwersalna Książka Kucharska,* Maria Ochorowicz-Monatowa indicates that while *bigos* may be costly to prepare it is well worth it. "It is best to prepare it for some large gathering. That way you can utilize any leftover ham, poultry, or game which will enhance the taste of the bigos. The more variety of meat, the better the bigos." Her recipe also called for the addition of a glass of Madeira at the end.

The mixture of kraut, meat, and additives was cooked over a slow fire for most of the day. Like many foods, *bigos* always tasted better the day after it was cooked when all the flavors had a chance to blend together. This made it a favorite dish to prepare when a crowd of guests was coming by or for the day after Christmas such as St. Stephen's Day, which was considered another holiday in Poland, and very little work was done in the kitchen. On this day people visited their friends and family, either as invited guests or simply dropping in, and the main meal on this day was *bigos* made from leftover meats and sausages. Legend has it that the best *bigos* has been left to stand two weeks for the flavors to fully develop. It also says that the only other thing served with *bigos* is unbuttered bread and a jigger of rye vodka or glass of red wine.

Most country households had barrels of sauerkraut prepared for the winter. They also collected and dried mushrooms and had some herbs and spices to add to their *bigos*. Large amounts of meat were unheard of in those situations so that their *bigos* may have been limited to some smoked sausage and bits of rabbit or duck. While it may not have been loaded with lots of meat, it was cooked just as carefully and enjoyed just as much.

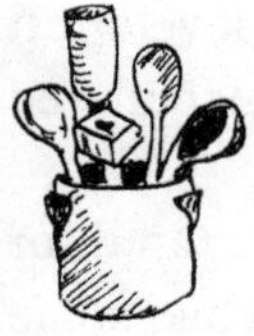

# BIGOS

*I use a Crock-Pot to achieve the slow cooking traditionally used for bigos. Not only does it taste great but doesn't require constant attention. However, a heavy duty Dutch oven that can simmer on top of the stove or be placed in the oven works just as well. You can substitute any cooked leftover meats for the pork in this recipe and omit the browning. Just layer your meat between the sauerkraut.*

*I always serve boiled potatoes on the side or lots of fresh rye bread and butter.*

4 pounds (2 quart jars) sauerkraut
½ cup pearl barley or green or yellow split peas, uncooked (optional)
1 pound fresh whole or sliced mushrooms or ½ ounce dried mushrooms
2 to 3 bay leaves
1 teaspoon allspice or peppercorns
2 tablespoons vegetable oil or bacon drippings
1 to 2 pounds of pork loin or pork chops
1 medium onion, chopped
½ pound cooked fresh Polish sausage
½ pound smoked Polish sausage, cut into thick pieces

1. Empty sauerkraut into colander and rinse under running water. If you enjoy very tart kraut this step can be omitted. If a milder taste is preferred, rinse once or twice, and squeeze out water with hands and place in large bowl. Barley or split peas can be added at this stage.
2. Place fresh mushrooms in 4 cups water and cook for 10 to 20 minutes. Drain, saving liquid to add to sauerkraut. If using dried mushrooms, cook them in 1 cup water for 5 to 10 minutes. Drain, saving liquid to add to sauerkraut and discarding any sediment or dirt that may settle on the bottom. Slice the mushrooms into strips and add to sauerkraut. Add bay leaves and allspice or peppercorns.
3. Place oil in large frying pan or Dutch oven and brown pork loin or chops lightly in the frying pan with the chopped onions for a few minutes on both sides and place in the bottom of the Crock-Pot or Dutch oven. Spoon ⅓ of sauerkraut mixture over meat.

4. Lightly fry fresh sausage in frying pan for 1 to 2 minutes on each side and add to Crock-Pot or Dutch oven. Spoon ⅓ of sauerkraut mixture over meat. Place sliced smoked sausage on top and cover with remaining sauerkraut.
5. Allow Crock-Pot to cook on low setting for 8 to 10 hours. Or put Dutch oven in a 325°F oven for 3 to 4 hours. If it begins to look a little dry as it cooks, add a little water to keep moist. Allow to stand overnight in refrigerator. Reheat next day and serve.

SERVES 8 TO 10 GENEROUSLY

By the end of October all preparations for the upcoming winter were coming to a close. The geese would have been slaughtered by now, the feathers plucked, washed, dried, and stored in the attic to be stripped later in the heart of winter. The geraniums from the flower garden were safely potted and placed on the kitchen sill. All the dead vines and leaves in the cottage garden were tilled into the soil where they would secretly and quietly enrich the earth for next year's seedlings.

❖ LUCY'S HOUSEHOLD HINTS: Another method of killing mice and rodents: In areas where mice and rodents tend to frequent place two saucers. On one, place some regular, clear water. On the other, place some finely crumbled gypsum or plaster. Cover this with a small handful of flour and leave for the night. The mice will eat the plaster with the flour, become thirsty, drink the water. Plaster with water is indigestible and will cause the mice to die.

❖ LUCY'S HOUSEHOLD HINTS: When eggs are hard to come by in fall and winter, use pumpkins as a substitute. One cup of mashed pumpkin will take the place of a dozen eggs. Dough must be worked very well and it cannot be used without yeast.

# WINTER

Źima

The onset of winter with its drifting blowing snows and unpredictable weather provided another challenge for the Polish farmer. Many small Polish villages consisted of a cluster of cottages that were isolated from other villages or hamlets by miles of poorly kept roads. Travel in the winter was generally on foot or by horse and sleigh and quick changes in the weather could become dangerous for anyone caught in a storm. As a result family life centered round the fireplace and stoves that drove away the cold. Any solitary traveler forced to seek aid or shelter would find the inhabitants ranged around the stove trying to stay warm and occupied by simple indoor tasks. The man of the house could be whittling clothespins for his wife or mending a harness. The housewife would be spinning wool or flax or stripping feathers.

The dropping in of a neighbor or unexpected traveler stranded on the road was met with pleasure as it often provided a welcome respite from the monotony of the same old faces and stories. Lacking other forms of entertainment, people often got together to sing, gossip, and help each other with tasks. While the summer and fall had provided some social contacts when people had gotten together for haying, threshing, and producing oil, the inactivity of winter provided endless hours of free time to meet their social needs.

One of the chief tasks of a country housewife during the winter was to spin wool or flax to make thread for weaving. The women often spent long hours in front of the fire with their drop spindles or spinning wheels deftly twisting raw materials into threads that would later be woven, knitted, or crocheted into much needed items. It was common for a few women to take turns meeting at one another's houses with their spinning wheels to share gossip, sing Advent songs, share recipes and gossip, or retell ancient legends and stories as the children gathered round to listen.

The other major activity was stripping feathers to make a pillow or a *pierzyna*—a down comforter. Preparation for this began much earlier in the year when the ducks or geese were plucked of their feathers at the end of May. The feathers were washed and dried and placed in a cloth or burlap bag and hung in the attic. If a home had a lot of daughters, the housewife thought ahead to the time when the daughter would need a dowry. Daughters were expected to bring something advantageous to a marriage, whether it was in the form of money, livestock, or household goods. Warm feather comforters and pillows to fight off the winter cold were considered indispensable and when winter advanced, the women of the house invited others in for *skubanie pierza*, the stripping of feathers of their quill. Each daughter could take a pillow and a well-stuffed feather tick as part of her marriage dowry.

As a reward for their help or camaraderie, the housewives in Śląsk region offered potato pancakes or a *kartoflak*, a baked potato casserole to those who came to help strip feathers or to share an evening of spinning wool.

*Feather-stripping during long winter evenings in Beskid Śląsk region, 1958. Photo by Stefan Deptuszewski. Courtesy of the National Ethnographic Museum, Warsaw.*

# Potato Casserole

*(Kartoflak)*

3 pounds potatoes, peeled and grated
1 small onion, grated
5 slices bacon, diced
½ cup hot whole milk
3 eggs, beaten
1 tablespoon parsley
2 teaspoons salt
½ teaspoon pepper
Sour cream (optional)

1. Preheat oven to 400°F. Mix together the grated potatoes and onion.
2. Fry the bacon until crisp. Crumble the bacon and pour fat and bacon over the potatoes. Add the hot milk, eggs, parsley, salt, and pepper.
3. Pour into a greased 10-inch cast-iron skillet or oven-safe casserole. Bake for at 400°F for 15 minutes. Reduce heat to 375°F and bake for 45 to 60 minutes longer.
4. Cut into wedges and serve hot with sour cream, if desired.

SERVES 8

# Beer Toddy

***(Grzane Piwo)***

*This quick drink was offered to someone who needed to warm up quickly because of excessive exposure to cold or frostbite. My mother always gave us half a cup when we had the flu, a severe cold or got caught in a cold rain. After drinking this she bundled us up under the* pierzyna *to make us "sweat." Did we ever!*

1 egg yolk
2 tablespoons sugar
One 12-ounce bottle beer

1. In glass measuring cup, mix sugar and egg yolk well.
2. Heat beer slowly in a saucepan but do not bring to a boil. Add 2 tablespoons of the hot beer to the egg yolk mixture and mix. Add another 2 tablespoons and mix again. Pour the egg yolk mixture in a thin stream into the heated beer and heat through. Serve immediately.

MAKES 1½ CUPS

## Wigilia

The most important and memorable day of the entire winter season in a Polish country cottage was Christmas Eve. Christmas Eve marked the last day of Advent, a period of forty days of quiet reflection and fasting. The proverb, *Jak będzie Wigilia, tak będzie cały rok* (As is wigilia, so is the entire year), denotes the importance of the entire day. Whatever an individual did on this day would be the same the following year. As a result it was approached very carefully, imbuing even everyday chores, such as drawing water from the well or bringing in wood, with careful consideration. There was an atmosphere of anticipation, of something special about to happen and as a consequence everyone spoke in subdued and respectful tones toward one another. The waiting, the anticipation, that sense of something special intensified as the day gave way to dusk when the all-important Christmas Eve supper called *wigilia* would begin. In some parts of Poland the Christmas Eve meal was called *wilia*. In the Kurpie region of Poland, north of Warsaw, it was called *zilija*. The word *wigilia* comes from the Latin word *vigilare* or "vigil" meaning to watch, to await. All await the birth of Jesus Christ on this night.

The day is a busy one nonetheless. The men of the family hitched up the horse and sledge and traveled into the woods to gather branches of spruce and fir. The evergreen branches were nailed to the door of the house or barn. The tip of a spruce tree was brought inside the house and hung from the ceiling upside down over the table where the *wigilia* meal was to be eaten. This was called a *podłaznik*. In even earlier times this decoration had been made of stalks of grain such as wheat or rye but eventually gave way to the changing times of bringing greenery into the home. The *podłaznik* was decorated by the children with fruit, nuts, and homemade ornaments made from wheat and paper.

*Wigilia in the Kurpie region, 1953. Photo by Jerzy Baranowski. Courtesy of the National Ethnographic Museum, Warsaw.*

The Christmas tree as we know it today did not make an appearance in Poland until the 19th century. Polish ethnographer Zygmunt Gloger wrote: "From the Prussians, there is the custom in Warsaw of a special treat for the children—a fir tree decorated with candy, walnuts covered in gold foil, apples and loads of candles. Sometimes among the branches there is a *szopka*, a manger scene, depicting the birth of Christ. There is an image of the Christ Child cleverly carved from wax lying in a manger and watching over Him is the Virgin Mary and St. Joseph. Breathing over Him is an ox and a mule. Angels and shepherds are in attendance, too." From the cities the custom of decorating a tree spread out to the countryside replacing the old customs.

The room where the meal was to be eaten was carefully decorated. According to ancient tradition, large sheaves of wheat, rye, or oats were placed in the four corners of this same room. Oftentimes hay was strewn on the floor in remembrance of the stable where the Christ Child was born. In some homes it was enough to place a thin layer of hay or straw on the table. This was then covered with the best white linen tablecloth. An empty place was set at the table in case a stranger or traveler happened to stop by. This is also a very ancient custom carried over from long ago when it was felt that dead ancestors visited their homes on this night. Families wanted them to know that they were remembered and welcome, and so set out food for them. Over time, the empty place came to mean different things including the possibility that any beggar or traveler who stops by on this night could be the Christ Child in disguise.

Housewives thought about and prepared for the meal long in advance of the day. Tradition dictates that this be a meatless dinner, and very long ago even milk and milk products were avoided. Today dishes prepared with milk are included but a real traditionalist today will cook without any meat fat at all, using vegetable oils such as canola and sunflower. Tradition also dictates that there should be an uneven number of dishes served. In the more well-to-do homes this was eleven or thirteen, with thirteen being the preferred number as it represented the number that sat down to the Last Supper. In more humble cottages, five or seven different dishes graced the table. For those of truly reduced circumstances, of which there were many throughout Poland, dish often consisted of simply tasting a piece of food. For example, the family would share a piece of fruit. Everyone received a slice, and this counted as one of the dishes. The number and type of dishes were supposed to foretell plenty in the year to come. The more dishes, the more abundant the harvest next year.

Each region of Poland had their preferred dishes and quite frankly, served whatever their mothers and grandmothers had served in previous generations. Up until the World Wars in some areas of Poland, this meal was eaten from a common bowl and in candlelight.

Traditional Christmas Eve dishes in the town of Przeworsk, Rzeszów region, would consist of:

1. Sauerkraut with peas *(Kapusta z grochem)*
2. Sour soup with peas *(Barszcz z grochem)*
3. Marinated mushrooms *(Marynowane grzyby)*
4. Dumplings with dried fruit *(Pierogi z suszonymi owocami)*
5. Noodles with honey and poppy seeds *(Kluski z makiem i miodem)*
6. Dumplings with potato filling *(Pierogi z ziemniakami)*
7. Millet groats with prunes *(Kasza jaglana ze śliwkami)*
8. Dumplings with sauerkraut *(Pierogi z kapustą)*
9. Noodles with plum jam *(Kluski z powidłem)*
10. Whole wheat berries with honey and poppy seed *(Kutia)*
11. Stewed Fruits *(Kompot z owoców)*

In the Śląsk (Silesia) region of Poland a typical menu would consist of:

1. Hemp soup (*Siemienotka*, also called *konopiotka*)
2. Pea soup *(Zupa grochowa)*
3. Boiled potatoes *(Kartofle)*
4. Millet *(Kasza jaglana)*
5. Millet with plums *(Kasza jaglana ze śliwkami*, also called *garus)*
6. Sauerkraut with peas or mushrooms *(Kapusta z grochem lub grzybami)*
7. Fried carp *(Karp smażony)*
8. Stewed fruit *(Kompot z owoców)*

Another typical menu:

1. Mushroom soup *(Zupa grzybowa)*
2. Sauerkraut with mushrooms, green peas, or barley *(Kapusta z grochem lub grzyby)*
3. Barley *(Kasza jęczmienna)*
4. Boiled potatoes served with herring in sour cream *(Ziemniaki ze sledziami w śmietanie)*
5. Noodles with poppy seed *(Kluski z makiem)*
6. Poppy seed roll or pastry *(Makowiec)*
7. Pickled beets *(Buraki marynowane)*
8. Dumpling stuffed with cheese, mushroom, sauerkraut, or cheese and potato *(Pierogi z sera, grzyby, kapusta lub ziemniaki i ser)*
9. Stewed fruits *(Kompot z owoców)*

As part of the solemnity of the day and as the last day of Advent, many people abstained from eating throughout the day and looked forward to breaking their fast. The meal generally began with a soup. It could be a mushroom soup, a red beet soup with mushroom-filled dumplings, or an almond soup. In the Radom region of Poland as well as in Silesia, a very ancient soup was one made from cooked and grated hemp seed with the addition of onions, a little bit of rye flour, a bay leaf, and sometimes a few bits of whole cinnamon.

The soup dish was followed by fish. Fish has been the symbol of Christ and Christianity for centuries and plays a role in the *wigilia* meal if it is available. Carp is credited with being the fish of choice on Christmas Eve. The aristocracy stocked private ponds with the fish in order to have it available but the truth of the matter was that almost any local freshwater fish was served on this night if it was available. It was served up in its entirety with beady eyes and tail intact after having been poached in beer or a variety of sauces. Perch was available from the waters of the mighty Wisła River. Tench, salmon, trout, eel, and pike were also obtained from local rivers, lakes, and ponds. The fish were baked, fried, stewed, or made into cutlets or aspics, depending on preference. Many families did not have access to or the money to buy fresh fish and made do with the readily available herring. Teamed up with hot boiled potatoes, it was both filling and inexpensive.

Cereals and grains figured largely in the Christmas Eve meal, more so than fish. The housewife often saved fine wheat flour for making bread and noodles on this special night. Noodles called *paluszki* were made from scratch. These were dumplings sprinkled with poppy seeds that were shaped long and thin because it was believed that the grains would be just as thick on the stalk in the coming year. In central Poland, the preferred dish was noodles and poppy seed. Other regions enjoyed a dish of noodles and stewed fruit or jam. Another variation was a bowl of cooked millet with butter, cinnamon, and sugar. In eastern Poland a dish called *kutia,* made of cooked wheat berries, poppy seeds, honey, and nuts was preferred above all others. A sauerkraut dish of some kind was also universal throughout Poland on Christmas Eve. For dessert there was a simple platter of apples and nuts in their shell. For those who could afford it there were honeyed cookies, a poppy seed pastry or bread or a small platter filled with raisins, walnuts, almonds, figs, and dates. In Upper Silesia the preferred dessert was baked apples with jam, eaten either hot or cold. Most meals were concluded with a simple compote made from dried fruits—plums, apples, pears, prunes, raisins, blueberries, cherries, or whatever dried berries could be reconstituted.

# FRIED FISH

***(Smażona Ryba)***

*My mother always served fried fish on Christmas Eve with hot boiled potatoes topped with butter and sour cream. In later years she liked to prepare a potato salad as a change from the boiled potatoes.*

1 to 2 pounds fresh or frozen and thawed fish of choice
Salt and pepper
1 egg
1 to 2 cups bread crumbs
Vegetable oil for frying

1. Cut fish into desired serving portions. Lightly salt and pepper to taste.
2. Beat egg very well in dish or shallow bowl. Place bread crumbs in another plate or platter. Dip fish into egg mixture and then into the bread crumbs.
3. Fry in hot oil in frying pan on both sides until cooked. Serve immediately or transfer to cookie sheet and place in warm oven until ready to serve.

SERVES 4

## POPPY SEEDS

For centuries Poland, as well as the rest of Eastern Europe, has been using the rich, nutty seeds of the poppy plant in cakes, breads, pastries, and noodle dishes. The edible bluish-black poppy seeds are produced by *Papaver somniferum*, or the opium poppy, also the source of opium. In many parts of Poland, poppy seeds were grown as a cash crop but many a housewife planted it for use in her own cooking and baking. The seeds of poppy are collected from the seed heads just as they are beginning to turn a gray-brown color and small holes appear just underneath the flat tops. They were cut and put head down into linen bags and shaken until the seeds dropped out and then stored away from the light.

Whole poppy seeds can be made into a paste for pastries by boiling the poppy seeds in milk to soften, draining well, and then grinding in a small food processor or meat grinder or crushing by hand with a wooden spoon. Another method is to scald the poppy seeds with boiling water and set aside to drain overnight. In Poland, poppy with honey is often used as a sweetener.

# Poppy Seed Roll

***(Makowiec)***

***This is an exceptionally light but flavorful poppy seed roll.***

4 cups flour
1 cup (2 sticks) butter, at room temperature
3 tablespoons granulated sugar
3 eggs, separated
One ¼-ounce package active dry yeast
1 cup warm water (115°F)
One 12-ounce can poppy seed filling

Frosting
One 3-ounce package cream cheese
2 tablespoons butter, melted
2 cups confectionary sugar
½ cup chopped walnuts

1. Mix flour, butter, and sugar with a pastry blender in a large bowl until pea-size crumbs form. Add egg yolks and mix well. Reserve whites.
2. Dissolve the yeast completely in the warm water and add to the dough mixture. Mix well until you obtain a slightly sticky dough. Place in tightly covered container and chill overnight.
3. Next day, bring the reserved egg whites to room temperature and beat until stiff.
4. Divide the chilled dough into two balls. On lightly floured board, roll out one of the balls of dough into a 13-inch circle. Spread half the can of poppy seed filling over the circle. Spread half the egg white over the poppy seed filling. Roll up like jelly roll. Transfer to one side of lightly greased 11 × 16-inch cookie sheet.
5. Repeat process with second ball of dough and transfer to other side of cookie sheet. Cover lightly with cloth and let stand in warm kitchen for 1 hour until risen.
6. Preheat oven to 350°F and bake for 35 to 40 minutes. Cool.
7. To make frosting beat cream cheese, melted butter, and confectionary sugar. Add extra confectionary sugar if too thin. Spread on both poppy seed rolls. Top with chopped walnuts.

EACH ROLL SERVES 8 TO 10

# Noodles and Poppy Seeds

*(Kluski z makiem)*

One 16-ounce package medium-size egg noodles
4 tablespoons (½ stick) butter, melted
One 12-ounce can poppy seed filling
1 tablespoon lemon juice
4 teaspoons grated lemon peel
1 tablespoon honey

1. Preheat oven to 350°F.
2. Cook noodles according to package directions. Drain and toss with butter while still warm.
3. Mix poppy seed filling with lemon juice, lemon peel, and honey.
4. Add to noodles and mix well. Place in baking casserole and heat through about 20 to 30 minutes.

SERVES 4 TO 6

## *KUTIA*

*Kutia*, one of the most ancient Christmas Eve dishes, must be honored for its age alone. It goes back thousands of years in Polish history combining two of the oldest foods known to man—wheat and honey.

A dish of whole or cracked wheat (or sometimes rice) softened in water, cooked, and sweetened with honey and flavored with nuts and/or dried fruits is served on Christmas Eve and has been known in many cultures. In the Middle East, a similar dish is called *kahmieh*. In Armenia it is called *anoushabour*. The Old English Christmas puddings called *frumenty* (from the Latin *frumentum*, "wheat") are part of the same tradition. It is known in Russia, Lithuania, and in the Ukraine where it traditionally begins the Christmas Eve meal. The wheat berries were replaced by rice when it became readily available. Maria Estreicherówna in her *Życie Towarzyskie i Obyczajowe Krakowa w latach 1848–1863* (Social Life and Customs in Cracow in 1848–1863) mentions *kutia*: "The meal began with chocolate soup, eaten only once a year on this day, followed by four types of fish and then *kutia*, only modernized—prepared not with wheat but rice mixed with honey and poppy."

# Kutia

*Whole wheat berries can be found in most health food stores and co-operatives.*

1½ cups whole wheat berries
4 cups water
1½ cups raisins
1 cup poppy seeds
2 cups water
½ cup honey
½ cup chopped walnuts

1. Rinse wheat berries. Drain and place in heavy saucepan. Place in water and bring to a boil. Reduce heat to low, cover tightly, and simmer until wheat berries are tender. This may take up to an hour or more. If the berries are still hard and the water is evaporated, add additional water.
2. When tender drain whatever water is left over and set aside to cool.
3. Place poppy seeds in bowl filled with 2 cups of water and allow to stand a short time. Drain off any impurities that may float to the top. Place poppy seeds in saucepan and cover with 3 cups of water and simmer on stove until they begin to disintegrate when rubbed between fingers. Drain poppy seeds and when cool, grind in meat grinder or food processor.
4. Mix wheat berries with ground poppy seeds, honey, and chopped walnuts. For a very traditional look, serve in large wooden bowl.

TIMESAVER: To eliminate extra step of cooking and grinding poppy seeds, use one can (12-ounce) poppy seed filling.

SERVES 6 TO 8

## FRUIT

It is known through existing documents that 4800 oranges entered Poland through Gdansk in 1795. To receive an orange at Christmastime, even among the wealthy, was a rare treat. It is also known that by 1860, grapes, watermelons, and pineapples were being imported from Russia. These, too, were destined for the tables of the wealthy. Among the poor, most Christmas Eve meals concluded with a stewed fruit dish called *kompot*, or compote. Compote is one of those dishes that is eaten throughout the year in Poland both as a refreshing drink and as a dessert. During the bounty of summer it can be made from sweet and sour cherries, strawberries, blueberries. Compote made from plums, apples, pears, rhubarb, gooseberries, and currants was extremely popular. It was also an important traditional dish for Christmas Eve because the entire meal had to reflect the bounty of everything from the fields, forests, lakes, meadows, and trees. At this time of the year when fresh fruits were not available, the compote was made from fruit that had been dried earlier in the season and saved for winter use. In my mother's home, the apples were peeled, sliced, threaded through a string, and hung to dry across the front of the stove. When all the moisture was removed, the dried apple slices were stored away so that they could be enjoyed in a compote on Christmas Eve.

# COMPOTE

*(Kompot)*

*Even though we now have lots of fresh fruit to choose from in the winter, this recipe calls for the traditional fruits. If you'd like you can add dried raisins or prunes for additional variety.*

3½ cups water
¼ cup sugar
2 or 3 whole cloves
2 apples
2 pears
1 cup dried, pitted prunes or ½ cup dark raisins (optional)

1. Place water in medium-size saucepan, add sugar and cloves, stir together, and bring to a light boil over medium heat.
2. Wash fruit, quarter, and peel. Remove inner seeds and cut into slices. Add fresh and dried fruit to the lightly boiling sugar water. Bring mixture to boil again and cook lightly for 3 minutes. Remove from heat, cover with lid and allow to cool. Serve cold in small bowls or fruit cups.

SERVES 4

When the house was ready and the food prepared, the housewife made sure that everyone was dressed in their very best. The youngest child of the family was sent to watch the gradually darkening sky for the appearance of the first star. As dusk descended, the candles or kerosene lamps were lit, and the housewife prepared for the most important moment of the meal by placing a blessed wafer called *opłatek* on the nicest plate that she owned.

When the first star was sighted, the entire family and guests gathered around the table. The evening that celebrates the birth of Jesus Christ, the triumph of light over darkness, can begin. It is the time of *wigilia*, the very core and essence of Christmas Eve throughout Poland.

## *OPŁATEK*

Today and in yesteryear, the Christmas Eve meal called *wigilia* begins with a prayer. Everyone knelt or stood around the table, blessed themselves with the sign of the cross and prayed together out loud, grateful for all the blessings of the past year. Having done that, they shared the *opłatek*, one of Poland's most cherished traditions.

*Opłatek* is essentially unconsecrated bread wafer of the type used for holy communion in many different Christian religions. It has been suggested by Polish ethnographers that the sharing of this bread wafer at the *wigilia* table is a modification of what was once the sharing of a ritual bread called *podpłomyk*. This was a thin, flat bread traditionally baked before placing loaves of bread in the oven. It was eaten by the inhabitant of the house but also sent to neighbors as a goodwill gesture. Over time it evolved into today's *opłatek*—a thin, white rectangular wafer. White bread wafers were made for human consumption, while pink, red, and green wafers were given to the animals. The sharing of the wafer between family and friends was and still is conducted with great solemnity and care.

The male head of house began the solemn ceremony by taking the *opłatek* and turning to his wife, wished her good health for the upcoming year, success in her housekeeping, the fulfillment of her heart's desires, and perhaps—if there was strain between them—to forgive him his faults and that the year ahead of them be a good one.

At his conclusion, she expressed her thanks, broke off a piece of the wafer that was extended to her and consumed it. She then offered her husband a piece of her bread wafer, responding to him in kind: wishing good health and fortune, that they all be together at the next *wigilia* dinner and, because in the sharing of the *opłatek* one overlooks any ill-feeling, forgets hurts, and ends any enmity or unfriendliness, she accepts his words of reconciliation and asks that he, too, overlook her deficiencies. The husband would then break off a piece of the wafer extended to him, and eat it. The wafer was then shared with any older relatives present, honored guests, and then with the children, starting with the oldest and so on down the line. Everyone, down to the youngest child present, had the opportunity to say a few words and exchange good wishes. One of the wishes commonly offered was "*Życzę ci zdrowia, szczęścia i wielkiej fortuny a po śmierci w niebie koróny*" (I wish you health, good luck, and great fortune, and after death, a crown in heaven). Sometimes the wishes were simple and to the point, i.e., that the next holiday be a better one, that there be no lack of food or shortage of heat.

The *opłatek* has to be shared with a warm and willing heart free of any rancor or hostility. That is its essence. It is a time of sharing, of forgiveness, reconciliation, and goodwill. In olden days powerful and rich lords broke *opłatek* with their humble servants. Master craftsmen shared it with their apprentices. It was a bridge that united estranged family members. Anyone seeking entrance on this night would not be denied, even if he was one's worst enemy. Indeed, if your worst enemy appeared that night, it was often a signal that he wished to make peace. And neither time nor distance prevented people from sharing the *opłatek*. As families and friends migrated from Poland to countries throughout the world, a piece of *opłatek* was sent in a letter to say "I share this with you on Christmas Eve."

After everyone had had an opportunity to share the wafer and express what was in their hearts, the supper could begin. When the meal was concluded everyone stood together again to bless themselves and express their thanks with "*Dziękujemy ci Panie za Opatrzność Twoją*" (We thank you Lord for your providence). The plate with the *opłatek* was left on the table throughout the twelve days of Christmas and shared with anyone who visited. Some families believed in sharing the *opłatek* with their animals and took some along with left-over food out to the barn to feed their dog, cat or cow.

If you cannot find *opłatek* locally, a source for buying it is listed in the last chapter.

## The Twelve Days of Christmas

The time between Christmas day and the Feast of Three Kings (January 6) was a festive season in Poland filled with many rich traditions that included caroling and enacting various plays and pageants. The young boys carried *szopka* from house to house, knocking on doors, asking if they could come in and entertain those within by reenacting the Nativity as well as singing traditional Christmas carols. The *szopka* were portable manger scenes made by the children themselves with the help of adults. Sometimes one of the boys accompanied the singers by playing the harmonica or fiddle.

Other youths visited from home to home and sometimes village to village dressed in costumes, performing dramatic plays about King Herod and his edict to kill the infant Jesus. In the Silesian area of Poland, shepherd boys would remove the bells from the necks of their animals and attach them to their clothes. Adding chains and other clanging and jingling objects to their garb, they traveled from house to house singing and blowing on trumpets and recorders. For their entertainment efforts the children and youths often received a few coins but more often they were invited into the house and rewarded with something to eat and drink. One of the most frequently offered treats was the very popular and aromatic *piernik*. Every housewife strove to have plenty of these honeyed cookies to offer the children.

From the very oldest time in Poland, a plain cake of flour and honey called *miodownik* (honey cake) was made. It wasn't until much later that Poland enjoyed its first *piernik*, which differed from the *miodownik* in that it contained spices.

The first known "cake" with spices in Europe resembling gingerbread is credited to the Germans. Soon after the Crusades, the city

*Christmas carolers with a* szopka *in Kraków region, c. 1950. Photo by B. Czarnecki. Courtesy of the National Ethnographic Museum, Warsaw.*

*Christmas postcard, 1913. Archives of the National Ethnographic Museum, Warsaw.*

*Christmas postcard, 1947. Archives of the National Ethnographic Museum, Warsaw.*

of Nuremberg in Germany became the center of the spice trade as tons of ginger, pepper, and cinnamon came over the Alps from Venice. Gingerbread making as a trade came to Poland from Nuremberg when German bakers first took their wares to Torun. From Torun, gingerbread making spread to Kraków where in 1611 the first gingerbread guild arose under the Latin name Contubernium Cuchlororum, and then another arose in Warsaw. All the guild members were German and it was not unusual for the Germans to prevent Poles from entering the profession. It wasn't until 1842 that the name of a Pole by the name of Jan Wroblewski first enters the list of honey dough bakers.

It was the sole prerogative of the guilds to make and sell the honey cakes and they made tremendous amounts of money in the process. The older the dough, the better the honey cake. It got so that aged gingerbread dough was as good as money in the bank. There was a man by the name of Johann Wesse who gave his 18-year-old daughter in marriage endowed with 150 barrels of honeyed dough that had been put down the year of her birth.

Strategically located in the very center of Europe and on the major crossroads of all trade routes east and west, the spices eventually made their way into Poland. With the addition of spices, which were called *piernej* in Old Polish, the mixture of flour, honey, and spices came to be called *pierniki* and then nicknamed into the shorter *piernik.*

The baking of *piernik,* or gingerbread, began in the large cities of Toruń, Gdańsk, Kraków, and Tarnów and was developed by the gingerbread guilds during the Renaissance in much the same manner as they had been with the Germans and Czechs. Initially, only the rich aristocracy had the privilege of enjoying the taste of a honey cake laced with aromatic spices. Wooden molds which were intricately carved and detailed by artisans. Everyday scenes from the lives of the rich such as nobles in full regalia, fancy horse-drawn carriages, women in fancy dress, and coats of arms were sculpted, filled with dough, baked, and sold by the gingerbread guilds. Peak development in making *pierniki* in very detailed wooden molds occurred in the 16th and 17th centuries. The ingredients and methods used to make the dough were secrets passed down by masters to their students and zealously guarded against competitors.

In the 18th century, the market for gingerbread expanded to include the wealthy bourgeois. At the same time, the intricately carved wooden molds gave way to a simple form in which only the outer contours were cut out and the details were marked with the help of a brush and glazes—what we today call icing—on top. There began to appear scenes appropriate for the major holidays such as the Madonna and Child, angels, and St. Nick at Christmas, and the Crucifixion and lambs at Easter.

By the 18th century, little gingerbreads were selling at church fairs and market days, finding their way into the daily lives and small celebrations of country folk. Images of peasant life began to appear in the form of figures of animals especially the rooster, stork, bear, and deer. Eventually, the *piernik* took the function of a greeting card. Cut into heart shapes, names like Hania, Zosia, or messages such as "*Kocham cię*" (I love you) or "*Z serca*" (From the heart) were written on the surface for a boy to give to his sweetheart. Girls were more likely to buy a *piernik* that depicted a man on a horse for their loved one.

Over time, spices which initially had been available only in the larger cities, began filtering down into even the remotest villages. With the increasing availability of cinnamon, cloves, and ginger, housewives could now bake their own *pierniki* and not have to wait for the traveling peddlers who visited the villages on foot or set up their stalls at church fairs and market squares. Folk tradition called for the baking of *pierniki* from fine rye flour which was browned and leavened with warm virgin honey and spices. It was sometimes steeped in spirits. The dough was rolled out and cut into shapes or, if the housewife could not afford the cut outs from the tinsmith, cut into circles with a knife. In some regions of Poland, an almond was pressed into the top of the *piernik*. While it was decorative, it was also the ancient symbol for fending off evil and protecting against ill fortune.

Old references and recipes for *pierniki* almost unanimously agree that the secret of a good *piernik* is to let the unbaked dough rest or age for a whole week or even longer in a cool place. In order for it to take on the best flavoring it should be prepared before or on the feast of St. Lucy (December 13) or on the feast of St. Andrew (November 29). It was carefully baked in a stove that was neither too hot nor too cold, with the best results obtained in an oven "in which bread has just been baked." The cookies were distributed to carolers, given to neighbors as gifts, and exchanged between the male and female youths of the village.

*St. Nicholas gingerbread baked at Christmas. Southwestern Poland. Photo by Krzysztof Chojnacki. Courtesy of the National Ethnographic Museum, Warsaw.*

# Honey Cookies

***(Pierniki)***

*This is the recipe my mother used every Christmas to make dozens of cookies and store them in clear gallon jars. She called them* całuski *or little kisses, which referred to them being exchanged by the boys and girls of the country villages. Topped with a whole almond, they are simple and delicate tasting. The type of honey used makes a significant difference in the final flavor of the honey cake. Buckwheat honey will give the cookies a very distinctive dark color and taste. Clover honey will give it yet a different flavor.*

2 cups all-purpose flour
½ teaspoon baking soda
¼ teaspoon ground cinnamon
¼ teaspoon ground cloves
2 tablespoons butter
1 egg
3 tablespoons sugar
½ cup honey
1 egg yolk
30 whole almonds

1. Combine flour, baking soda, cinnamon, and cloves. Set aside.
2. In a large mixer bowl beat butter with egg, sugar, and honey until well blended. Add flour mixture and beat until combined. Cover and chill overnight for flavors to blend.
3. Preheat oven to 350°F.
4. On a lightly floured surface roll out half the dough at a time to ⅛-inch thickness. Keep remaining dough chilled. Cut with 2- or 2½-inch round cookie cutters or glass. Place on lightly greased cookie sheet. Lightly brush cookies with beaten egg yolk. Press 1 almond into center of each cookie.
5. If desired, use a drinking straw to make a ¼-inch hole near the top of the cookies before baking. After baking and cooling, thread ribbon through the hole and tie a bow or make a loop for a tree ornament. The cookies can also be finished with an icing instead of an almond for decoration.

6. Bake for 8 to 10 minutes, until golden. Remove from sheet and cool on wire racks.
7. Store in airtight container. If cookies harden, place a few slices of apple in the container until they soften.

MAKES APPROXIMATELY 2½ DOZEN COOKIES

## Recipe for What Ails You

Winter could be very difficult time for the very young and very old in Poland. Food privations, scarcity of heat and inadequate clothing all contributed to weakness and susceptibility to illnesses including colds and inflammations of the chest. Medicines were hard to come by and folk remedies didn't always rectify the problem. When someone was gravely ill, sometimes the last resort was to kill a chicken and ply them with chicken soup. This was no small matter since selling eggs was a source of cash for purchasing items that couldn't be produced at home such as salt or kerosene. In Galicia, the part of Poland that was under Austro-Hungarian rule during the time of the partitions, it was a test to give an ill person chicken soup. If the chicken soup did not help, it meant that the person was sure to die. This certainly gives you an idea of the restorative value placed on chicken soup!

If a chicken was sacrificed for the sake of a loved one, it made several meals. The broth was given to the very weak to build strength. The broth served over noodles, groats, or rice was a meal unto itself. The boiled meat served with boiled potatoes and a vegetable was a meal fit for a holiday. My mother used to buy her chickens live at Curley's Poultry Market. Hundreds of clucking hens in their cages! The noise! The stench! She killed the chicken herself, plucked the feathers, disemboweled it, and singed the pin feathers over the gas flame. I watched her do it so often I could do it myself (but please don't make me do it! Just the memory of those singed feathers makes my nose curl!) Chicken fat was never thrown away or seen as a bad thing. It was the fat that gave strength and restoration. A jar of rendered chicken fat was always lurking in the back shelf of our refrigerator next to a jar of goose grease which she rubbed on our chests when we had bad colds. And please don't remind me of the cod liver oil she forced down our gullets in wintertime!

# Chicken Broth

**(Rosół)**

*My mother always added the brown outer skins of the onion to the cooking pot. It gave her chicken soup a beautiful golden color.*

1 pound bony chicken pieces (backs, necks, wings)
2 quarts water
½ medium onion, cut in half
1 stalk celery with leaves, cut up
1 large carrot, cut in pieces
1 bay leaf
2 teaspoons salt
1 teaspoon pepper

1. Place rinsed chicken parts in a stockpot with the water. Add onion, celery, carrot, bay leaf, salt, and pepper and bring to a boil. Simmer, covered for 1 hour. Lift out chicken pieces with a slotted spoon. Pick over the bones and save any meat for another use.
2. Strain stock by pouring through a colander or sieve. Discard vegetables.

***Variation***: Follow step 1 but return any meat to pot with vegetables. Pour over cooked noodles or rice as a soup.

MAKES ABOUT 6 CUPS CLEAR BROTH

# Chicken Soup from Beef and Chicken

***(Rosół z wołowiny i kury)***

*This soup is made from combination of chicken and beef the way my mother did. We had this meal for Sunday dinner both winter and summer. It always conjures up the image of my entire family eating Sunday dinner while listening to the Polish mass that aired from St. Stanislaus Church in Buffalo, New York from 12 to 1 P.M.*

1 chicken, cut up
1 pound meaty beef bones or back ribs
3 quarts water
½ medium onion, cut in wedges
1 stalk celery with leaves, cut up
3 large carrots, cut in half and sliced lengthwise
2 bay leaves
2 teaspoons salt
1 teaspoon whole peppercorns
Cooked noodles or rice
Hot boiled potatoes
Butter
Sour cream
Chopped fresh dill (optional)

1. Place rinsed chicken and beef in a stockpot with the water. Add the onion, celery, carrots, bay leaves, salt, and peppercorns and bring to a boil. Simmer, covered, for 1 hour or until beef is tender.
2. For first course of dinner, pour broth over cooked noodles or rice and serve as soup.
3. For second course, remove meat and carrots from pot and arrange on platter. Serve with hot boiled potatoes topped with butter, sour cream, or fresh dill if it's in season.

SERVES 6

❖ Lucy's Household Hints: To handle frostbite of feet, hands, nose and ears, melt a tablespoon of fat from a goose, add a tablespoon of oatmeal and heat until it browns. Press through a sieve and allow to cool. Apply the mush as a salve for frostbitten areas.

## CARNIVAL *(Zapusty)* AND FAT *(Shrove)* TUESDAY

The French call it *Mardi Gras*. The Germans call it *Fasching*. The Poles called it *karnawał*, *ostatki* or *mięsopust* or *zapusty*. All refer to carnival time, which began anytime after February 2, also known as Candlemas.

The last week before Lent was the most active beginning with Thursday and ending with the last day called Fat Tuesday or Shrove Tuesday. It is a time before the fasting and rigors of Lent when all meat and dairy products were eliminated from the diet. Subsequently, the last few days before Lent were generally high in consumption of foods rich with butter, eggs, cream, and fats—all foods that were strictly avoided during the time of fast. The rich foods were shared with family, friends, and neighbors and the eating was accompanied by singing, dancing, and masquerading.

Traditional foods eaten during this time were crepes stuffed with cheese or meat, *chruściki*, (a type of fried dough) as well as doughnuts and pancakes of any kind including potato pancakes. Pancakes come under various names and guises in Poland. *Placki, racuchy, pampuchy,* or *pępuchy* were pancakes made with yeast and various types of flour. The preferred flour was wheat but many families made them from buckwheat and potato flour. Because they were all made with yeast they were sometimes called *drożdżaki*, or yeast cakes. The yeast dough was fried in fat and then sugared. The children ate them hot off the frying pan. *Racuchy* were eventually replaced by doughnuts.

### DOUGHNUTS

The Polish word for doughnuts is *pączki*. The word comes from the verb *pęcznieć*, "that which swells." It is known that doughnuts were being eaten in Kraków during the reign of King Jan Kazimierz (1648–1668). These were heavy and less appetizing than their later form when French and Viennese cooks came to Kraków in the second half of the 18th century and gave them their light consistency. The distinguished writer and historian, Reverend Jędrzej Kitowicz (1728–1804) wrote: "Nowadays the doughnuts are so plump and light that if you squeeze one in your hand it springs back to its original size like a sponge and a light wind would whisk it off the platter."

Doughnuts were extremely popular items during carnival time but traditionally were made the week before Ash Wednesday. Łukasz Gołębiowski mentions them in his writings. "Universal are doughnuts made with marmalade or plum jam. If the statistician of the Kuryer Warszawski is correct there were 31,000 of them sold at Lour's Bakery. They were also being sold at Minie at the corner of Freta Street and at Calstemur's in Old Town that were being sold for 4 to 6 pennies each. This isn't even mentioning the ones fried in private homes." The fillings included almond paste, jams, and preserves made from plums, rose hips, apricots, and cherries.

## Doughnuts

***(Pączki)***

4½ cups unbleached flour
3 egg yolks
2 eggs
Two ¼-ounce packages active dry yeast
1 cup milk
¼ cup (1 stick) butter
⅓ cup sugar
1 teaspoon salt
1 teaspoon vanilla
One 12-ounce can prune filling (also called *lekvar*)
Oil for frying
Confectioners' sugar

1. Bring flour and eggs to room temperature. In large mixing bowl combine 2 cups of the flour and the yeast.
2. In a saucepan heat milk, butter, sugar, and salt until butter melts. Cool down to 110° to 115°F.
3. Add liquids to flour and yeast mixture. Add vanilla, egg yolks, and eggs. Beat on low until mixture starts to come together. Stir in remaining 2½ cups flour ½ cup at a time until it is incorporated into the dough by either using a dough hook or by kneading on lightly floured surface. Continue kneading until smooth for 4 to 5 minutes.
4. Place dough in a greased bowl and turning once to grease surface. This is important to keep dough from drying out while rising. You can work a little extra oil over the surface of the dough with your fingertips.
5. Cover with a thick towel and allow to rise in a warm place away from draft, until doubled in bulk, about 1 hour.
6. Punch dough down, cover, and allow to rest for 10 to 15 minutes.
7. On lightly floured surface, roll out one half of the dough to ¼-inch thickness.
8. Using a 2½-inch round biscuit cutter or glass, cut out 24 circles. Trimmings from the dough can be re-rolled but do not re-roll too often or it will make doughnuts tough. Place completed circles on lightly floured baking sheet. Cover and let rise in a warm place until doubled in bulk, about 1 hour.

9. In deep-fat fryer or large heavy saucepan, heat at least two inches of oil to 325°F. Fry 4 or 5 doughnuts at a time for about 45 to 60 seconds on each side or until golden brown. Remove from pan with slotted spoon and drain on paper towels.
10. With a thin knife, cut a small slit on one end of the doughnut, going to the center of the doughnut. Wiggle the knife back and forth to create a pocket for the filling. Spoon the prune filling into a pastry bag fitted with ⅛-inch-round decorating tip. Insert pastry tip into slits in doughnuts and pipe some filling into each doughnut. Sift with confectionary sugar.

***Variation***: For unfilled doughnuts, follow steps 1 through 8 but with lightly floured doughnut cutter, cut out doughnuts. Re-roll "holes" and trimmings (or fry "holes" separately). Follow steps 9 through 11.

MAKES 24 DOUGHNUTS

# Apple Fritters

***(Jabłka w Cieście)***

*When my mother made fritters she used any apple that was on hand. After slicing into rings she cut the core and seeds out of the middle of the apple slice with her sewing thimble!*

2 to 3 winesap apples
1 cup flour
½ teaspoon salt
2 teaspoons baking powder
1 large egg
⅔ cup milk, at room temperature
2 tablespoons unsalted butter, melted
Oil for frying
Confectioners' sugar

1. Peel the apples and slice into ¼-inch-thick rings. Remove center core and seeds using a knife or very small biscuit cutter.
2. Mix flour, salt, baking powder, egg, milk, and melted butter lightly with spoon or whisk. Do not overbeat.
3. Heat enough vegetable oil in kettle or cast-iron frying pan to 3 inches in depth and bring to 375°F. Use a candy thermometer to measure temperature. This is important because if temperature is too low it will result in a soggy fritter. If it is too hot the batter will burn on the outside and remain uncooked inside.
4. Dip apple slices in batter to coat and fry until golden brown on both sides. Remove to plate covered with paper towels to absorb excess oil. Sprinkle with confectioners' sugar.

MAKES 12 TO 15 FRITTERS

# Crepes with Cheese

*(Naleśniki z serem)*

*I use an 8-inch, well-seasoned cast-iron frying pan to make these crepes. It makes it easy to swirl both the oil and batter over the surface of the pan as well as flip the crepe over to brown on the other side.*

Crepe Batter
3 eggs
1 cup flour
¼ teaspoon salt
1 tablespoon sugar
1 cup milk
1 tablespoon rum or whiskey
Oil for frying
1 to 2 tablespoons butter

Crepe Filling
1 pound farmer's cheese
1 egg yolk
3 tablespoons sugar
Yellow or dark raisins (optional)

1. Beat eggs in mixing bowl until frothy. Add flour, salt, and sugar and beat well.
2. Gradually add the milk. Beat well until you have a thin batter. Add rum or whiskey. Allow the batter to rest for at least 10 minutes before frying.
3. Place ½ teaspoon of oil in frying pan over medium heat. When hot, add a scant ¼ cup of batter to the frying pan. Holding the frying pan slightly above the stove, quickly swirl the batter until it reaches the outer edges of the pan. Allow to brown slightly for 30 to 45 seconds. Using a spatula, flip the crepe to other side for same amount of time. Remove to plate or platter.
4. Repeat step 3 until all batter is used up.

5. *To Make the Filling:*
   Mix the cheese, egg yolk, and sugar together thoroughly.

6. *To Fill and Fold the Crepes:*

   *Method 1.* Spread 1 to 2 heaping tablespoons cheese mixture on half of a crepe. Fold crepe in half and in half again.

   *Method 2.* Spread 1 to 2 heaping tablespoons cheese mixture in center of crepe and spread to within 1 inch of the sides. Fold ⅓ of the crepe over the filling and then fold over the other ⅓ of the crepe. Fold in ends to form a small packet.

   *Method 3.* Spread 1 to 2 tablespoons of the cheese mixture on half of the crepe. Roll the crepe into a cylinder.

7. When finished folding crepes, melt the butter in a frying pan. Place as many crepes, seam side down, as will fit into your frying pan. Fry over medium heat for 4 to 5 minutes until heated through and golden brown. Transfer to ovenproof platter and place in oven to keep warm until all crepes are fried. Serve with sugar, syrup, or fruit.

MAKES 12 TO 14 CREPES

## HOW TO FOLD CREPES . . .

**METHOD #1** • SPREAD 2-3 TABLESPOONS FILLING OVER THE INSIDE HALF OF A CREPE. ROLL CREPE

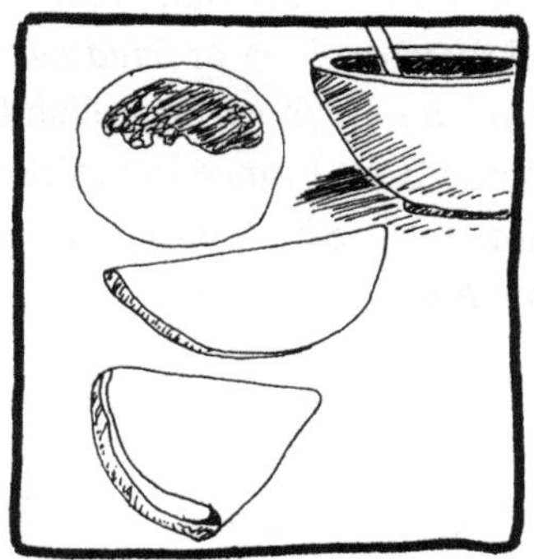

**METHOD #2** • SPREAD 2-3 TABLESPOONS FILLING OVER THE INSIDE HALF OF A CREPE. FOLD CREPE IN HALF, THEN IN HALF AGAIN.

**METHOD #3** • SPREAD 2-3 TABLESPOONS FILLING OVER CENTER OF CREPE, LEAVING A 1-INCH BORDER. FOLD 1/3 CREPE OVER FILLING, THEN FOLD IN OTHER 1/3 CREPE. FOLD ENDS IN TO FORM A SMALL PACKET.

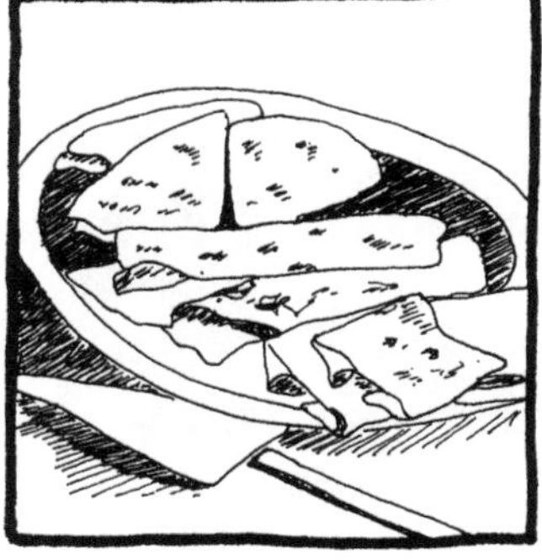

SAUTÉ CREPES OVER MEDIUM HEAT ABOUT 3 MINUTES ON EACH SIDE OR UNTIL EVENLY BROWNED.

## FRIED DOUGH

Almost every nation has its version of fried dough. The Dutch called them *kulljes*. Russians call them *hvorost* or *khvorost*, a word used to denote firewood or kindling because they look like branches covered with snow. Ukranians call them *verhuny or werczuny*. Americans call them *crullers* or *fried twists*. The Poles call them *chróst*, *chrusty, chruściki,* or *faworki*. Polish historians claim that *chruściki* came to Poland from France in the 1800s when all things French were highly valued. Here in America, Polish Americans call them *angel wings* or *bow ties*.

# Fried Dough

***(Chruściki)***

*My mother always called out merrily* "Chrusty, chrusty na zapusty" *when she mixed the dough for chrusciki, always adding a small jigger of my father's favorite Kessler whiskey to the ingredients. I loved listening to her stories about how all the neighbors would get together to make them. One neighbor brought eggs, another flour, and the third the fat to fry them in.*

4 eggs
4 egg yolks
1½ cups confectioners' sugar
2 tablespoons whiskey or rum
3 cups all-purpose flour
3 to 4 cups vegetable oil or shortening for frying

1. In large mixing bowl beat eggs, yolks, and ½ cup of the confectioners' sugar with electric mixer until light and fluffy.
2. Add the whiskey or rum along with the flour. You should obtain a stiff, slightly sticky dough.
3. On a well-floured surface, gently roll half of the dough into a 12 × 6-inch rectangle. Cut into 1½-inch-wide strips and then cut along the strips at an angle. You can make your *chrusciki* long and substantial (as my mother did) or shorter for a daintier look. Make a small slit in middle. Carefully pull one end of strip through the slit. Repeat with remaining strips.
4. Heat oil in wide pan to 375°F. Fry 2 to 3 *chruściki* at a time in hot fat, 15 to 30 seconds on each side or until golden. Remove with slotted spoon and drain on paper towels. Repeat with remaining strips. When cooled, place the remaining cup of confectionary sugar in a small strainer and shake lightly (or more heavily depending on preference) over the *chruścicki.* Best if eaten same day. Can be stored in airtight containers.

MAKES 4 DOZEN

❖ LUCY'S HOUSEHOLD HINTS: One of the most important concepts in making good *chruściki* is to prevent the dough from lying around and drying out. The oil should be slowly heating as you make the dough.

• CHRUSCIKI •

COMPLETED BOW TIE, ANGEL WING

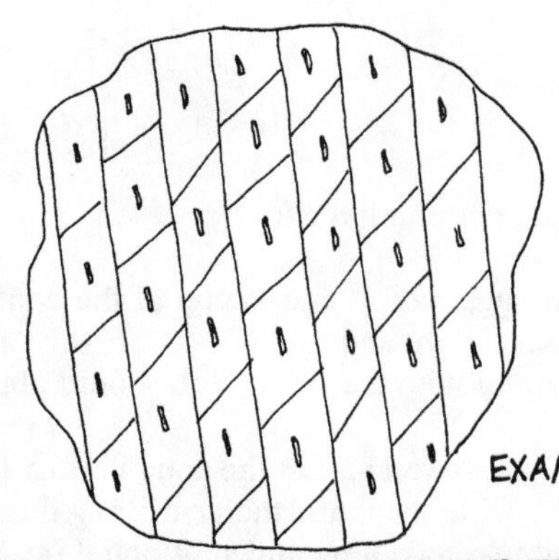

EXAMPLE OF CUTTING DOUGH FOR CHRUSCIKI

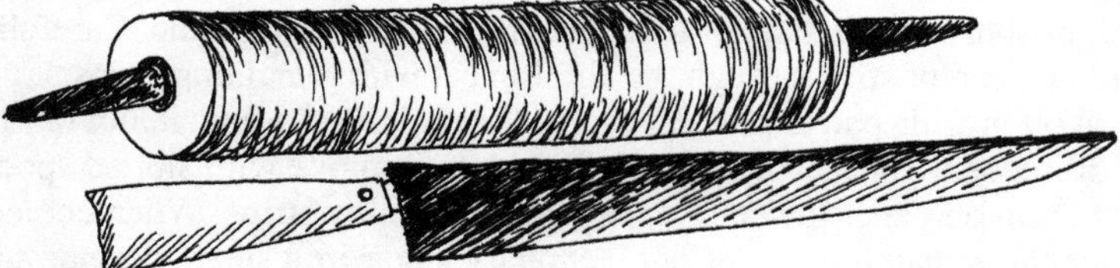

Other traditional foods served during carnival time were fried or boiled eggs. This has been preserved in Polish folk song:

*Jak cię nie żałować*
*mój miły zapuście*
*Jedno jajko w grochu*
*A drugie w kapuście.*

If you're not too stingy
My dear carnival
One egg in the peas
Another in the sauerkraut.

# Fried Eggs and Noodles

***(Jajka z kluskami)***

*I love this simple dish. My mother served it all the time for a quick and filling supper. When she had leftover noodles or macaroni of any sort, she heated them up on her own rendered lard with cracklings, called* smalec, *for added flavor. She served peas or her home-canned green beans on the side.*

2 tablespoons butter or bacon drippings
One 12-ounce package medium-size noodles, cooked
6 to 8 beaten eggs
Salt and pepper

1. In large frying pan, melt butter or bacon drippings on low heat. Add noodles and slowly heat through.
2. Add eggs and stir through the noodles until eggs are cooked. Salt and pepper to taste and serve immediately.

SERVES 3 TO 4

## BRAISED BEEF

Like chicken, beef was not a meat that country folk tasted very often. It had to be a truly special situation to warrant the cost. *Zrazy* is beef that has been generously cooked with fat and cracklings, onions, and a thick sauce made from browned flour, spices, and mushrooms. There were numerous types of *zrazy*: flat, rolled and stuffed with onions, pickles, horseradish, or mushrooms. There was also chopped beef made in its own sauce with onions and mushrooms. There is *zrazy à la Nelson*, supposedly named after Admiral Nelson, layered with potatoes, and *zrazy à la Napoleon* with layers of beef and vegetables covered with a white wine and sealed in a dough.

# Braised Beef

*(Zrazy)*

*This meat dish was something my mother served for Sunday dinner with buckwheat groats and hot grated beets on the side.*

1 to 2 pounds thin-cut sirloin or top round
1 teaspoon salt
1 teaspoon pepper
½ cup flour
2 tablespoons vegetable oil
1 medium onion, chopped
1 quart (4 cups) water
½ pound fresh mushrooms, sliced
1 beef bouillon cube

1. Cut meat into desired serving portions. Mix together salt, pepper, and flour and place on plate. Dredge the meat in the flour.
2. Heat oil in Dutch oven. When oil is hot place meat pieces and onions inside and allow to brown. The flour will stick to the bottom of the pan. This is perfectly alright. You want the flour to brown along with the meat. It will give your gravy a nice brown color. Stir the meat to keep it from burning yet allowing it to brown.
3. Add the water and stir. The liquid will thicken due to the flour. Add mushrooms and bouillon cube.

Allow to cook for at least an hour or until meat is tender. If gravy thickens too much, add small amount of water to reach desired consistency.

SERVES 4 TO 6

## Ash Wednesday and Lent

As Fat Tuesday drew to a close, the housewives scalded their larders, pots, and pans to free them of any traces of fat in preparation for the meatless days of Lent which began the very next day on Ash Wednesday.

During the Middle Ages there were 192 fast days in Poland throughout the calendar year. This included the long fasts of Lent and Advent, Fridays, the evening before most popular holy days and sometimes even on Mondays. Besides not eating meat for 51 days of the year, they were unable to eat eggs, milk, and butter during the fasts. In spite of these rigid restrictions, the people of Poland adhered strictly to the rules of the church. It was said that "A Mazur (someone from Mazowsze) would sooner kill someone than break his fast."

The most rigid fast period was that of Lent when even milk and milk products were forbidden. If a housewife had a cow and milked regularly, the milk was made into cheeses and dried. The cheese was stored and consumed during harvest season when farm work was at its peak and left little time for cooking.

The chief source of food during the Lenten season was fish. It was eaten fresh or preserved, either salted, dried, or smoked. Salted fish in barrels was one of the main Lenten dishes of the servants and officials in the court of Jadwiga and Jagiełło. The fish most often dried were roach, bream, and gudgeon. They were placed in a heated oven on a bed of straw until sufficiently dried and then stored in bags and hung in attics.

The most popular fish consumed during Lent was herring. According to a document from the Małopolska region of Poland, it was already being sold as an import along with fabric and salt in 1264. Herring was one of the items of distant trade, entering at Gdansk and transported down the Wisła and its tributaries. It was then further transported on land and subsequently appears on the records of customs-houses. By the 15th century it was one of the main items sold in village and town marketplaces. In large cities there were even special areas in the market place designated just for the sale of herring. Two things accounted for its popularity. The first was that it was fairly cheap. At the end of the 14th century, 100 soaking herring cost 10 *złoty* (coppers or pennies). Unsoaked, the price rose to 12 *złoty*. The second reason was that it was valued for its saltiness which, unlike today, was considered desirable.

## *ŻUR*

One of the other main foods consumed during Lent was a soup called *żur*, a meatless soup made from fermented rye flower. It was also made from wheat or wheat bran that was common in Kujawy, Kraków region, and that portion of Poland called Galicia during the partitions of Poland. Oats were also used to make the *żur* in southern Pohale region. In southern Podlasie the country people had their own version of soured buckwheat called *kwas*. To confuse matters even further *żur* was also called *kwaśny barszcz* or simply, *barszcz*. The terms were used interchangeably.

To make *żur* the housewife mixed rolled oats or coarsely ground oat or rye flour with warm water in a special 2-liter crock made from unglazed pottery called a *żurownik*. Sometimes a piece of rye bread was thrown in to aid the fermenting process. Garlic and salt were added to improve the taste. The crock was covered with a clean cloth and placed near a warm stove to ferment for at least two days.

When it came time to make the soup, the mixture was strained through a cheesecloth, especially if rolled oats were used, and heated. It could also be poured over cooked grains or plain boiled potatoes for breakfast, lunch, or dinner or served just about any time of day to fill a hungry stomach. At times other than Lent, salt pork, milk, or cream were added. The Polish ethnographer, Łukasz Gołębiowski, claimed that the Russian people had the equivalent of *żur* but they called it *kisiel*. It was much thicker than *żur* and sometimes chilled and cut with a knife.

# SPRING

Wiosna

*Easter postcard, 1932. Archives of the National Ethnographic Museum, Warsaw.*

## EASTER

Easter, the feast of the Resurrection of Christ, is the greatest holy day of the Polish year. Pope Leo the Great called it the feast of feasts, regarding it as the most joyous observance of the Church. Its importance was highlighted by a long period of fasting during Lent and by the special observances of Holy Week.

## HOLY WEEK

The period of Holy Week is extremely rich in customs and traditional recipes. The week begins with Palm Sunday. In the Christian calendar, Palm Sunday celebrates the triumphant entry of Jesus Christ into Jerusalem and ushers in the most important days of the church year. Everyone attended Mass and all the churches were filled with the earliest greenery. In Poland, pussy willows were among the first shrubs and trees to release their buds or catkins. Easily found throughout Poland along streams and growing wild in the fields, Polish people brought the newly budded branches to church, and over the centuries they have come to be synonymous with a Polish Easter. However, there were numerous other types of greenery in Poland's history that were used as palms. These include alder buckthorn, boxwood, yew, hazelwood, pine, and juniper. After being blessed, the "palms" were brought home and tucked behind holy pictures or into vases and placed on "God's corner" or the table or dresser that acted as the home altar. It was believed that the blessed palms protected the home against lightning and hail, and protected the inhabitants within as well. It was even customary to swallow one of the catkins as a means of assuring good health for the following year.

The first days after Palm Sunday were devoted to scrubbing and decorating the main room of the house. The housewife washed her windows and hung new curtains. Flowers were made from tissue paper and tucked behind holy pictures. The bed linens were freshened and the best pillow coverings were slipped on. *Wycinanki*, brightly colored paper cut-outs, were pasted to the walls. This was especially critical if her house was chosen to be the one where the priest visited to bless the baskets.

After putting the house in order, the housewife began the serious business of cooking and baking. Since most homes were self sufficient, planning and preparation had occurred long before this day. The pig for hams and sausage would have been slaughtered weeks, even months, ahead and been smoking or curing for some time. The fine white flour was saved for the special baking. Butter was staying fresh in the springhouse or cellar. There was some homemade beer, vodka, or wine, and teas from rose hips which she had been saving. In the end, whether well-to-do or poor, the Polish country housewife would prepare the best she could with what she had available.

## *ŚWIĘCONKA*

*Święconka* is the name given to the basket of food that is taken to church to be blessed on Holy Saturday. *Święconka* is also the name given to the Easter morning breakfast that is eaten after returning home from the early morning Resurrection Mass because the breakfast consisted of the food that was taken to church to be blessed on the previous day. When the Polish housewife planned her Easter menu, she was essentially planning what foods were going to be taken to church to be blessed on Holy Saturday and then consumed the next day on Easter Sunday.

There were numerous variations on the quantity of food prepared for Easter *święconka* in Poland or the way it was prepared. Much depended on what a person could afford. When you strip it down to its bare bones, however, traditionally it consists of some type of pork—either whole roasted pigs with an apple or hard-boiled egg in their mouth and served up on a bed of greenery, or whole smoked hams and/or sausage. Sausage, or *kiełbasa*, has been a perennial favorite at the Polish Easter table for centuries. In the second half of the 17th and beginning of the 18th century, twelve different kinds of sausage could be found on the tables of the very rich. Among nobles and magnates there were as many as twenty-four varieties! It was served fresh, smoked, as small links, as enormously long rings, or sliced in soup.

The other foods that are traditional are eggs. These could be stuffed, prepared in aspic, and a million other forms. The Polish country peasant liked his egg hard-boiled and eaten plain. Indeed, even the tables of the rich and famous boasted plain hard-boiled eggs along with a host of other methods of preparation. There were also homemade cheeses and breads made of the finest wheat flour, or hearty rye, sourdough, or potato breads. There were special cakes in the shape of a lamb, or a loaf cake called *placek*, and/or a cake called a *baba* studded with raisins.

In the Opole region, a traditional Easter wreath was made of braided yeast bread studded with colored eggs and decorated with boxwood. In the Cieszyn region, the braided yeast bread was covered with chopped nuts. Another characteristic bread from this area was one that was baked with pieces of ham or sausage inside. In the Opole region, these breads were called *szołdry,* while in the Cieszyń region they were called *marziny*. The girls would present the young men with these bread delicacies on dyngus day, Easter Monday. There were condiments such as horseradish or horseradish mixed with grated cooked beets called *ćwikła*.

On Good Friday and Holy Saturday, the housewife began cooking and baking until the house was fragrant with the sweet and spicy smells of baking ham, bread, and cakes. The goal of the housewife was to have everything done so that the food would be ready to be blessed by Saturday afternoon.

## *The* **Święconka** *Basket*

The *święconka* basket was (and still is) filled with food that has been blessed by a priest. The housewife chose a basket as small or as large as she needed. In these modern days baskets are fairly common and inexpensive, but in old Poland, if someone did not have a suitable basket, a large wooden bowl was substituted or even a small drawer from a dresser was used.

When she had her food prepared, the housewife lined the bottom of the basket or bowl with a piece of homemade linen or special cloth that she had woven, crocheted, embroidered, or inherited. The most traditional foods that were neatly arranged in the basket or bowl were bread, hard-boiled eggs, butter, sausage, horseradish, and salt. Anything else was dependent on the whims of the housewife such as wine, a pastry, or a sweet cake called a *baba* or *babka*. Some housewives included a favorite item such as honey or a cheese tied with a red ribbon. Others liked to tuck a small bundle of pussy willows or bits of greenery such as boxwood around the coiled sausage. Sometimes housewives added potatoes or flax seeds. The most humble of baskets contained a few hard-boiled eggs, butter, and cheese and were decorated with bits of greenery such as moss or branches of huckleberry. The basket was then covered with a clean cloth, a piece of embroidered linen, or a fringed scarf. It was ready to be blessed.

### *Symbolism of Foods in the* **Święconka** *Basket*

Centuries have passed since the first blessing of the food on Holy Saturday and the Catholic church has ascribed special meanings and symbolism to the food placed in the Easter *święconka* basket.

*Paschal Lamb*—a representation of the Lamb of God, it is usually of butter, cake, or sugar and is the centerpiece of the foods brought to church to be blessed.

*Eggs*—a symbol of new life, of rebirth.

*Meat*—a symbol of prosperity, especially pork such as ham and sausage (kielbasa). It is also reminiscent of the Old Law of the Old Testament which forbade pork. Christ fulfilled the Old Law and subsequently pork is eaten on the day of that fulfillment.

*Horseradish*—a bitter herb that signifies the bitterness of the suffering of Christ and the gall given to Christ on the cross.

*Salt*—a basic spice and preservative. In Polish tradition offering guests bread and salt is a sign of hospitality.

*Greenery*—a symbol of the awakening and greening earth at this time of year. Boxwood has been traditional.

*Bread*—a symbol of the bread of communion, the bread of the Last supper. The round loaves are usually topped with a cross.

## THE BLESSING OF FOOD

When all was prepared on Holy Saturday, the housewife was ready to have her food blessed. The blessing of the food was a critical necessity. Writing in 1904, an ethnographer documenting the Easter customs of the Nowy and Stary Sącz regions of Poland states "they bless what they have. Besides common foodstuffs, they also bless salt and lard or butter. The blessed salt they pour on fire during times of lightening and storms."

Polish ethnographers have documented that initially the custom was for priests to visit the homes and bless the baskets. Sometimes he went from home to home, being careful not to omit even the most humble cottage. In some regions it was the custom for one of the homes in the village to be chosen as the gathering place for the blessing of the baskets and everyone would assemble there to await the priest. All the baskets and bowls were placed on the table or on benches gaily decorated with greenery such as periwinkle or boxwood.

In regions where there was only one parish for numerous small villages and hamlets, there was a known designated spot for everyone to bring their baskets. This could be at a roadside shrine at some major crossroads. Mothers and children would walk or ride to the nearest site clutching their baskets, anxious so as not to miss the priest.

In her book *Rok Polski*, Zofia Kossak portrays food being blessed at a small village:

*Blessing of food. Date and location unknown. Archives of the National Ethnographic Museum, Warsaw.*

*Country women from the Kraków region waiting for the priest to arrive to bless their food baskets. Date unknown. Archives of the National Ethnographic Museum, Warsaw.*

*Blessing of food on Holy Saturday in Sarzyna near Leżajsk. Photo by K. Chojnacki. Courtesy of the National Ethnographic Museum, Warsaw.*

*Blessing of food in the village of Olszewnica outside of Warsaw, 2000. Photo by Krystyna Bartosik.*

*At the church cemetery, under a bare linden tree, the women sat in a circle holding a basket with food. At the bottom (of the basket) was a snow white cloth on which was placed bread, the basic staff of life, butter, a cheese as round as the moon, salt, sweet bread and sausage—everything beautifully decorated with painted eggs, the blue flowers of periwinkle and the green leaves of boxwood.*

Sometimes the basket of food was blessed at the church immediately after the Resurrection mass. This makes sense when one considers the distance that sometimes had to be traveled to get to church on foot or by horse and wagon. Taking the food to church on Holy Saturday was a much later version of blessing of food and it was this custom that was brought to the United States by Polish immigrants and continues to be one of the much loved customs of Holy Week.

After returning home from being blessed, the basket was placed on the table in God's corner. The food would be eaten the following morning after the sunrise service.

## Easter *Święconka* I

Cold Baked Ham
Fresh Sausage with Marjoram
Smoked Sausage
Thickly Sliced Rye Bread
Butter Lamb
Beet Relish *(Ćwikła)*
Hard-Boiled Eggs
Almond Pastry, Babka, Krupnik

## Easter *Święconka* II

Red Beet Soup with Uszki
Thinly Sliced Cold Ham
Fresh Sausage with Marjoram
Smoked Sausage
Hard-Boiled Eggs
Basket of Assorted Breads
Homemade Horseradish and Mustard
Lamb Cake
*Placek*
Iced Vodka

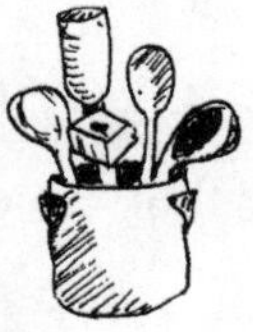

# Hard-Boiled Eggs

*Hard-boiled eggs with the shells removed are at the heart of the* święconka *basket and at the* święconka *breakfast. Never boil the eggs to doneness. If eggs are boiled or overcooked, the yolks will turn an unattractive greenish gray around the whites.*

1 or 2 eggs per person

1. Put the eggs in a saucepan roomy enough to hold them without overcrowding and cover with cold water by at least an inch or two.
2. Heat water with eggs until completely boiling.
3. Remove the saucepan from heat, cover tightly, and let stand for 15 minutes.
4. Pour out the hot water and run cold water over the eggs. It will make peeling easier.
5. Crack the egg against a flat surface. Peel the eggs under running cold water, beginning at the large end. Store shelled eggs in a tightly covered container in the refrigerator, after taking to church to be blessed, to prevent drying out.

## EGG DECORATION

Coloring eggs for Easter is a very old and ancient tradition. On Holy Thursday or Good Friday, the women of the house sat down to color eggs. There were different ways of decorating the eggs. For *kraszone* or *kraszanki*, a single color was applied by using roots and herbs. The earliest egg decorating utilized vegetables, fruits, spices, and tea. In the Orawa region, the housewife often used dyes made from boiling onion skins and the grains of rye. Household items such as vinegar and alum were used to make the colors hold.

## NATURAL EGG DYES

These were the most commonly used items to produce colors:

Yellow onion skins—dark yellow to copper
Beets—light pink
Blueberries—blue-gray
Dried hibiscus flowers—lavender
Turmeric—golden yellow
Teas—mellow terra-cotta brown

As the name implies, *malowane* or *malowanki* were eggs that were painted with a colorful design on top. These were sometimes called *byczki*. Another style was *oklejane* and *nalepianki* when the outside of the egg was decorated with colored paper, ribbon, straw, or yarn. The most famous type of egg decorating was *pisanki*. This was and still is an ancient Polish folk art form of decorating eggs with various designs. The root word for this form of Easter egg decorating comes from the Polish word *pisać* which means "to write." It was a craft passed on from one generation to another, very often mother to daughter, but men became involved in decorating eggs also. Various designs were drawn on the surface of an egg using a pin or nail dipped in hot wax. After the design was drawn, it was placed in a dye bath or solution. The wax protected the design beneath it. When the design was completed, the wax was removed by holding the egg near a candle flame and the wax wiped from the egg. Some individuals worked for hours making the most exquisite designs. Making *pisanki* is the subject of numerous, readily available books so I will not dwell on them here and refer you to the source list in the appendix for further information.

## EASTER LAMB

The Easter Lamb is the most significant symbol of a Christian Easter. The *Agnus Dei*, (Latin for "the lamb of God") with a banner of victory or the depiction of a lamb balancing a cross on one of its hooves, became a symbol of Jesus and the Resurrection. The Easter lamb became an important focus of Christian art and eventually became popular as a symbol among Easter decorations.

The custom of placing a lamb on the Easter table was introduced by Pope Urban V (1362–1370). This particular custom began to be initiated in Poland during the reign of King Zygmunt III Waza (1587–1632) when he placed a lamb made of gold on his Easter table. In 1685, an Italian by the name of Alfierini presented a lamb to Queen Maria, wife of King Jan Sobieski (1674–1696). It was covered with the down of a swan made to look like wool and had an 8-inch banner on which the word *alleluja* was written 18,250 times! The number represented the number of days that the queen had lived. On pressing a spring, the lamb would rise. In return, the Queen gave the Italian a ring on which the word *alleluja* was spelled out in gems. Wealthy nobles began copying the royal family with lambs made of alabaster and studded with precious and semiprecious stones.

Over time it became more and more customary for people from all ranks and socioeconomic status to have a symbol of the lamb of God on the Easter table. Country folks initially made their lambs out of butter, a commodity they had immediate access to. In later years, when it was cheaper and more widely available, sugar was used and then the two combined into the form of a cake. Subsequently they were made of numerous other materials including chalk, wax, and gypsum but the lambs made of butter remained consistently popular.

*Easter postcard, 1923. Private collection of Krystyna Bartosik.*

Butter lambs were shaped by either using a mold or free form. The lamb was placed on a "field" of bittercress (*Cardamine pratensis*), one of the first types of greenery to appear in the meadows of Poland. In the Opole region it was traditional to make a cake in the shape of a lamb. By the 17th century there wasn't a home in Poland that didn't celebrate the Easter holiday with a symbol of the lamb of God, affectionately called *agnuszek.* Long ago it was typical for the faithful to eat lamb on Easter Sunday. Father Newerani wrote of this custom in 1739 "the blessing of the lamb represents the real Lamb of Christ and his triumph, that is why it is customary to place a victory banner on a baked lamb." In the 17th century, de Labourer wrote "Everyone on this day has a baked lamb on the table."

A lamb is still one of the most prominent features of the Easter table. Every family can choose their particular medium for the Easter lamb for their Easter table. I offer here two traditional forms that were typical in a country cottage: the homemade butter lamb and the lamb cake.

*Easter postcard, 1918. Archives of the National Ethnographic Museum, Warsaw.*

# Butter Lamb

*When the women of Poland made their butter they added a bit of juice from a carrot to make it more yellow if it was too pale. In the Podhale and Spisz region it was customary for the women on Good Friday to make their butter while dressed in their nightshirts. No one today can enlighten us as to why. They called it* Wielkopiątkowe masło *(Good Friday butter).*

1 stick butter

1. Allow the butter to soften almost to room temperature.
2. Place on plate, and using a paring knife, cut off ¼ piece and place on top of the remaining piece. This will form the rough shape for the lamb.
3. Begin shaping the neck of the lamb by scooping out where the two pieces meet along all four sides. Place the scoopings against the bottom piece of butter along the front, sides, the back end or on the top. This will begin filling out the body while giving shape to a neck.
4. Round out the edges of the head using the knife and continue to place the scrapings on the top of the smaller piece to give round shape to the head.
5. To make the ears, load the tip of your paring knife with a little bit of the butter and shape it along the tip of the knife being careful not to cut yourself. Then place the knife with the point facing downward at the side of the head and draw the knife upwards.
6. Use cloves or peppercorns for eyes.
7. By this time the butter will be sufficiently soft. Using a toothpick, make a circular forward and backward motion in the butter along the sides, back of the lamb as well as the back and sides of head for a fleecy look.
8. Using the tip of your toothpick, imbed a very small piece of parsley where the mouth would be. This gives the appearance that the lamb is partaking of some spring greenery.
9. Place a piece of thin red ribbon around the neck and cross over at the base of the neck. It will stay in place by virtue of sticking to the butter.
10. Make the red banner out of construction paper or ribbon that is 1½ inch wide. Make a white cross on the banner with white paper or thin white ribbon. The cross can also be bought at craft stores. Glue the banner to a white cocktail straw, bamboo stick, or whatever is on hand that is suitable.
11. Tuck greenery around the lamb (curly parsley, alfalfa sprouts) to give the impression of a lamb on a newly greened meadow.

## • EASTER BUTTER LAMB •

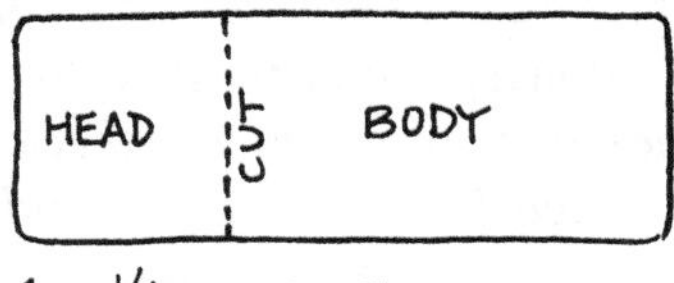


1• 1/4 LB. BUTTER

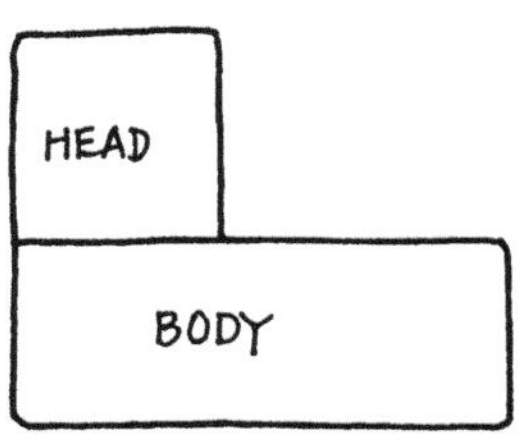


2• PLACE CUTOFF PIECE ON TOP FOR HEAD.

3• SHAPE INTO LAMB AND DECORATE.

# Lamb Cake

***(Agnuszek)***

*This cake recipe requires a two-part metal mold in the shape of a sitting lamb. The mold is approximately 10 inches long at the base and stands 7¾ inches tall from the base to the top of the head. Some families have passed this mold down from generation to generation. If you'd like to start the tradition in your own home, check with better culinary stores. They can also occasionally still be found in antique stores or flea markets.*

*The batter fits perfectly into the face portion of the mold and makes for a delicious, firm cake that can withhold the rigors of popping out of the mold with everything intact.*

¾ cup granulated sugar
½ cup shortening
2 eggs
1 teaspoon vanilla
1¾ cup all-purpose flour
1½ teaspoons baking powder
¼ teaspoon salt
⅓ cup milk

1. Preheat oven to 350°F. Grease insides of both parts of the lamb mold very well, paying special attention to the tip of the nose and the ears. Dust inside lightly with flour.
2. In large mixing bowl beat sugar with shortening until light and creamy. Beat in 1 egg at a time, beating well in-between. Add vanilla and beat well again. Add flour and baking powder. Continue beating. Add salt and milk and beat again. Batter will be thick.
3. Pour batter into face portion of the mold beginning with the face and ears and then rest of body. Shake mold against solid surface to make sure batter settles into all the small crevices.
4. Cover with second half of mold and place carefully on rack in oven.
5. Bake for 45 to 50 minutes. Test for doneness by inserting a wooden skewer into the holes in the back portion of the mold. If skewer is still damp or wet, bake an additional 5 to 10 minutes.

6. Remove from oven. Carefully take off the back portion of the mold. Cool in mold for 5 minutes and then carefully remove cake from second half of the mold.
7. Place on platter or cake plate covered with paper or cloth doily. Allow to cool completely. Brush any loose crumbs from the cake carefully with soft pastry brush. Lamb can be left plain or apply a frosting of your choice.
8. Place a piece of thin red ribbon around the neck and cross over at the base of the neck. It will stay in place by virtue of sticking to the frosting. Or, if you have one, string a small bell on thin ribbon and tie at the back of the neck.
9. Make the red banner out of construction paper or ribbon that is 1½ to 3 inches wide. Make a white cross on the banner with paper or thin ribbon. Glue banner to a cocktail straw, bamboo stick, wooden skewer, or whatever is on hand that is suitable. The cross can also be bought at craft stores.
10. Tuck greenery around the lamb (curly parsley, alfalfa sprouts) to give the impression of a lamb on a newly greened meadow. Use small gum drops, jellybeans, peppercorns, whole cloves, or star anise for eyes.
11. Decorate around the lamb with colored eggs, *pisanki*, and a sprig of pussy willows or yellow forsythia.

SERVES 8

## *BABA*

In Polish vocabulary the word *baba* conjures up many different meanings. It is the name given to an old married woman and to a midwife. It was also the name given to a type of pear that grew in Poland at one time. The word *baby* is also an old-fashioned Polish word for a constellation of stars. It is most well-known, however, as the name for a special yeast cake baked for Easter that was made of fine wheat flour, raisins, eggs, and sometimes cheese, called a *baba* or *babka*.

Many believe that it takes its name from the Polish word for old woman because it is baked in a traditional fluted baking pan that resembles a woman's thickly gathered skirt that fans out towards the bottom. Some say that the origin of Poland's *baba* however, is attributed to Polish King Stanislaus Leszczynski, who was at one time exiled in Lorraine, France. After partaking of that country's *kouglhof* he thought it too dry and improved upon it by adding rum. He is said to have named his creation after his favorite hero, Ali Baba from *The Thousand and One Nights*. The recipe was supposedly a great success and was taken up by cooks and French pastry chefs.

Whatever the source of the name, the *staroploska baba*, or old Polish *baba*, was a rich golden yeast dough studded with raisins. The golden color came from the use of saffron. The *baba* recipes of old called for as many as 60 egg yolks, the whitest flour, freshest butter, and the addition of costly spices such as saffron and other expensive ingredients such as raisins. A *baba koronkowa* was an Easter *baba* made from 24 egg yolks along with butter, flour, sugar, and yeast.

Polish historians claim that the traditional *babas* were baked in clay or copper molds in the shape of a Turk's turban. *Baba* forms made from stoneware were preferred as they cooled slowly and decreased the possibility of the cake falling flat and causing the housewife embarrassment. *Babas* were also baked in well-oiled clay or terra-cotta flowerpots. According to Polish ethnographer Zygmunt Gloger, the petty gentry baked their *babas* in pots that had to be broken in order to remove the cake. Sometimes a pan surrounded with paper forms was used to give the dough extra room to rise. These paper forms were up to two feet high and called *podolskie*.

In his book *Lud Polski*, Gołębiowski states that in the 1800s "the bakeries were making all kinds of babas—from almonds, from rye flour and even from three colored doughs—white, pink and dark dough."

We know that the traditional Polish *baba* was made from yeast, a leavening agent that can sometimes be capricious and quirky even in today's modern times. In the early days, the baking of the Easter *baba* took on the elements of a genuine melodrama. The prepared dough was placed under a *pierzyna* (down comforter) to provide adequate warmth to make the dough rise. While it nested in this cocoon of feathers, it was forbidden to open a door or window to let in cold draughts of air. Everyone walked gingerly and avoided any sudden movements which would cause the rising dough to fall. There was great ceremony in putting the risen dough in the oven and then pulling it out later. After baking, it was delicately treated until completely cooled. Then it was either left plain or frosted and decorated. A beautifully turned out *baba* was a housewife's pride and was used as a major centerpiece for the Easter morning breakfast table. Needless to say, a soggy, burnt, pale, or misformed *baba* was considered a major household tragedy.

I've made my own version of the Polish housewife's method for keeping the dough warm to help it rise. Into a large round coiled basket, I place an old feather pillow that's become too loose and floppy to use on the bed. I've kept this old pillow over the years because it brings to mind the many winter evenings my brothers and I stripped feathers under my mother's watchful eye in order to make it. She made a *pierzyna* and two feather pillows for each of us. On top of the pillow, I place my bowl with the dough and cover it with a thick dishtowel. Here are my other secrets for making baked goods that call for yeast: (1) I use unbleached flour as opposed to the all-purpose bleached variety. It works better with yeast. Because it is unbleached it can spoil faster, so it should be kept refrigerated. (2) Always bring your flour, eggs, and butter to room temperature. The cold of the ingredients can affect the yeast.

# Easter Baba

***(Baba Wielkanocna)***

*This recipe makes a nice small* baba, *perfect for including in the basket taken to be blessed on Holy Saturday. If you are going to use a terra-cotta flowerpot (7 or 8 inches across the top), season the pot first by brushing the inside with vegetable oil, then place it on a baking sheet and heat in a 450°F oven for 1 hour. Cool, wash, and dry the seasoned pot before using it. If the flowerpot has a hole at the bottom, line the bottom with circles of lightly greased parchment before inserting the dough.*

2 cups unbleached flour
4 whole eggs
½ cup (1 stick) butter
¾ cup golden or dark raisins
¾ cup hot water
One ¼-ounce package active dry yeast
3 tablespoons warm water
3 tablespoons sugar
½ teaspoon salt

1. Bring flour, eggs and butter to room temperature.
2. Soak raisins in ¾ cup hot water for 15 to 20 minutes until plump.
3. Sprinkle yeast over the 3 tablespoons of water that has been warmed to 110° to 115°F. Mix together until dissolved.
4. In large mixing bowl mix together flour, sugar, and salt. Add yeast mixture and mix. Add one egg at a time mixing 1 to 2 minutes after each addition. Then add softened butter 1 tablespoon at a time until mixed.
5. Drain raisins well and add to dough. Dough will be sticky.
6. Butter and flour a *baba* pan, Bundt pan, or terra-cotta flowerpot. Place dough evenly in bottom of pan. Cover with clean cloth and place in warm area to allow dough to rise until double in bulk, about 1 hour.
7. Preheat oven to 350°F. When dough has risen, place carefully into oven and bake for 20 to 30 minutes until golden brown.
8. Allow to cool in pan for 5 to 10 minutes, then turn out onto a cooling rack.
9. Leave plain or decorate with frosting.

SERVES 6

# Baba au Rhum

**(*Baba z Rumem*)**

*The egg yolks give this* baba *a golden yellow color without the use of any artificial coloring.*

2 cups unbleached flour
6 egg yolks
½ cup (1 stick) butter
½ cup golden or dark raisins
½ cup hot water
½ cup milk
One ¼-ounce package active dry yeast
½ cup sugar
½ teaspoon salt
Peel from 1 orange

Rum Syrup
½ cup sugar
¾ cup apricot juice or water
1 teaspoon lemon juice
½ cup rum or less

1. Bring flour, egg yolks, and butter to room temperature.
2. Soak raisins in the hot water for 15 to 20 minutes until plump. Drain and squeeze raisins lightly to remove excess fluid.
3. Warm the milk to 110° to 115°F in a small bowl or 2-cup measuring glass. Sprinkle yeast over the warmed milk. Add 1 tablespoon sugar and mix in ½ cup of flour. Leave in warm place for approximately ½ hour until it begins to proof (expand).
4. In another mixing bowl, beat the butter and remaining sugar until light and fluffy. Add egg yolks beaten with the salt, the orange peel, flour, and the expanded yeast mixture. Mix well until smooth, about 10 minutes. Add raisins and mix through.
5. Grease and flour a *baba* pan if you have one. A regular tube pan will do nicely also. Fill the pan with the dough. Cover with clean towel and place in warm area, free from drafts, until it doubles in size, about 50 to 60 minutes.

6. Preheat oven to 350°F. Bake 30 to 40 minutes and allow to cool completely. Remove from pan.
7. While the cake is baking, make the rum syrup. In small saucepan cook sugar and apricot juice until sugar dissolves. Add lemon juice and rum, mix together, and remove from heat. Allow to cool slightly.
8. With a long, thin skewer make holes along top of *baba*. Pour rum syrup slowly over the *baba*. Let stand for a few hours or overnight. This *baba* tastes best the next day.

SERVES 10

## PLACEK

To Polish Americans, the term *placek* conjures up the image of a sweet yeast bread with a crumbly topping of flour, butter, and sugar baked in a rectangular loaf pan. Polish ethnographers studying the preparation of food and its consumption among country folk feel that *placek*, the name given to a cake made of yeast that was baked for special occasions, is the modern day evolution of the ancient *kołacz*, the special bread baked for weddings. Ethnographer Jan Bystron states, "In certain parts of Poland the *kołacz* is called *placek*. This is a baked item made from white wheat flour with cheese and raisins."

The *kołacz*, made from the finest wheat flour and eggs, was essentially a round bread baked for most weddings well into the late 1800s. The name *kołacz* stems from the Polish word for "circle" and defined the traditional look of wedding bread—a hand-shaped round loaf. Two things happened in the late 1800s to change the shape and texture of the wedding bread. The first was the availability of yeast which became common in country villages during that time period. The second was the development of metal baking forms, especially the rectangular loaf pans that could be seen everywhere in country homes. At the same time there began a greater availability of what had previously been luxury items—cane sugar, beet sugar, and its substitutes such as beet molasses, as well as spices. The country housewife began using yeast to obtain a finer textured dough and added milk, oil, eggs, cinnamon, some type of sweetener, and sometimes saffron to the wedding bread. And what housewife doesn't love a new gadget or pan for the kitchen? Instead of shaping by hand into a round loaf the old-fashioned way, the new rectangular loaf pans were used. By 1890, wedding breads and special occasion holiday breads were being made in the new baking pans. Polish ethnographers add that it wasn't until the time period between the two World Wars that women began topping their *placeks* with the crumbly mixture of butter, flour, and sugar.

*Placek* was another baked good that was often taken to be blessed on Holy Saturday. It was tied with a blue ribbon around the middle with a small twig of greenery such as myrtle (*Myrtus communis*) tucked in it.

# Placek

3 eggs
4 cups plus 4 tablespoons unbleached flour
½ cup golden yellow or dark raisins
½ cup hot water
Two ¼-ounce packages active dry yeast
½ cup warm water
1 cup sugar
1 cup milk
½ cup (1 stick) butter
1 teaspoon salt
¼ teaspoon nutmeg
1 teaspoon vanilla

TOPPING
⅓ cup sugar
3 tablespoons flour
2 tablespoons butter
⅛ teaspoon nutmeg
⅛ teaspoon cinnamon

1. Bring eggs and flour to room temperature.
2. Soak raisins in the hot water for 30 minutes or until plump. Drain and squeeze raisins lightly to remove excess fluid.
3. Place ½ cup warm (110° to 115°F) water into a 2-cup measuring glass or a bowl. Sprinkle yeast over water and mix together. Add ½ teaspoon of the sugar to the yeast mixture and the 4 tablespoons of the flour to make a thin batter. Set aside to rise for 15 to 20 minutes. It should become bubbly and frothy.
4. Scald the milk in small saucepan, remove from heat and add the butter, salt, nutmeg, and vanilla. Cool to lukewarm (110° to 115°F).
5. In large mixing bowl, beat the eggs and remaining sugar until pale yellow. Add the lukewarm milk mixture and then the yeast mixture.
6. Gradually add the remaining 4 cups of flour, beating well. Add the raisins and mix through. The dough will be somewhat sticky.
7. Place in warm area and allow dough to double in bulk for about 1 hour.

8. Grease and lightly flour two 9 × 5-inch or 8 × 3¾-inch loaf pans. Distribute dough evenly between the pans. Cover with cloth and let rise again for 30 minutes.
9. While the dough is rising, make the topping. Place dry ingredients in small bowl and cut the butter into flour and sugar with a pastry blender until it looks like coarse meal, as if making a pie crust. Or, place ingredients in food processor and pulse together to achieve same effect.
10. Preheat oven to 350°F. Sprinkle topping evenly over the dough and bake for 30 minutes.

MAKES TWO 9 × 5-INCH OR 8 × 3¾-INCH LOAVES

## SAUSAGES AND HAM

There is no denying that the central focus of the Easter meal was pork in some shape or form. In the more well-to-do homes, hogs were killed in the early spring to assure that there would be plenty of sausages, either fresh or smoked, for the Easter morning breakfast.

*Kiełbasa przez pas*
*Nadziana kiska*
*Osolić, opieprzyć*
*Będzie pełna miska.*

Sausage as long as your waist
Stuffed blood sausage
Salted, peppered
Will fill the platter.

See the recipe for fresh sausage in the fall chapter (page 78). If you don't wish to make your own sausage for the Easter table, visit a Polish meat market for ready-made cold smoked meats, hams, and sausages. The choices are numerous: *szynkowa* (ham sausage), *myśliwska* (hunter's sausage), *kabanosy* (a thin dried sausage), *baleron* (marbled Polish ham), *krakowska* (Kraków Type), and *polędwica* (smoked pork tenderloin). Any domestic fully cooked ham will do or look for a canned Polish ham like Krakus which can be found in the refrigerated section of your local supermarket.

## ALL ABOUT *BARSZCZ*

*"Ten kraj pachnie jak dymiąca waza gorącego barszczu z grzybami i szpikem w rurze."*

Stanisław Brzozowski

—Sam ws'ród ludzi

"This country smells like a simmering pot of hot beet soup with mushrooms and marrow bones."

The term *barszcz* has appeared in Polish chronicles as far back as the $16^{th}$ century when Simon Syreński (1540–1611), a physician and philosopher, documented that the people of Poland made a sour soup called *barszcz* and that it was useful both as food and medicine. In those days and perhaps even much earlier, *barszcz* was the name given to a plant from the Heracleum family (supposedly *Heracleum sphondylium*) that grew wild in the fields and flowered in June. Today, we know this plant as cow parsnip and it is better known for its medicinal qualities than as a food. Much later, when beets became available and the people began to make a soup based on fermented beets it, too, was called *barszcz*.

The importance of beets in the life and diet of people of Poland is undeniable. Polish historians indicate that long ago both red and white beets were used in Polish cooking. Souring white beets was universal in Poland throughout the Middle Ages. Red beets did not make an appearance in Poland until the $16^{th}$ or $17^{th}$ century. Soup made from the juice of fermented beets was commonly found not only among the poor and petty gentry but it was also favored by rich nobles. Red beets were cut into round slices, packed into small barrels, and covered with a brine. This was mixed with a little beet sugar, a piece of rye bread was added and allowed to ferment. These pickled beets gave off a sour juice that was something close to vinegar. "Among the wealthy," writes Zygmunt Gloger, author of the four-volume *Encyklopedia Staropolska*, "it was prepared in a wooden barrel covered with a cloth and the soured juice was used to make a soup enjoyed by lords and ladies, their guests, servants and the poor of the village." He went on to say that the soured juice was thought to be medicinal. He himself remembered that when people suffered from sore throats, they received a throat wash from the manor house made from the juice of soured beets mixed with honey. It helped everyone. Physicians recommended clear, unsalted beet broth to lessen a fever and it was supposedly very good for a hangover.

Eventually, *barszcz* became a generic term for two kinds of soups. The first type of *barszcz* was a soup made of fermented rye, oat, or sometimes wheat bran. This was also called *żur*, *kwaśny barszcz*, or *biały barszcz*. It was made of a mix of rye or oat flour and water that was placed in a crock and allowed to ferment near a warm stove. When done fermenting, it was strained through a linen cloth, salted and cooked.

The second type of *barszcz* was a soup made of red beets. To better identify it, it is often termed *czerwony barszcz*, or red beet soup. The beet soup was (1) cooked with beef marrow bones and served with small dumplings; (2) creamed with the use of sour cream and served with sausage; (3) served as a clear and meatless broth in the morning after a long night of dancing and feasting; and (4) served plain with barley and mushrooms for fast days. However, in some parts of Poland a beet soup was often made from fermented beets and also called *żur*. In some regions such as that of Kielce, *barszcz* referred to a soup made of sorrel with flour and milk. *Barszcz* was made from barberry, currants, cranberries, and gooseberries. It was also made from fermenting plums. Polish Americans often get into heated discussions about what constitutes *barszcz*. The terms were interchangeable and meant different things to different people in different regions.

Different parts of Eastern Europe also had their versions of the same soup. *Botwina* or *boćwina* was a soup made in Lithuania from young beet greens. It was also initially made from *Heracleum sphondylium* but the plant came to be named from the word *butwieć* which at one time meant "grows abundantly." The Ukranian version is filled with meat, beets, and other vegetables. The Ukranians also call sorrel soup *zeleni borsch* or green borsch. The Russian version has tomatoes and very little meat and is called *borscht*.

Overall, the basis for many Polish dishes was something soured. Numerous visitors to Poland commented on the fact that the people loved sour and tangy flavors. *Kwas* was another generic word for any dish prepared with fermented juice of fruits or vegetables. Pickle juice was another basis for summer soups. *Kwaśnica* was a broth made from the juice of apples to which was added mushrooms, pepper, and bay leaves and it was eaten with noodles or potatoes.

## Sour Juice from Beets

***(Kwas na barszcz burakowy)***

*Adapted from*: Lucyna Ćzwierczakiewicz's *365 Obiady*

METHOD 1

Take a fair amount of red beets, rinse and peel carefully. Cut larger ones in half and place in a small wooden barrel or large earthenware crock and pour in previously boiled and cooled soft water. Place someplace warm, for instance in the kitchen near the chimney. After four days it is ready to use. Then it should be taken to the cellar so that it stops fermenting and keeps its freshness. The fermented juice can be bottled soon after, preferably by the 6th day. Pour into bottles, top with oil and store in a cool place. It will remain fresh for a few months.

METHOD 2 (Faster)

Take a half a pound of coarse rye bread and a piece of finer sour rye and cut into pieces. Place in a half-gallon pot. Add six peeled chopped beets and cover with previously boiled and cooled soft water. Place overnight near a warm chimney and during the day in the sun. Stir the mixture a couple of times during the day. By the third day you will have the most excellent *barszcz*. The combining of the soured bread with the sugar in the beets results in an exceptional vinegar. Use this sour juice to make *barszcz* on some beef bones or meatless with mushrooms, three or four sprigs of parsley, chives and a bay leaf. Remember that the sour juice should be added last so that it doesn't lose its taste.

# White Barszcz

***(Chrzanówka / Żur Wielkanocny)***

*One of the traditional dishes was* żur wielkanocny *or* biały barszcz, *a hot soup made from fermented oats with dollops of sour cream, horseradish, quarters of hard-boiled eggs, and sausage. In the Orawa region the horseradish* (chrzan) *was laid on with a heavy hand and called* chrzanówka.

3 cups uncooked oatmeal
Large piece sour rye bread
4 cups hot water
1 pound Polish sausage
½ teaspoon salt
½ teaspoon pepper
1 tablespoon horseradish
Hard-boiled eggs, croutons, or potatoes

1. Combine the oatmeal, rye bread, and hot water. Allow to stand for 24 hours until mixture ferments.
2. Strain oatmeal mixture. Cook sausage in 4 cups water. Remove sausage (reserving liquid) and cut into slices. Add oatmeal liquid to sausage liquid and cook together over medium heat. Add salt and pepper. Add horseradish. Serve over hard-boiled eggs, croutons, or boiled potatoes.

SERVES 4

# Red Beet Soup with Little Ears

***(Czerwony Barszcz z Uszkami)***

*Red beet soup was always served for supper on Easter Sunday in our home. My mother saved the liquid from cooking the fresh sausage and used it as the base for the soup. The final flavor of the soup depends heavily on the spices and herbs used to make the sausage.*

*To give her beet soup a beautiful dark color, my mother would take half a raw beet, grate it, place it in a sieve, and submerge it in the stock just long enough for the color to bleed in. The grated beet was then discarded.*

1 to 2 pounds fresh Polish sausage (not smoked)
3 quarts water
Two 15-ounce cans whole beets or 2 pounds cooked fresh beets
1 clove garlic (optional)
1 tablespoon vinegar
Pinch of dill weed

1. Cook fresh sausage in water for at least an hour. Remove sausage from pot, allow to cool and store in refrigerator. Allow stock to cool and refrigerate. The next day remove fat that has risen to top and place the stock over medium heat.
2. Cut beets into thin julienne strips. When stock has started to simmer, add cut beets and juice from the beets. Mince garlic and add to soup. Add vinegar and bring to a light simmer. Do not allow the soup to come to a boil. It will lose its color.
3. Serve over pieces of sliced Polish sausage, hot boiled potatoes, hard-boiled eggs, or over little *uszka* (recipe follows). Garnish with a pinch of dill weed.

SERVES 6 TO 8

# Little Ears

***(Uszka)***

Dough

3 cups flour

One 8-ounce carton sour cream

1 egg

1 teaspoon salt

4 tablespoons (½ stick) butter or margarine, melted

Mushroom Filling

2 to 3 tablespoons butter

½ cup finely minced onions

1 pound fresh mushrooms, finely chopped

½ cup fine bread crumbs

½ tablespoon salt

¼ tablespoon pepper

1. Mix all dough ingredients together and work into dough. Knead until soft and smooth. Allow to stand a few hours or overnight in refrigerator.
2. The next day, bring to room temperature. On a lightly floured board, roll out and cut dough into 2 × 2-inch squares using a knife.
3. For the mushroom filling, melt butter in skillet. Add onions and sauté. Add mushrooms and cook uncovered for about 15 minutes or until most, but not all, of the water from mushrooms has evaporated. Add bread crumbs, salt, and pepper and mix together. The mixture should be moist but not runny. If dry, add a little bit more butter.
3. Place a teaspoon of filling in center of dough square. Fold each square in half to form a triangle. Bring the two long ends together and pinch closed. Continue until all the dough and filling is used up.
4. Drop carefully into boiling, salted water until the "little ears" float to the top about 2 to 3 minutes. Remove with slotted spoon to a platter. Do not allow to overlap or stick to one another. Cool completely and refrigerate. Just before serving, bring the "little ears" to room temperature. Place five or six little ears in a soup bowl. Cover with hot beet soup.

MAKES 3 TO 4 DOZEN

## HOMEMADE HORSERADISH

***(Chrzan)***

*Horseradish is an integral part of the Easter meal and can be offered plain or mixed in the very old-fashioned Polish style with coarsely grated or chopped beets.*

2 cups freshly grated horseradish root
½ cup wine vinegar or plain vinegar
½ teaspoon salt
½ teaspoon pepper
1 tablespoon lemon juice

1. Mix all ingredients together. Store in clean sterilized jar in refrigerator.
2. Offer as condiment to accompany beef, pork, or sausages.

MAKES APPROXIMATELY 2 CUPS.

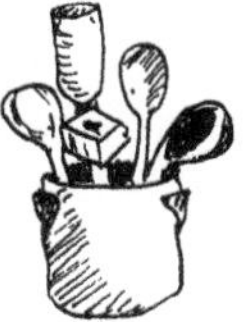

# Red Beets with Horseradish

***(Ćwikła)***

*My mother always grated her beets very fine to blend nicely with the horseradish and I do the same. Make it the night before to allow the flavors to come together. Serve in a small cut-glass bowl if you have one. The red color looks beautiful. Even lowly horseradish gets special attention on the Polish Easter table!*

1 tablespoon vinegar
1 tablespoon brown sugar
3 cups freshly cooked beets, peeled and cooled
¾ cup prepared horseradish
¼ teaspoon salt

1. Mix the vinegar and brown sugar together until dissolved.
2. Grate the cooked and cooled beets. Add the horseradish, the vinegar and sugar solution, and salt.
3. Serve as condiment to accompany the ham, sausage, or whatever cold meats you are serving.

MAKES 3¾ CUPS

# Red Beets

***(Buraki)***

*These beets are a great accompaniment to any beef or pork dish. My mother fixed it all the time using her own canned beets.*

6 to 8 medium-size cooked beets
1 tablespoon butter
½ tablespoon flour
1 tablespoon vinegar
½ teaspoon salt
1 tablespoon sugar
2 tablespoons sour cream (optional)

1. Grate the beets.
2. Melt the butter in a saucepan and add the flour, making a roux. Add the vinegar, salt, and sugar and mix together. Add the grated beets. Heat through until bubbly. Add the sour cream.

SERVES 4 TO 6

## Honeyed Vodka

***(Krupnik)***

*Na zdrowie!* (To your health!)

1½ cups water
1 stick cinnamon
1 whole kernel nutmeg
½-inch slice raw ginger root
½ vanilla pod
6 whole cloves
4 whole juniper berries
Peel of 1 orange removed by vegetable peeler
Peel of ½ lemon removed by vegetable peeler
2 cups honey
1 cup water
1 bottle (750 ml) 100 proof vodka

1. In a clean, unchipped enamel or stainless steel pot combine the 1½ cups water, spices, and peels and bring to a boil.
2. Remove from heat, allow to cool, cover and set aside in cool place to steep for 7 days.
3. Strain mixture carefully through coffee filters several times until clear. Discard spices.
4. Boil honey with the 1 cup of water. Remove any material that may rise to the surface with slotted spoon. This makes for a clearer brew. Cool.
5. In a large, clean 1.75-liter bottle, combine the spice liquid with the honey liquid. Mix together. Fill the rest of the bottle with 100 proof vodka or substitute a lower proof vodka to make a less potent cordial. Wait one month before serving for flavors to pull together.

MAKES APPROXIMATELY 1.75 LITER BOTTLE

## DECORATING THE TABLE

The Easter table reflected the importance of the day when the housewife covered it with her very best white tablecloth. In the middle of the table she placed a vase of pussy willows, the symbol of spring, or a plate of *pisanki*. Perhaps her centerpiece was a beautifully baked lamb cake surrounded by gaily colored eggs or an image of the Easter lamb made of sugar or butter. The food was laid out on the table in as decorative a manner as possible. She arranged large platters containing sausage, a pork roast, a ham, or veal. On another platter or small basket she placed hard-boiled eggs and then placed bowls with condiments such as horseradish, butter, vinegar, and if she could afford it, a bottle of wine or vodka. Perhaps there was a bottle of homemade liqueur or *krupnik*, a honeyed vodka. Braided breads, *babas*, all richly made with eggs and wheat flour appeared along with other sweets including pastries made of nuts, cheese, or almond paste. In the Opole region, a yeast bread braided in the form of a wreath was placed on the table, filled with colored eggs, and decorated with branches of boxwood.

The Easter morning breakfast always began with a special ritual around the consumption of the eggs that were blessed the previous day. In this simple but almost sacred act, the blessed egg was cut into quarters and perhaps again into eighths. The head of the house offered a piece to each of the family members and friends present with everyone wishing each other joy of the Easter day and blessings for long life and happiness. In certain parts of Poland, the egg was eaten with a dab of horseradish in memory of the bitter gall offered to Christ on the cross. The long Lenten fast was over and when everyone had wished one another good wishes, health, and prosperity, the people began the serious business of eating the hams, sausages, and all the other delicacies on the table. When everyone had eaten their fill, they continue to sit around the table having another glass of tea or perhaps a glass of wine, enjoying conversation and the special day.

While the *święconka* breakfast was traditionally a cold collation, the other meals of the day could be a variety of dishes. Dinner that day usually consisted of *barszcz* (either red or white), a broth made of beef served with noodles, and sauerkraut soup with sausage. Supper consisted of meat, eggs, baked breads, and sweets. In poorer homes, a chicken may have been sacrificed, made into soup and eaten with homemade noodles.

From the notebooks of a wealthy housewife we receive a sense of the opulence of the Easter breakfast:

Easter Breakfast for 18

| | | |
|---|---|---|
| Baba. | Large with saffron | 2 |
| Baba. | Koronkowa | 1 |
| Baba. | With raisins | 1 |
| Placek. | With white frosting | 1 |
| Placek. | With pink frosting | 1 |
| Placek. | With almonds and raisins | 1 |
| Placek. | Another, filled | 1 |
| Mazurek. | With almond paste and preserves | 1 |
| Mazurek. | Macaroon-type | 1 |
| Ham. | Smoked | 1 |
| Veal. | Side of | 1 |
| Lamb. | Stuffed and Baked | 1 |
| Piglet. | Stuffed and Roasted | 1 |
| Sausage. | Fresh, on a platter | 1 |
| Sausage. | Fried | 1 |
| Turkey. | Stuffed or in aspic | 1 |
| Pate. | Cold | 1 |
| Eggs. | Hard-boiled for around the lamb, piglet, and sausage | 60 |

Have available: fresh butter, anchovy butter, Swiss cheese, peppermint and anise vodka, lemons, mustard, vinegar, oil, bread, rolls. Bouillon and hot wine before the breakfast in glasses or goblets.

## EASTER MONDAY

The Monday after Easter is called *dyngus* day in Poland. On this day and the next, Easter Tuesday, the housewife did little cooking. Enough food had been prepared ahead of time to simply reheat quickly. She served up leftovers such as cold meats, hard-boiled eggs, soups, and bread or cakes. *Bigos* is a perennial favorite on this day, especially if Easter falls early on the calendar year when the day is cold. Then something hot is much appreciated. Made ahead of time to allow the flavors to blend together, it is heated up and offered to family and visiting friends and guests.

❖ LUCY'S HOUSEHOLD HINTS: Working around fires and stoves, a housewife is very likely to experience burns. Shake bicarbonate of soda over it or spread the yolk of an egg over it. In the event it should blister, cover it with a patch of cloth soaked in spirytus (100 proof alcohol). When it breaks, soak in gray soap mixed with chamomile and cover with a cloth soaked in flax oil mixed with lime (stone) water.

❖ LUCY'S HOUSEHOLD HINTS: One of the best methods for filtering water is passing it through charcoal. Break up wood charcoal into tiny pieces and rinse through cold water. Spread thinly between two pieces of flannel or thick felt. Run water through.

# SUMMER

## Lato

# Preharvest Time

*Jak kwitnie bób, to największy głód*
When the fava bean blooms, the greatest hunger

The above Polish proverb refers to one of the most difficult periods for the Polish country kitchen. From March to the time of reaping the first grains was a period called the *przednówek*, or the period preceding the new harvest. If the previous fall harvest happened to be poor, the larder was lean. It wasn't until July, when poppy was in seed and the early potatoes could be dug that people saw the end to privation and said to each other "*Jak już kwitnie mak, to już nie tak*" (when the poppy blooms, it's not like it was). But until then, the springtime presented a very sparse period.

Small wild game such as wild ducks, geese, partridges, or European thrush were hunted down and often cooked on the spot in a very old method. The bird was plucked cleaned of entrails and feathers, covered with a thick wet clay with a small opening left for steam to escape. The whole thing was placed in a bed on hot ashes from a bonfire. When deemed cooked, the clay was broken and the roasted bird eaten.

The fields and meadows were searched for wild herbs and plants, which were consumed to prevent starvation. This included common goutweed and other pig-weeds, sow-thistle, wild charlock, and nettles. The young leaves of nettle were gathered, scalded with boiling water, then cooked and squeezed out by hand. The mass was then mixed with milk, cream, or pork drippings. Seasoned with flour or egg, this "green soup" was considered a luxury. Nettle was felt to clear the blood and act as a spring tonic. From the grated root of horseradish, a soup was also made which was eaten with potatoes and bread. Other wild plants such as couch grass and heather were used in baking bread and making pancakes. Couch grass was especially popular during times of famine. It was washed, dried, crumbled, and ground with wheat and oat grains for a bread extender. Many felt that besides adding sweetness to the bread, it was a strengthener. Fields were searched for frozen potatoes, which were washed, dried, and then ground into flour to make noodles. Some people like to eat the early tiny tender leaves of nettle or sorrel in salads along with other greens.

## Sorrel Soup

***(Zupa szczawiowa)***

1 pound fresh sorrel leaves (15 to 20 leaves)
2 tablespoons butter
6 cups light chicken stock
¼ cup sour cream
1 tablespoon all-purpose flour
Cooked rice, potatoes, or hard-boiled eggs (optional)

1. Remove stems and wash sorrel leaves thoroughly. Sauté in butter in frying pan until wilted and soft. Press the cooked leaves through a sieve and add to the saucepan containing the chicken stock. Bring to a simmer.
2. In a separate bowl, mix the sour cream and flour together thoroughly. Combine with the chicken/sorrel stock. Heat through but do not allow to boil. Serve plain or over cooked rice, potatoes, or hard-boiled eggs cut in quarters.

SERVES 4

# SUMMERTIME

High summer was a good time for the Polish peasant. The danger of starvation was past as the earth yielded its wonderful gifts. Among the first gifts to be gathered were wild berries from the meadows and woods. According to Polish folk tradition, the berry season was begun on the feast of St. John the Baptist on June 24. It was believed that the saint not only blessed the waters of the rivers and lakes but the berries in the woods as well. After this date the berries were known to be sweeter and healthier. These included elderberries, blueberries, raspberries, blackberries, and huckleberries (also called whortleberry), a type of blueberry. All of these were picked for home use and also for sale in the marketplace. When my mother sent my brothers and I out to the meadows and forests looking for berries she always liked to tell us the story of how she and her younger brother Peter picked enough wild blueberries to buy themselves a pair of shoes for school.

Blueberries were given the generic name of *czarne jagody*. At home the blueberries were eaten with milk or a dollop of cream, made into a cold blueberry soup, made into cakes and cobblers, and folded into pierogi. The juice was extracted and made into a syrup to sweeten tea during the cold winter months. *Famuła* was a type of blueberry soup with milk. Blueberries were also dried to be cooked later in the winter in compotes. The dried berries were also stored in the medicine cabinet and used in the treatment of diarrhea.

*Garus* was a soup made from cooked pears and apples or cooked plums. Flour was added as a thickener and sometimes it was served with milk. It was eaten with cooked grains or potatoes. Another soup was *fafuła*, made from elderberries with flour and milk.

## FRUIT CAKES

The table of Poland's Queen Jadwiga was graced with lovely tortes and sweetbreads with cheese inside. But the queen's table was often similar to that of her humble subjects. Special holidays called for special baking and more expensive ingredients but summertime called for whatever fruit was in season. There was no lack of fresh fruit such as sweet and sour cherries, plums, pears, and apples. These were often offered at the end of a meal. If the home could afford it the fruit was sweetened with honey and teemed up with a flour batter. Cakes and tortes made of fruit are still extremely popular in Poland.

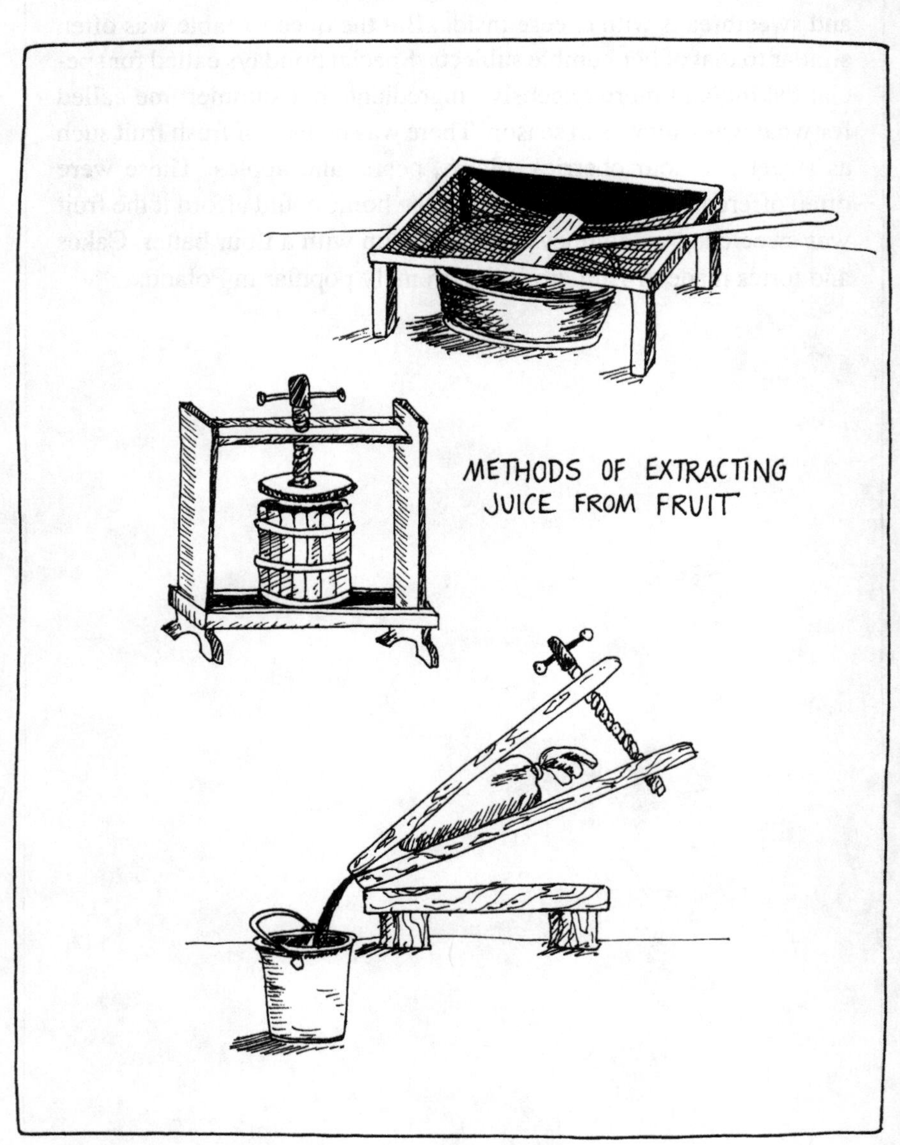
METHODS OF EXTRACTING
JUICE FROM FRUIT

# Plum Cake

***(Ciasto z śliwkami)***

*This was one of my mother's all-time favorite summertime dessert cakes. I used to help her mix the batter by hand with a wooden spoon. My arms would get tired! Then one year she bought herself a golden yellow electric hand mixer. Oh the wonders of electrical appliances!*

2½ cups all-purpose flour
One ¼-ounce package active dry yeast
½ cup milk
⅓ cup butter
⅓ cup sugar
½ teaspoon salt
2 eggs
5 ripe Italian plums, halved and pitted
Confectionary sugar (optional)

1. Mix together flour and yeast in large mixing bowl.
2. In medium saucepan place milk, butter, sugar, and salt and heat until just warm (110° to 120°F). Add to yeast mixture along with the eggs. Beat with electric mixer, scraping along the sides of bowl frequently for a few minutes. Batter will be sticky and stiff.
3. Spread dough into a 9 × 13-inch greased baking pan. Arrange plums neatly, cut side up, in rows on top of dough. Cover and let rise in a warm place until almost double, about 30 to 40 minutes.
4. Preheat oven to 375°F oven and bake for 30 to 35 minutes. Cool completely. Sprinkle lightly with confectionary sugar.

SERVES 10

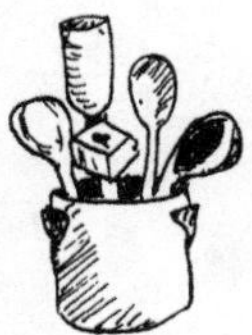

# Fruit Cake

***(Ciasto z owocami)***

*If company is on the way and there's not enough time to wait for a yeast rising, a regular sweet bread recipe can be substituted for the dough. The minimum of ingredients allows it to be pulled together very fast an hour before someone stops by for coffee or tea. I like to use peaches and ¼ teaspoon of ground nutmeg or cinnamon in the batter.*

1 cup all-purpose flour
½ cup granulated sugar
1 teaspoon baking powder
¼ teaspoon ground nutmeg or cinnamon
2 large eggs
⅓ cup milk
3 tablespoons vegetable oil
3 to 4 ripe peaches

*TOPPING*
2 tablespoons sugar mixed with ¼ teaspoon ground cinnamon

1. Preheat oven to 375°F. Grease and flour an 8-inch square pan or one 9-inch round cake pan.
2. Mix flour, sugar, baking powder, and nutmeg or cinnamon into a bowl of electric mixer and blend together.
3. Add eggs, milk, and oil. Beat until thick and smooth. Pour into prepared pan.
4. Halve and pit the peaches. Arrange them in slices on top of the batter. Sprinkle with the cinnamon and sugar topping.
5. Bake 40 to 45 minutes until it is well browned and crisp on top and a wooden pick inserted into the center comes out clean. Cool at least 10 minutes before serving.

***Variation:*** Substitute blueberries or apples for the fruit.

SERVES 4 TO 6

## MILK AND BARNYARD PRODUCTS

The barnyard played an important role in rural peasant kitchen. Making butter was a universal occupation throughout all of Poland and was made from the milk of three different animals: cow, sheep, and goat. With the exception of the Carpathian Mountains where butter was made from a mix of cow and sheep milk or just sheep milk, butter was generally made from cow milk. Polish writers of the 16$^{th}$ through 18$^{th}$ centuries constantly wrote of sheep milk, milking, and the dietary value of sheep milk and its by-products. A wide array of documentation testifies that up until the end of the 19$^{th}$ century, it was common practice to milk sheep and that the milk was considered to be on an equal basis with that of a cow. Equally well thought of was goat milk. These were usually found in smaller villages among families who were too poor to even own a cow but also among the people of the Beskid Sądeckim mountain region who sent them out to pasture with the sheep. A source written in 1809 claimed "one good goat could take the place of three weak cows" with the milk chiefly used to make butter and cheese.

The cow was a symbol of family life. Milking, feeding, and taking the cow to pasture often made men and women out of small boys and little girls. Cows were milked twice and sometimes three times a day and produced very important products for sale and consumption.

The production of butter began from the moment of gathering the milk, which would be left in a cool place such as the root cellar or any cool room away from the rays of the sun, until the cream rose to the surface, which generally occurred 24 to 48 hours after the milking. According to village housewives, the gathered cream should "sour" for a while. Instructions left from the 17$^{th}$ and 18$^{th}$ centuries admonished housewives not to allow the milk to sour to long "for from soured cream the butter is inferior and unstable." The cream was then made into butter with the help of butter churns.

In the 19th and 20th centuries, a variety of butter churns were utilized. Different types were preferred in different regions, but there were essentially three kinds. The first was a butter churn where the cream was beaten in a container with the help of a rotary paddle. The second type was a cylindrical, rocking container with a handle where the cream flowed and beat against the sides of the container. The third type was a tall standing, unmovable container made of wood or pottery with a paddle that was raised up and down. These butter churns had a variety of names depending on the region. In areas around Kraków it was called *maślnica*. In Poznań, Mazowsze, and in the Carpathians it was called *kiernice*. In Podlasie, it was called *tłucki*.

In Polish peasant life, butter made infrequent appearances at the table. More likely to be seen was rendered fat from chicken, pork, or beef. Bread was eaten plain or with lard or jam. Freshly churned butter was designated to be sold to buy items that could not be made at home such as sugar, salt, spices, lamp oil, or other critical necessities.

Butter designed for sale was made as attractive as possible. It was taken to the marketplace in special containers or in special forms called *osełki* which consisted of butter molded into a cylindrical shape, flat on the top and bottom, and decorated on top with the use of a template made especially for this purpose. The butter was taken to market wrapped in a large cabbage or horseradish leaf. Each block of butter generally weighed about 1 kilogram (2.2 pounds).

At the end of the 19th century, butter molds became very common. It is believed that these molds came to Poland through the Germans and Moravians. They were initially used extensively in the Kaszuby and Śląsk regions and then spread to other parts of Poland by the second half of the 19th century and remained in popular use until World War I.

Carpenters made the butter molds out of blocks of birch or linden wood and less frequently out of poplar, alder, and sycamore. The inside was turned on a lathe or gouged out and a pattern carved out at the bottom and sometimes along the sides. The molds were rectangular, square, or round in shape and were often richly carved. Sold at the local marketplace, the oldest of these were round, but the rectangular shapes were the more popular. The butter was packed into the mold, leaving a decorative impression on top when it was released. The molds also

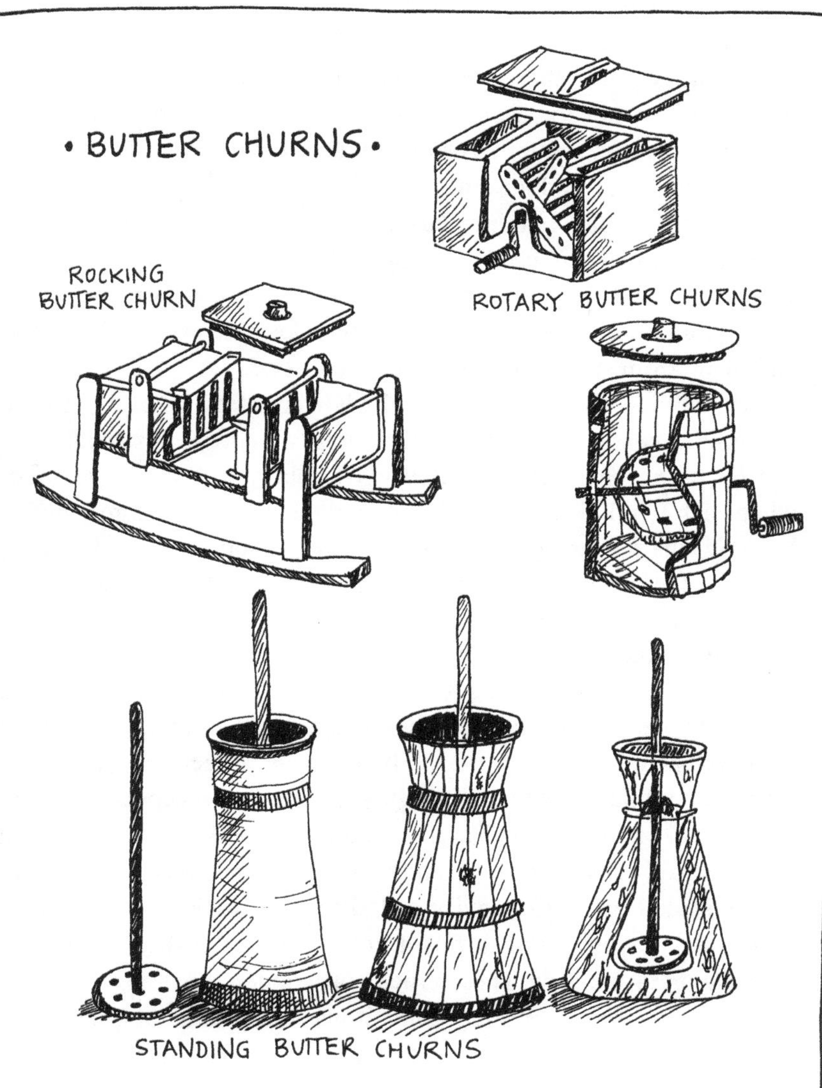
• BUTTER CHURNS •
ROCKING BUTTER CHURN
ROTARY BUTTER CHURNS
STANDING BUTTER CHURNS

reflected weights of quarter, half, and one pound. In Opole, these molds were also called *kwartki* (quarter pound) and later *połfontki* (half pound) which testified that the butter was a certain weight.

Also very common were fitted molds composed of two halves. Unlike press molds, these were strictly for decoration, particularly in the shape of lambs for Easter but also chickens, roosters, and fish. In the Słupsk region, butter lambs were also made for weddings to be eaten by the bride and groom.

There were also butter rollers and carved, flat pieces of wood or templates which were used to decorate the top of butter that had been shaped by hand. Besides the use of butter molds, small crocks and wooden tubs were also popular. The wooden tubs were called *faski* and made from staves or from a block of wood.

Butter was often preserved for the winter, a time when cows gave less milk. Even in the most humble cottages, there were special utensils for conserving butter. This was especially true in earlier times when each family was self-sufficient and the plenty of summer had to last until the following spring. Butter was preserved through salting from the 17$^{th}$ century to the time between the two World Wars. Butter churned in May was considered especially good for this purpose. It was supposed to contain the best flavors and tended to preserve well.

After a thorough rinsing, this spring butter was salted down with the use of a wooden spoon in a bowl so that the salt was distributed evenly throughout the butter. Then it was placed in a crock or wooden tub that had been thoroughly washed and steeped in boiling water, packed down very carefully so as to allow no air to remain which would cause it to spoil. At the top, more salt was packed on or it was sealed off with heavily salted water. Sometimes the salted butter was covered with a fat of some kind to ensure against air entering and ruining it. These crocks or wooden tubs ranged from a half-liter to twelve-liter sizes. Then it was taken to a cool, dry place such as a cellar and used during the winter to flavor dishes.

Gifts of food were very precious. A small crock or jar of herbs steeped in pork or chicken fat was exchanged among housewives at Christmas. The butter was placed in a small bowl or crock. The top was decorated in a variety of ways using a spoon or knife, or cutting a design onto a sliced potato or turnip and pressing onto the top.

• BUTTER MOLDS •

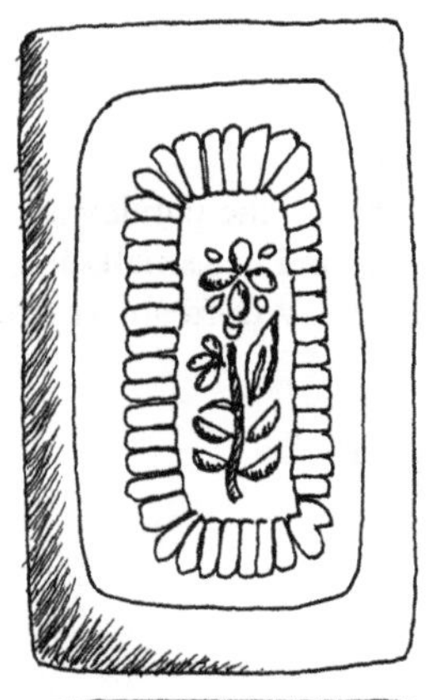

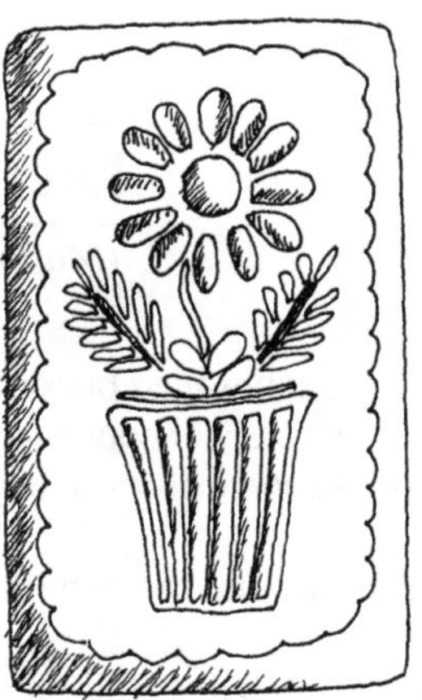

## Parsley-Chive Butter

*(Masło z zieleniną)*

½ cup (1 stick) unsalted butter, softened
1½ tablespoons chopped parsley
1½ tablespoons snipped chives
1 tablespoon lemon juice (optional)

1. In a small bowl, stir the softened butter with the parsley and chives (and lemon juice, if desired) until blended. Mound in a small dish and set aside for a few hours for flavors to blend. Serve with fresh rye bread.

MAKES ½ CUP

## Dill Butter

*(Masło koperkowe)*

½ cup (1 stick) unsalted butter, softened
1 tablespoon finely chopped fresh dill leaves
½ tablespoon chopped fresh parsley

1. In small bowl, stir the softened butter with the dill and parsley until blended.
2. Mound in a small dish and set aside for a few hours for flavors to blend.

MAKES ½ CUP

## EGGS

Another product that came from the barnyard was eggs. Eggs were rarely eaten except for very special holidays. They were also sold or bartered for other necessary items. For the winter, eggs were stored in crocks in the cellar.

## SUPERSTITIONS

The barnyard had its own list of superstitions, beliefs, and practices:

- ▶ Before making butter wipe out the butter churn with mugwort.
- ▶ Churning butter on Monday will cause crickets, cockroaches, and bedbugs to breed.
- ▶ Do not sell or lend milk after sunset or the cows will go dry.
- ▶ If milk should boil over on the stove, sprinkle a little salt on the spilt milk or the cow's udder will crack.
- ▶ If you mix your milk with that of a neighbor, it will spoil.
- ▶ On the day a calf is born, don't lend anything from the house or the cow will lose her milk and mice will make much mischief.
- ▶ When setting a hen on eggs, try to put the eggs in a man's hat or cap and then transfer them to the nest. Try to do this on a Sunday or a holiday, at a time when people are coming out of church.
- ▶ On the day the housewife separates the cabbage plants in the garden, she shouldn't sell eggs or sweep her house.

Other beliefs included:

- ▶ Hazel tree branches that have been blessed on the Feast of Our Lady of the Herbs (August 15) placed in the thatch of the roof will protect the house against lightning.

- ▶ If a broom is placed at the doorstep of the house, a witch cannot cross over the threshold.

- ▶ If you're sweeping the floor, don't give the broom to someone else to finish the job because you're giving up good luck.

- ▶ Water should not boil by itself for a long time on the stove because it will cause bad luck (a death in the family).

- ▶ If a fork falls at the time of setting the table, it is a sign that someone will arrive during dinner. If someone's spoon falls to the ground while eating, it's a sign that someone hungry will arrive.

## BUTTERMILK

Buttermilk is the liquid remaining after the cream has been churned to butter. The word *buttermilk* seems to suggest things that are bad for your arteries, yet its calorie count and fat content is approximately the same as the milk it originally came from and retains the valuable calcium, riboflavin, and protein as well. In the Polish country kitchen, buttermilk was one of the main drinks of the house, used in making a variety of dishes at any time of day or night and even fed to the pigs for fattening up. Buttermilk pancakes served for noonday meals and for supper were a perennial favorite and made from everything imaginable including buckwheat groats, ground hemp seed, broad beans, potatoes, or fruit such as apples, pears, plums, and wild berries. These had to be eaten the day they were made as they dried and hardened quickly. During times when iron skillets were still unknown the pancakes were cooked in a very primitive manner. A flat rock was heated over hot coals till white, greased with a piece of fat stuck on a stick, and the pancake mixture poured on the heated rock. This was a method that could be done anywhere anytime, even by armies on the march.

TIMESAVER: Today most buttermilk is produced by fermenting pasteurized skim milk with a bacterial culture. It has a long refrigerator shelf life but can separate as it sits. Always shake well before using. Sour milk can be substituted for buttermilk. Add 1 tablespoon of fresh lemon juice or distilled white vinegar to 1 cup of room-temperature milk. Let stand for 20 minutes until the milk begins to form a firm curd.

# Buttermilk and Mashed Potato Supper

***(Ziemniaki z maślanką)***

***This is one of my mother's quick and easy Friday suppers that appeared more frequently during Lent with a vegetable on the side.***

1 quart buttermilk
2 tablespoons fresh chopped dill or chives
2 to 3 pounds potatoes, peeled
1 teaspoon salt

1. In a pitcher, mix buttermilk and dill or chives and refrigerate for an hour.
2. In a medium-size pot of water, cook potatoes with salt until soft, 25 to 30 minutes. Drain potatoes, return them to the pot, and mash with potato masher or mixer.
3. Mound portions of the mashed potatoes on individual plates. Make a well in the center of the mounds and pour buttermilk into the well and over potatoes.
4. Serve with green beans, carrots, beets, green salad, or vegetable of choice.

SERVES 4

# Buttermilk Pancakes

*(Maślane placki)*

*Good for breakfast, lunch or dinner.*

1¼ cups all-purpose flour
1 teaspoon baking powder
2 teaspoons sugar
½ teaspoon salt
1 cup buttermilk
½ teaspoon baking soda
2 eggs, slightly beaten
2 tablespoons butter or margarine, melted or vegetable oil
Vegetable oil for frying

1. In medium-size bowl mix flour, baking powder, sugar, and salt.
2. Mix buttermilk with baking soda. Add eggs and butter, margarine or oil. Blend wet and dry ingredients together. If too thick add buttermilk in small increments until desired consistency.
3. Heat heavy cast-iron griddle or frying pan with 1 to 2 tablespoons oil.
4. When hot, spoon batter onto hot pan to make individual pancakes. Fry until golden on each side. Serve with fruit syrup, maple syrup, or sugar.

MAKES 12 TO 14 MEDIUM-SIZE PANCAKES

# Buttermilk and Herb Dressing

***(Maślanka z ziołami)***

*This buttermilk dressing is great on salads as well as on partially cooked and chilled vegetables for a summer side dish. Arrange vegetables such as tomato slices or wedges, zucchini, yellow and green bell peppers, baby beets, and cucumbers on a platter covered with bed of greens. It can be made up to three days ahead.*

⅓ cup mayonnaise
¾ cup buttermilk
1 small green onion, finely minced
1 medium-size clove garlic, minced
½ teaspoon salt
½ teaspoon ground pepper
1 teaspoon freshly minced parsley
1 teaspoon freshly minced dill

1. In medium-size bowl, whisk together the buttermilk, mayonnaise, onion, and garlic.
2. Whisk in the salt, pepper, parsley, and dill.
3. Place in a sealed jar and refrigerate overnight for best flavor.

MAKES APPROXIMATELY 1 CUP

## Cold Summer Soups

Cold soups prepared from fresh vegetables, abundant in the garden and made quickly, were an important part of cooking in the summer when it was too hot to stoke up the stove. Vegetables and buttermilk were teamed up for a delicious cold soup that could be kept chilled in a stream bed or root cellar until time to eat. According to Gołębiowski, the Lithuanians made their chilled beet soup with beet greens based on sour beet juice and prepared with sour cream. It was simmered with pieces of crayfish, veal, turkey, or capon—all of it added to the soup chopped in small pieces. Hard-boiled eggs and cucumbers were added. Later, asparagus became popular.

# Cold Beet Soup

***(Chłodnik)***

1 small bunch (5 or 6) fresh, medium-size beets
2 quarts cold water
1 medium-size cucumber, chopped
2 small dill pickles, chopped
4 tablespoons chopped scallions or chives
5 red radishes, thinly sliced
2 cups buttermilk
3 tablespoons cider or white vinegar
2 tablespoons finely chopped fresh dill leaves
1 teaspoon salt
Hard-boiled eggs (optional)

1. Wash any dirt off beets until completely clean. Cut off green leaves 1 to 2 inches above the beetroot (if you cut into the beetroot while raw all the color will leak out during the cooking) and cook beets in the water until soft. Cooking time will vary depending on the size of the beets. Test for softness with a fork as you do for a boiled potato.
2. When cooked, remove beets from water into separate bowl and allow to cool completely. Save the cooking liquid, as this will form part of the stock for the soup.
3. When beets have cooled completely enough to handle, slip off the skins and dice the beets. Place all chopped vegetables in large bowl or clean cooking pot. Add 2 cups of the cooled beet liquid, the buttermilk, vinegar, dill, and salt and stir together.
4. Cover the bowl or pot securely and refrigerate overnight for the flavors to blend together.
5. Stir soup and serve plain or place a quartered hard-boiled egg in the center of soup bowl and ladle soup over the egg.

TIMESAVER: Good quality canned beets or a quart jar of bottled borscht found in larger supermarkets can be substituted for fresh beets. Just add rest of ingredients and chill.

SERVES 6

# Making Cheese

Cheesemaking was another important by-product from milk and was a chief means of livelihood in southern Poland in the Tatra mountain region. Here, where farming gave a meager and uncertain livelihood, the mountain men and women reared cattle and tended sheep. High up in the mountains beyond the villages were open clearings suitable as pastures for grazing sheep called *hale*. These areas were often owned by an entire village or a group of villagers whose ownership was tied to ancient land grants which remained acknowledged through the centuries.

The art of Carpathian cheesemaking was brought to Poland from the Balkans by migrating shepherds known as Walachians, who had been appearing on Polish territory since the 14th century, migrating westward with their flocks of sheep, goats, and cattle.

The entire village, or a group of owners, hired a lead shepherd called a *baca*. This was a position that became a tradition within a family, passed on from generation to generation. The *baca* was an expert cheesemaker whose job was to take the sheep to the grazing pastures and carry out cheesemaking. Contracts with the *baca* began in the spring and were generally verbal in nature. It was very clear, however, how much the *baca* was to be paid and what he had to pay in the way of recompense in case of damages. The *baca* was saddled with the responsibility for the flock of sheep placed under his care. He also had the help of a group of underlings called *juhasy*. For every fifty sheep he needed one helper and since a flock of sheep generally consisted of 150 to 200 sheep, he generally hired three to four helpers. Payment to the helpers was also traditional. An adult helper received payment in so many cheeses, usually one per day while on the job. A younger helper received half a cheese. If the grazing was very successful and the helper pleased the boss, he was also rewarded with clothing, boots, or shoes.

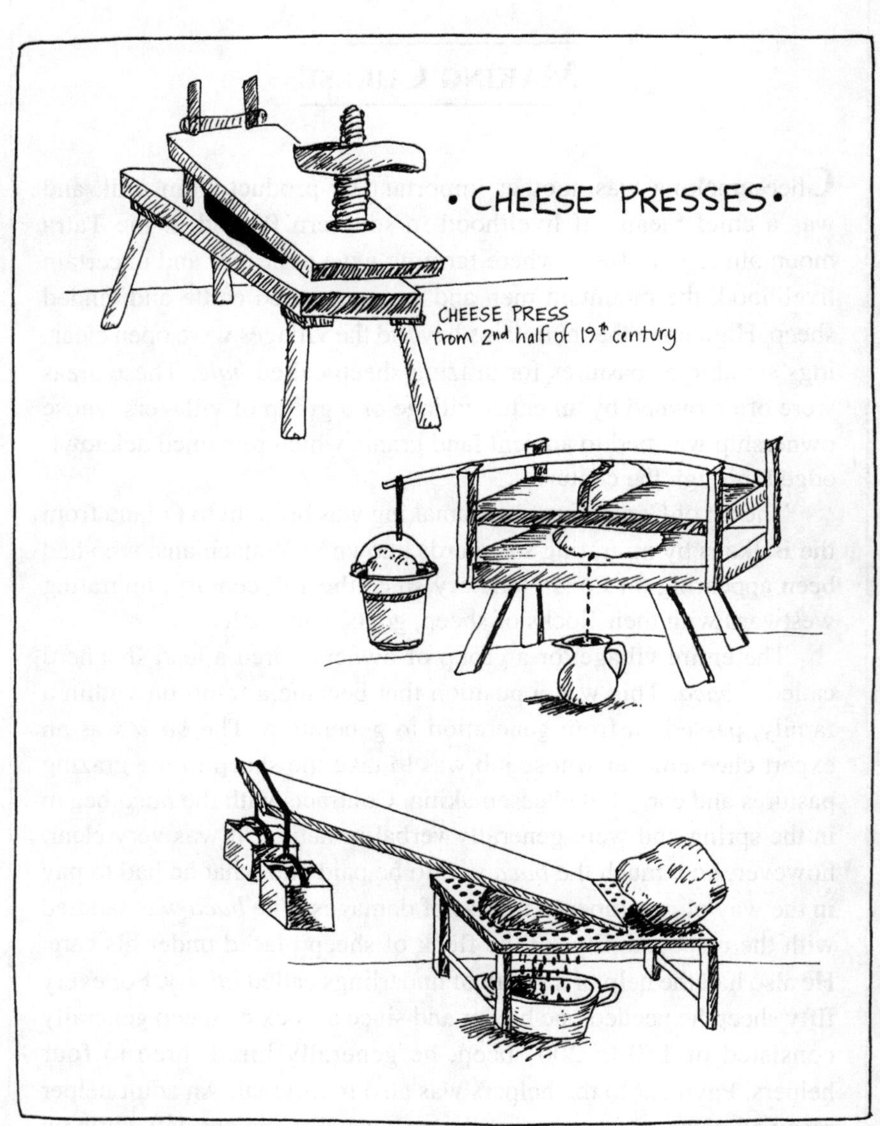
• CHEESE PRESSES •
CHEESE PRESS
from 2nd half of 19th century

• CHEESE DRYING •

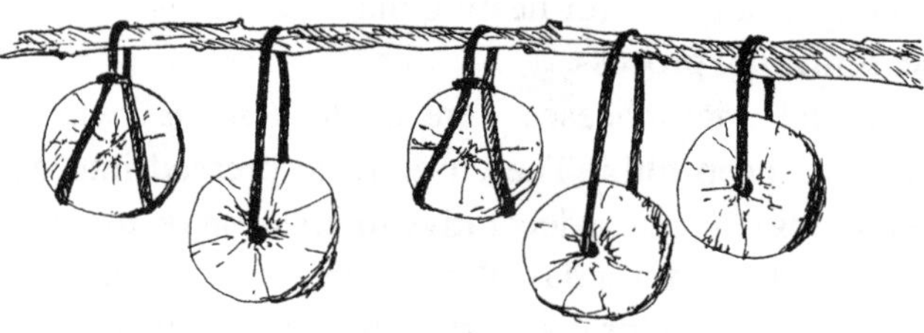

CHEESES DRYING IN THE SUN

CHEESE
HANGING IN NET
MADE FROM LINEN THREAD.

NET WOVEN FROM STRAW
FOR DRYING CHEESES.
( RADOM REGION )

The *baca* and his helpers slept and worked in rough mountain huts called *szałas*. The huts had all the necessary utensils needed to carry on the work of milking and making butter and cheese. All the equipment was made of wood because it was felt that metal containers changed the taste of milk. In the center of the hut was an open fire contained by rocks. Hanging over it from a hook in the rafter was a large copper pot used for heating the milk that was the first step in the cheesemaking process.

Fresh and dried cheeses were made. *Oscypek* was made from the curds of sheep milk. The curds were pressed into oval-shaped wooden molds to create a decorative impression on the surface. After immersion in brine for a day, the cheese was then smoked for up to six days giving it a color that varied from golden to a dark chocolate. Another cheese called *bryndza* was also made. To make *bryndza*, partially ripened cheese curds were broken up by hand, generously salted, doused with a generous dose of *spirytus* (alcohol) and packed into wooden barrels with yet more salt. Sheep butter was also made.

The whey left over from making the cheese was the principle foodstuff and drink of the shepherds. It was heated in a wooden copper pot to just about boiling. With a wooden ladle the *baca* scooped up the thick fatty coating that rose to the top which had the consistency of thick cream. This was cooled, allowed to ferment slightly, and was drunk sour. Sometimes this thick coating was made into butter in the same manner as cow butter.

For breakfast, the shepherds ate cheese and drank cold whey and an oat or barley cake with sheep butter. A hot dinner was prepared twice a week. There were potatoes cooked in the glowing embers of the fire dotted with sheep butter or bacon fat. They were eaten with spoons from a common bowl and washed down with whey. Sometimes dumplings were made from wheat flour and they, too, were smothered in sheep butter.

Meat was eaten in the huts only in unforeseen circumstances when a sheep was maimed or met with some unfortunate accident. The carcass was cooked or boiled into a broth. The shepherds gathered mushrooms for mushroom soup and foraged for wild berries. Sausage and alcohol only made rare appearances—usually when someone made the trek up to the pasture to visit. At various times

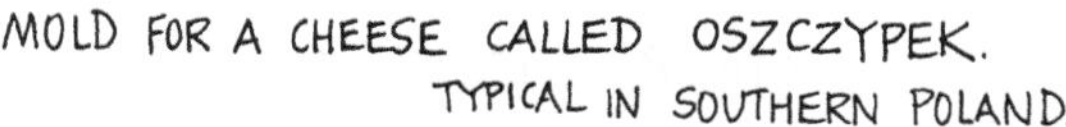
MOLD FOR A CHEESE CALLED OSZCZYPEK.
TYPICAL IN SOUTHERN POLAND.

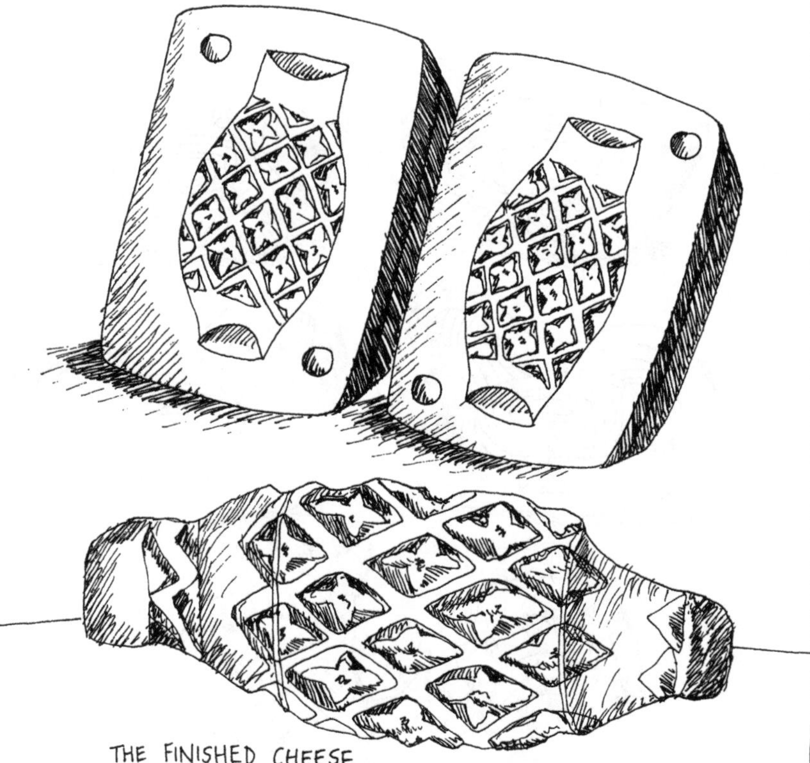

THE FINISHED CHEESE
MADE FROM OSZCZYPEK MOLD.

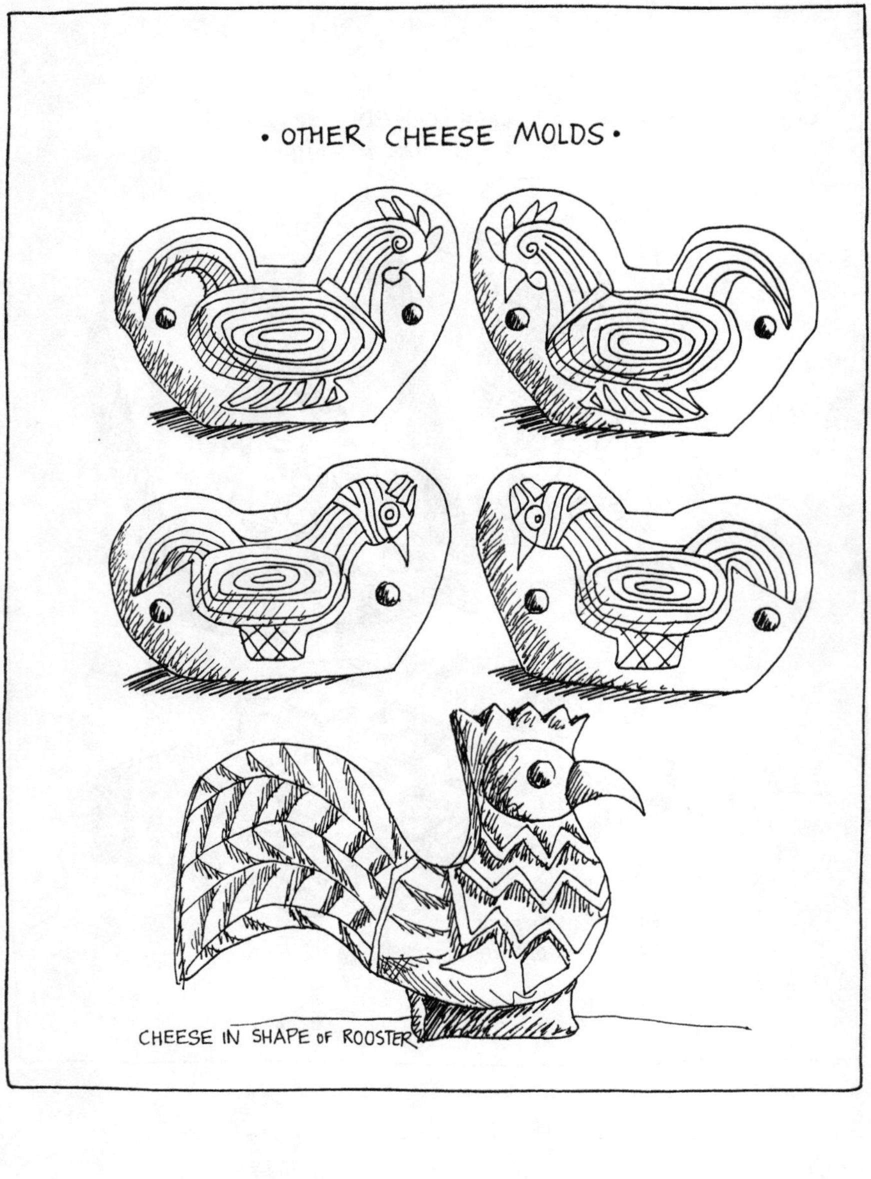

## • OTHER CHEESE MOLDS •

CHEESE IN SHAPE OF ROOSTER

throughout the spring and summer, people would travel up to the mountain pastures to take away the perishable cheeses and butter to be sold or bartered at the next market day. On the Feast of St. John (June 24) the shepherds always held a small celebration. They were often gifted with eggs which were fried over an open fire.

Outside of the Tatras, cottage cheese was often made from cow milk. Freshly made cottage cheese was eaten with dumplings and in *pierogi*. In the Kurpie region, for instance, an afternoon snack called *podwieczorek* consisted of bread with cottage cheese, sour cream, or honey washed down with cool milk. Very popular suppers in summer were based on milk such as potatoes doused with buttermilk or sour milk. Sometimes cheese curds were wrapped in cloth and squeezed by means of a homemade press. One such cheese was *gomółka.* It was a small round cheese, usually the size of a hen's egg, salted and flavored with caraway seed and/or white mustard and then dried in a linen bag or a net made from twisted linen threads or straw ropes. Made in both peasant cottages and manor houses, it was a cheese for day-to-day consumption or for keeping through the winter.

Cheese was stored away and kept for very busy times like the harvest time when work was very intensive with little time for heating and cooking. They were often salted, sometimes sprinkled with poppy seeds. Many weighed 4 to 6 pounds. Most frequently, after being squeezed in a press, they were dried for a very long time near the stove in cloth bags or nets made from twisted linen threads or straw ropes. Sometimes cheeses were made especially for sale. Buyers traveled from village to village buying homemade cheeses to sell in big city markets or the women took them to market to sell or trade for other important items needed around the home.

## Bringing in the Sheaves

Most peasant farmers grew the grains that were ground into flour and then made into the bread that fed and nourished their family. Harvest time was a very demanding time of intense labor that required

*Bringing in the hay in the summertime, 1958. Photo by B. Czarnecki. Courtesy of the National Ethnographic Museum, Warsaw.*

the combined effort of the entire family. Men and women would cut the fields of grain with hand tools, bind the cut wheat into sheaves, stack them in shocks, and later thresh and winnow the grain. Polish wives worked right alongside the menfolk, binding the cut wheat or rye and stacking them in shocks on the open field. This left little time for cooking. Food preparation and consumption during this time was simple. Breakfast consisted of a quick meal of bread and butter or bread and cheese and then the family headed out directly to begin work in the fields as soon as it was bright enough to see. The day's meals were easily transported in baskets and eaten out in the open under a bit of shade. Dried cheeses, prepared way ahead of time just for this situation were softened in a hot oven and taken to the fields to consume for a second breakfast or late lunch. A pitcher of sorrel or beet soup, whitened with milk, buttermilk or sour cream was also taken to the fields and eaten with rye bread. If the housewife wasn't involved in the harvest, she sent out hot food to the working men in *dwojaki* filled with hot buckwheat groats seasoned with bacon, or hot potatoes sprinkled with dill and dab of butter or sour cream. Liquids were taken in the form of sour milk, buttermilk, or spring water mixed with homemade fruit syrup which had been kept cold in earthenware pitchers. According to ethnographer Gołębiowski in *Lud Polski,* one of the traditional foods offered during the harvest was potatoes with bacon, and *pierogi* with cheese or buckwheat. These two dishes were also offered on the Feast of St. Peter, the patron saint of harvesters celebrated on June 29.

Once the grain was cut and brought to the barns, the next phase of harvesting began—threshing and winnowing the grain. Many barns in Poland had a threshing floor called a *boisko*—a large wooden deck with carefully fitted boards so that there were no cracks for grains of wheat, oats, or barley to fall through. The sheaves of wheat were spread on the floor and the threshers would "flail" them until the grain was loosened from the heads. The most common design for the *cepa* or the flail, one in use since the early days of the Christian era, was simply two pieces of wood as thick as a shovel handle, one 6 feet long, the other 18 inches long, loosely attached to one another, end to end, with a leather thong. The short piece of wood, called the swigle would generally be made of hardwood.

The sheaves were unbound and placed in the middle of the threshing floor. The handle of the flail was raised until the swigle was shoulder high and then brought down firmly so that it struck full length against the straw until it shook off the grains from the heads. When all the grain had been shaken off the heads, the straw was removed and saved for mulching, composting, weaving into rope, or for thatching. The remaining grain, generally consisting of chaff and small bits of straw were ready for winnowing. In a steady wind, the grain was poured from one container to another until most of the straw particles were blown away, literally separating the wheat from the chaff. The grain could then be stored in sacks or barrels until ready to be ground into flour.

The grains of wheat, rye, or oats in raw form are inedible. The farmer was then faced with having to take his grain to the miller to be ground into flour. Smaller amounts of flour could also be ground at home. A mortar and pestle called a *stepa* was one of the earliest devices for crushing grains in Polish peasant cottages but yielded a coarse meal at best. Another method of grinding grain and cereals was by crushing them between two stones with an implement called a *żarna*, or quern.

The quern was a hand-powered mill consisting of two circular stones, the top stone turned by hand against a stationary bottom one. The upper stone rested on a spindle extending through the bottom so that there was about 1⁄16-inch space between the abrasive surfaces. As the top stone, or runner stone, turned against the non-moving stone, the grain was broken down and milled. A stick or lever was fastened to one side of the runner so the individual milling could turn the wheel easily. It remained in use in Poland for a very long time.

Water-driven mills for grinding grain first made their appearance in Poland in the 12th century. Their appearance and growth over the centuries throughout the Polish countryside did not eliminate the primitive methods of grinding grain using the mortar and pestle nor the use of a quern. There were many reasons why both primitive methods continued way into the 20th century.

First of all, not every village could boast a windmill or watermill. In many situations, the mill was located some distance away and required traveling time. Upon arriving at the mill, the *gospodarz* (farmer) could be greeted by the site of a dozen other farmers queued

*"On one's own field." Illustration from Kłosy, 1876.*

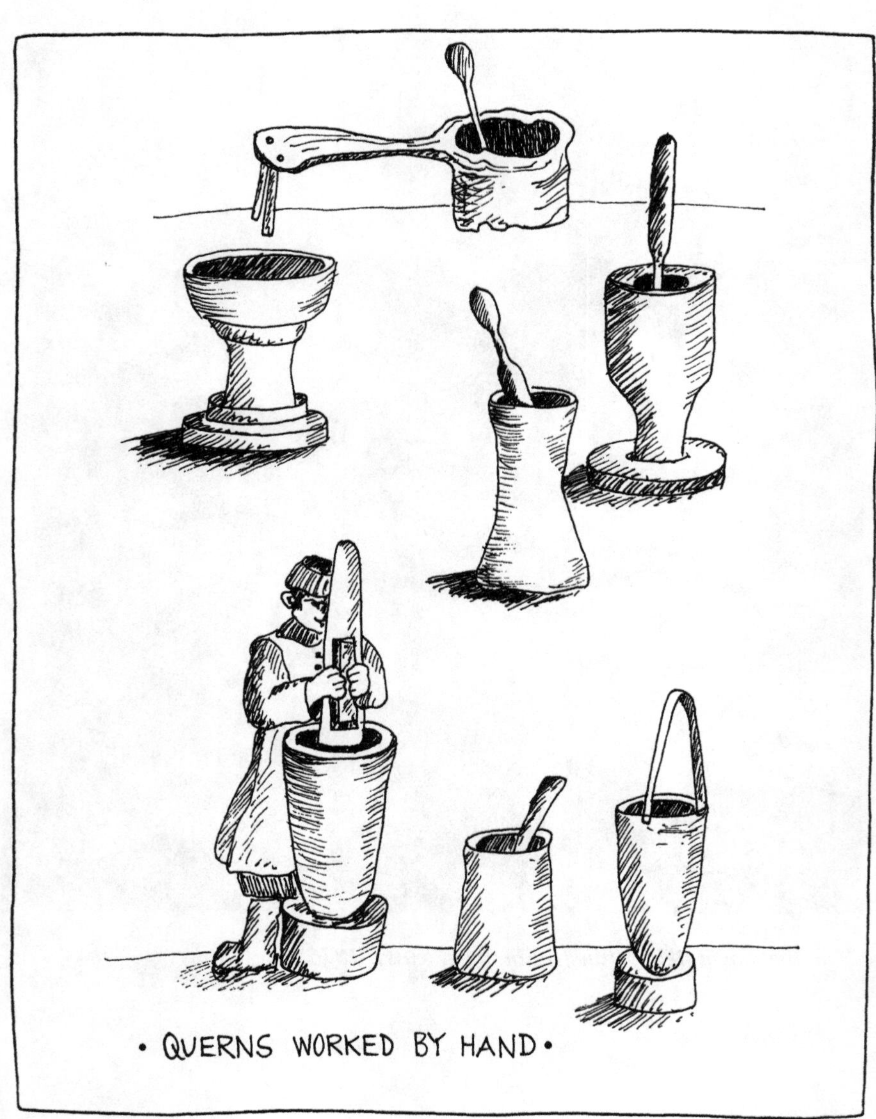

• QUERNS WORKED BY HAND •

•GRINDING QUERNS•

up in line for the same purpose. The *gospodarz* either had to wait his turn or drop off his grain and retrieve it at a later time. The entire activity could consume the better part of a workday or even a few mornings. Many felt this was a great waste of time and subsequently preferred to grind their grain on an as-needed basis at home.

Another deterrent to taking your grain to the miller was that you had to pay a certain amount for the service, either in money or a return on goods. The most accepted manner of payment was giving the miller a certain portion of the ground flour. Up until the last quarter of the 19th century, flour was not weighed but measured in special containers and receptacles. This often gave rise to anger and disputes. Was the receptacle to be filled level to the rim or with a nice mound rising in the middle? Many farmers felt the millers took gross advantage of the situation and declined the use of the miller in favor of grinding their own grain at home.

It is estimated by Polish historians that in the 15th and 16th centuries, close to 60 percent of all grains designated for human consumption in Poland were ground at home with mortar and pestle or quern. When watermills became more widespread, 30 percent of all the grains were ground with mortar and pestle or a quern. The massive destruction that occurred in Poland in the second half of the 17th century because of numerous wars led to the return of grinding grain at home. By the 19th century there is another decrease in home milling but the period of World War I brought on an unexpected rise in the use of the quern. The war once again caused the destruction of mills. The millers, their sons, and helpers were called up to serve in the military leaving people to once again fend for themselves. Food made with flour became extremely scarce and the Poles brought out their home querns in an effort to avoid starvation. In the regions of Poland under German rule, the use of the home quern was forbidden. Even though the punishment for grinding your own flour was extremely severe, the Poles continued to use their querns under great secrecy. They hid their querns in specially dug pits or in the brush and undergrowth of dense forests. In 1918 in Pułtusk (outside of Warsaw), when the German administration combed the woods and fields to uncover hidden querns, they confiscated more than 300 home querns but their owners remained unidentified.

History repeated itself again during World War II and more than one family avoided starvation by grinding their own grains at home on the simple quern or, if even that was lost in the war, through the use of a hand-turned coffee grinder.

## KASZA

*Kasza to matka nasza.*
Grain is our mother.

In Poland, the word *kasza* is a general term that can refer to any cereal grain including wheat, rye, oats, buckwheat, barley, or millet. Very often the word is clarified by using the name of the specific grain such as *kasza jaglana* (millet) or *kasza gryczana* (buckwheat groats). Grains such as wheat, barley, and millet were being used as food for both man and beast in ancient Egypt in 6000 B.C. and later by the Greeks and Romans. Archeological digs in Great Poland reveal that barley, wheat, and millet were being grown in Poland during the Stone Age as were peas, fava beans, and to a lesser degree, lentils. Rye and oats were latecomers to Poland. The earliest, most primitive types of foods were loose mixtures of ground grains mixed with water or milk and eaten as a porridge or gruel. In the 17th century, Szymon Syreński (Syreniusz) wrote: "Before people began eating bread, they ate ground barley and wheat." In his cookbook Czarniecki made note of the use of wheat, rye, and both the regular and pearl barley.

Grains and the eating of grains took place at every important holiday and family celebration so that throughout the centuries, the term *kasza* meant one of the more important moments in life. In Poland, Russia, and Bulgaria the word *kasza* was used to denote a birth or christening. To say *zapraszamy na kaszę,* "we invite you for kasza" was an invitation to a wedding. Over time the eating of ground grains at a wedding was replaced by the preparation of a loaf of bread called a *kołacz* or *korowaj*. Along the same vein, *babczyna kasza* was an invitation to a christening.

According to Gołębiowski, the terms *sałamacha* or *sałamata* were Tartar terms that were used interchangeably for a gruel or porridge made of oat flakes. Among white Russians, *sałamata* meant a sweet drink made of honey, vodka, plums, and cherries. In the Ukraine, it was a thin soup made from buckwheat with a little salt. Among the Cossacks, *sałamata* was a thick wheat porridge which was both a beverage and food.

*Mamałyga, małałyga,* or *małaj* are other terms used by Polish food historians. This is a dish made with wheat (some say with corn) and eaten with cheese. In some regions, *mamałyga* is the name for a thin soup of grain while in others it refers to a flat cake or pancake.

Among the Poles, *polewka* was a sour soup made from some type of crushed grain. *Zacierka* was also an old name for a soup made from grains. *Kruszobka* was a thin porridge eaten with grains. There were numerous other dishes made from grains such as *frejdka*, *muza*, *rozworka*, and *rawarka.* The names appear in various historical sources but how they were prepared has been lost to us.

## BUCKWHEAT

**H**ere in America when Polish Americans hear the word *kasza* it conjures up images of buckwheat groats. Besides being called *gryczana*, it was also called *hreczka* or *gryka.*

Buckwheat, unlike rye, wheat, and oats, does not grow as the tall grass that we are familiar with when we think of grains. It grows as a small bushy plant and is harvested late, after frost has killed the plant. Buckwheat groats are whole, hulled, triangular buckwheat seeds that are pale in color until toasted which gives them a brown appearance and nutty flavor. One of its chief advantages is that it will grow in poor soil and rocky areas, making it a favorite crop to grow in many parts of Eastern Europe, Poland, and Russia. Polish food historians believe that the Tartars supposedly introduced buckwheat to the Greeks and then to the Slavs who readily adopted it and also called the grain *tatarka.* The use of the grain as a food spread throughout the rest of Europe. Growing buckwheat was then adopted in America, especially in the southern states, where it was ground into an inexpensive flour for making buckwheat pancakes.

It is not surprising that buckwheat groats were an important staple of the Polish diet. It is highly nutritious and takes a shorter amount of time to cook than wheat. This saved fuel which was an important consideration during times when all cooking was done with wood. The cooked grain was served plain with milk and milk products, salt pork or meat, and gravies. The ground kernels resulted in a very desirable buckwheat flour. The flour was used to make buckwheat noodles, often thought to be the best type of noodles, cooked with milk. Some buckwheat noodles were made with yeast. Buckwheat flour was also used to make a flat cake called *tatarczuchy* and *prażucha*, a popular item at country fairs. A very ancient and traditional Christmas Eve dish in the Lublin area was cabbage leaves stuffed with buckwheat groats.

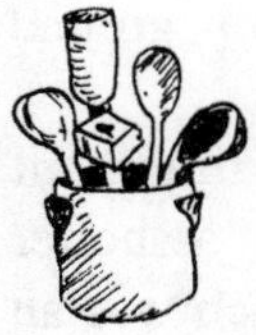

# Buckwheat Groats

***(Kasza)***

*Any leftover gravies are great over* kasza. *Add a vegetable for a satisfying meatless dinner.*

2 cups water or chicken, beef, or mushroom stock
1 teaspoon salt (optional)
¼ teaspoon pepper
1 tablespoon butter
1 cup buckwheat groats *(kasza)*
1 egg, slightly beaten

1. In a small saucepan combine the water or stock with salt, pepper, and butter and bring to a boil.
2. While that is coming to a boil, combine the buckwheat groats with the egg and mix thoroughly so that all kernels are coated with the egg. Transfer to a 1-quart saucepan and heat the groats over high heat for 1 to 2 minutes until groats appear dry.
3. Add boiling liquid to the heated kernels and stir through. Reduce heat and steam gently for 10 minutes until all liquid is absorbed.

SERVES 4

## MILLET

From sources written in the late Middle Ages, it is known that millet—dried, crushed, and baked in a hot oven—was taken on the road by Polish soldiers as war rations. It only required pouring boiling water or milk on it to reconstitute it into a satisfying gruel or porridge or to be baked on a hot rock to make a quick and filling flatbread. Over the centuries, millet, known as *kasza jaglana* or *proso* continued to dominate as major article of consumption.

Millet had a very important place in Polish peasant cookery. Along with barley it was one of the most frequently consumed grains followed by buckwheat, oats, and rough-ground rye. It was cooked and added to noodles and mushrooms or eaten with milk and drippings. Mixed with fried onions it provided a hearty filling dish. Served with raisins or sugar it really made a major statement at a country wedding. In Polesie, millet was one of the most important dishes served at a christening. Mixed with salt pork, it was eaten at the beginning of the celebration. The people in the Kaszuby region served millet mixed with honey at weddings.

Unlike buckwheat groats, which withstood the test of time and continued to be popular into the 20$^{th}$ century, millet began to fall out of favor when a newer grain called rice began to become available. Rice, called *biała kasza*, initially was considered so special that it was reserved for important feasts such as weddings. Currently, most people know millet only as birdseed.

## BARLEY

Barley is considered to be among the oldest cultivated grains. It was one of the earliest grains to be harvested by man and to be steeped in boiling water to make a crude porridge. It was the chief bread plant in the ancient world as well as for hundreds of years in Europe. Two types of barley called *jęczmień* were available for human consumption in Poland: the rougher peeled or hulled barley called *pęcak* or *pęczak*, and the finer, milled pearl barley called *perłowa*. Barley was eaten with soups, milk, buttermilk, or cream. The word *krupnik* can mean a barley soup but it also can refer to honeyed vodka. In Rzeszów and Kielce, barley dominated as a major foodstuff. *Spółka* was a barley and pea porridge. Barley flour was used to make noodles and bread and was often mixed with rye flour for the same purpose.

Barley was so important a foodstuff for centuries that it played a major role in all important festivities. In many parts of Poland the bride and groom had to eat a bowl of cooked barley which was to have the power of uniting them in thought and purpose. Over time the traditional grains were replaced by newer grains such as rice.

# BARLEY SOUP

***(Krupnik)***

*Polish ethnographers agree that krupnik along with* barszcz *and* kapuśniak *are considered true Polish soups. It is a mixture of many Polish staples—barley, potatoes, and mushrooms.*

½ pound beef bones or chicken backs and necks
2 quarts water
1 celery stalk, chopped
1 small onion, chopped
1 cup sliced fresh mushrooms
½ cup pearl barley
1 teaspoon salt
1 teaspoon pepper
2 large potatoes, peeled and diced

1. Rinse off bones or poultry pieces and place in the water. Bring to a boil. Skim off any foam that forms with slotted spoon. Add celery, onion, mushrooms, and barley. Allow to simmer for an hour or until beef is tender.
2. Remove bones with slotted spoon. Pick meat off bones and return to pot. Add salt, pepper, and potatoes and cook another 10 minutes until soft.

SERVES 4 TO 6

## BREAD

Historical records reveal a variety of baked goods made from flour in 14th-century Poland. For instance, crescent rolls, known as *rogaliki* were a favorite of Queen Jadwiga, wife of King Jagiełło. A sweet dough of flour and honey called a *miodownik* was also being made and a dough wrapped around cheese that we know today as *strucla*. There were pancakes made of cheese, poppy seeds, and saffron that were fried in oil. There were also various types of soft pretzels called *obwarzanki*.

In spite of a variety of different kinds of rolls and sweet dough, the main type of bread that was consumed was rye bread. White bread made of fine wheat flour, as we know it, was considered a true luxury seen only in the most prosperous homes or sometimes for special holiday baking. Rye bread, made from coarsely ground flour called *razowy*, was the norm throughout all of Poland from the 10th century on. Historical records reveal that dark rye bread served as the penance meal for King Boleslaw II (1042?–1082) during his pilgrimage of atonement to Hungary. Rye bread was also made from more finely ground rye flour that was called *pytlowy*.

Bread was often dried to a hard consistency in the oven and taken on trips. During times of war and long marches on foot or on sea or river voyages, or even in monasteries where fasting was very strict, dried bread, also known as *biscoctum* (biscuits or hard tack), was consumed. These dry biscuits were already being prepared in various ways in the 14th and 15th centuries.

Rye has always thrived in eastern and central Europe because it grows in poorer soil making it popular in Russia, Germany, Poland, and throughout the Scandinavian countries. It will thrive where wheat will not even survive. A mixture of rye and wheat was common in Lublin and the Małopolska. In the Beskid Mountains and Podhale, a combination of rye and oat flour was common. In Rzeszów, rye and barley was favored. Added to various flours were raw, grated potatoes or cooked mashed potatoes for added moistness. Pumpkin was added in Pomorze and Wielkopolska. Ground lentils, peas, bran, or cabbage and onions were also added to stretch the flour, especially in early spring when the larder became leaner and leaner. In times of extreme hunger and famine, chestnuts, acorns, and peas were ground and added to flour as an extender. During times of starvation, couch grass (*Agropyron repens*), pigweed (*Chenopodium album*), and even the root of trees were ground and added to the flour. They didn't necessarily add to the flavor of the bread but cheated the stomach into feeling full. The most frequent additive or extender to bread was potatoes. The potatoes were generally frozen ones, unsuitable for eating any other way.

Bread was baked from coarsely ground flour from the grains of rye, barley, wheat, oats, buckwheat, and sometimes corn. There were also combinations of various grains such as buckwheat flour and rye. Buckwheat was dried, ground, and mixed with salt and a leavening agent. This bread, often baked in clay pots, was best eaten fresh as it crumbled and fell apart after a few days.

One of the most primitive types of bread, called *moskol*, could be found among the *Górale,* the mountain people of southern Poland. This was bread made from oats or from barley. Sometimes cooked potatoes were added. The roughly ground oats or barley were mixed by hand with water and a pinch of salt. It was kneaded until hard, shaped flat by the palm of the hand, and baked on a flat metal sheet placed over glowing coals. The top of this oatcake or oatbread was fairly smooth but on baking and breaking in half to eat, it was as stiff and hard as a brush. Even this simple bread was considered expensive because it required a fair amount of flour and was subsequently only baked from time to time. This type of bread could still be found in the valleys around Nowy Targ in the period between the two World Wars. It was given to children for their lunch when they went to school and was prepared for adults during times of hard labor in the fields such as harvest time.

### *Bread Day*

In his book of collected proverbs, S. Adalberg collected 179 proverbs about bread. Some include:

*Chleb i woda to nie ma głoda.*
Water and bread, there is no hunger.

*Bez chleba, nie obiad.*
Without bread, there is no dinner.

*Chleb pracą nabyty, bywa smaczny i syty.*
Bread obtained through work is tastier and more filling.

*Komu chleb zaszkodzi, temu kij pomoże.*
Whomever bread troubles, perhaps a stick will help.

*Trzeba chleba i nieba.*
One needs only bread and heaven.

*Jest kromka chleba, a na cóż mi buły.*
If there is a piece of bread, who needs rolls.

*Na Św. Jakub (July 25th), chleba nie kup.*
On St. Jacob's (July 25th), no need to buy bread.

*Kto ma chleb, niech nie szuka kołaczów.*
Who has bread, need not seek cake.

In Polish tradition, bread was a symbol of plenty and success. Not everyone had their fill of it. In many situations it appeared at the table only on Christmas and Easter, or at a christening or wedding. According to Adam Chętnik, a Polish ethnographer who documented life of the Kurpie region, "the life of a Kurp is more than humble. He generally eats sauerkraut, potatoes, and beet soup. It requires a well-to-do home to find a piece of dark bread within." In some regions of Mazowsze and Podlasie, it was common practice among the country folk to lay a loaf of bread covered with a white linen towel on the table when entertaining guests.

The all-important task of breadmaking was usually done once a week and was an all day affair. Most breads made at home used a "sour" dough known as *kwas* as a leavening agent. Yeast did not

*Country woman with a braided bread called* kukiełka. *These breads were baked by a godmother for her new godchild. Village of Gostwica, 1965. Photo by B. Czarnecki. Courtesy of the National Ethnographic Museum, Warsaw.*

make an appearance in country villages until the late 1800s and even then was used only to bake special holiday breads. Baking powder as a leavening agent was the last to come along after World War I. For everyday consumption, the Polish housewife prepared her bread from sour dough.

In the first phase of this process, warm water was added to one-half or one-third of the flour used for that week's breadbaking. This was mixed in the dough bin for as long as needed until it looked like milk. Then the dough bin and its contents were covered with a clean cloth or a wooden cover and placed on a thin layer of straw so that the bottom could be warm and it was left overnight. This mixture was made active by taking advantage of the wild yeasts naturally available in the rye flour or in starchy foods such as potatoes, and became sour, hence the name sourdough. Sometimes it took longer to sour. In newer dough bins, it often soured for up to four days. In some areas the process was accelerated with the addition of whey, potatoes or potash. Each housewife knew her dough bin and took this into account as part of her preparations.

Sometimes, instead of starting from scratch with each baking, the housewife kept a steady supply of this soured flour and water mixture which today we call sourdough starter. Kept in a crock in a warm place, the housewife had an unending supply of leavening. Each time a portion was used for baking, an equal portion of the mixture was saved, more flour and water added, and then it was allowed to bubble up and "work" until needed for the next week's baking.

### *Dough Bin*

The dough bin used by Polish housewives was made from tightly woven straw or wood. The best dough bins were made of oak and if it wasn't possible to construct it entirely of oak at least a few strips of oak were used. The best dough bins were also those inherited from family members since they were well used and had successfully yielded good dough for bread. There were a lot of beliefs and folklore associated with the dough bin. There were dough bins who liked it quiet, some were averse to the cold. The dough bin could also be affected if sniffed by a dog, cat, or pig. Many housewives refused to lend to lend their dough bins, say for instance, if a neighbor lost one through fire, because a sloppy housewife could ruin it, that is, lose its ability to sour and because of the belief that "dough bins are afraid of strange thresholds." In situations where the dough bin was lent to a neighbor or family member, the borrower was required to return it with a piece of *podpłomyk* (bread) in it, covered with a clean cloth, and the borrower was to say "The Lord repay you." This would protect the dough bin from the evil eye. If, regardless of taking precautions, the dough refused to rise it could still be rescued. The dough bin could be incensed with blessed herbs such as those blessed on the feasts of the Assumption or Corpus Christi. Older beliefs stressed how a dough bin could be bewitched so that no matter what, the dough would not rise.

The dough bin was never washed. The old soured fragments of dough clinging to its sides were often the basis for the fermentation of the next batch of dough.

## *Preparing for Baking*

The next step in the breadmaking process was to inspect the watery dough for bubbling and a sour smell. If all was right, the second step of the process could begin. The rest of the flour was added, along with additional water and some salt and kneaded. It was again covered, kept in a warm place to rise until the next morning. The next day the housewife would knead it down, shape the loaves either freehand or with the help of coiled rye baskets into round loaves. In the Łowicz region, the loaves were placed in clean clay potsplaited straw, or *krążki* (what we today call a banneton) made from linden for the rising. While the dough was rising for a second time, the oven was prepared.

The bread oven was a small, enclosed fireplace with its own flue, leading into the main central flue. In order to heat it to the proper temperature, a fire of kindling was started on the oven floor and during the course of an hour or more, wood was constantly fed into the fire until the walls were glowing hot. (In some parts of Poland, a small

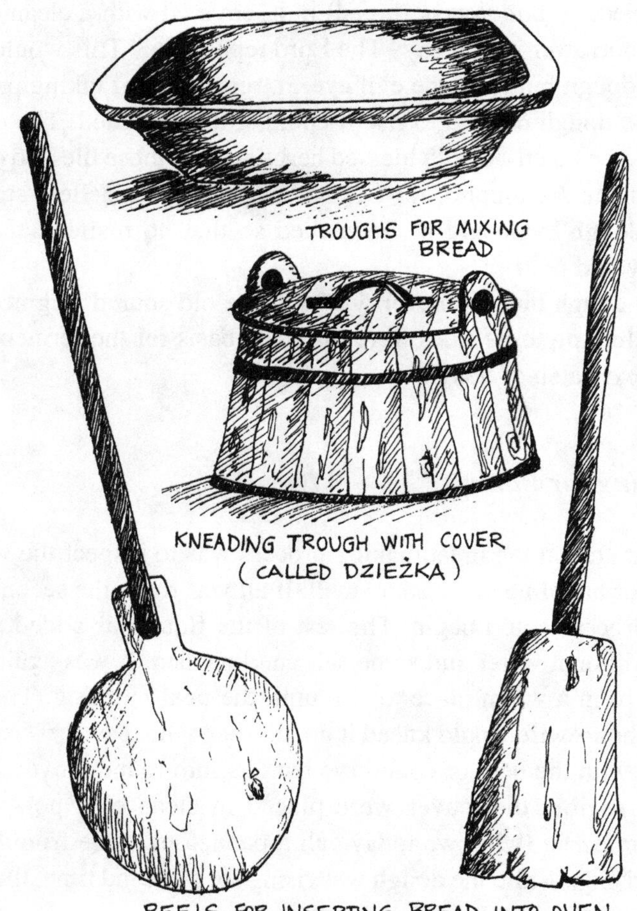
• UTENSILS FOR MAKING BREAD •
TROUGHS FOR MIXING BREAD
KNEADING TROUGH WITH COVER
( CALLED DZIEŻKA )
PEELS FOR INSERTING BREAD INTO OVEN
( CALLED ŁOPATA )

village would have a communal bake oven located outside in a central area or people could take the dough to a baker for final baking).

When the housewife decided the oven had reached the right temperature, she scraped out the ashes with what is called *kosiory* in Poland and swept the bottom until it was clean and then plugged the flue. Great loaves of coarse rye, wheat, or potato dough, sometimes weighing 7 or 8 pounds each, were placed on dampened horseradish, burdock, or cabbage leaves.

Before placing the risen dough in the hot oven, the housewife slashed the top of the bread with the sign of the cross. A long handled peal was used to place the rounded loaves into the oven, often rearranging the loaves to try and get them to bake and brown evenly. She then closed the oven opening with a wooden door and left the loaves to bake slowly. The bread would bake for 1 to 2 hours depending on the oven, and if potatoes were added to the bread, even more time was required. The housewife knew that it was done when tapping on top of the loaf produced a hollow sound.

A loaf of freshly baked bread, whether thick and coarse for everyday consumption or light and fine for high holy days, was treated with reverence. Even to this day many a country housewife who bakes her own bread will make the sign of the cross over it before cutting into it.

A well-baked loaf of bread was the pride of every housewife and a girl was not considered marriageable until she was able to bake a decent loaf of bread.

Aside from the usual large loaves of bread, small *podpłomyki* were made from the dough sticking to the sides of the dough bin. Many felt that these small pieces of dough were the most tasteful. In the center of these pieces of dough, small pieces of chopped onion with oil or butter were added or sometimes honey. Before placing it in the oven, the housewife scored the dough so that it would be easier to break in half or quarters after baking. This hot *podpłomyk*, baked on the edge of the oven was shared with neighbors or the children eagerly awaiting something fresh from the oven.

A• RAKES FOR PULLING HOT COALS OFF OVEN FLOOR (CALLED KOSIÓRY)
B• BROOM FROM STRAW C• FROM RAGS D• FROM PINE BOUGHS
FOR CLEANING OUT ASHES FROM STOVE.

# Sourdough Starter

*(Zakwas)*

3 medium-size potatoes
2 cups water
2 cups unbleached flour
2 tablespoons sugar
½ teaspoon active dry yeast

1. Scrub the potatoes and cook in the water until completely soft and falling apart. Drain, saving the water. Pick off potato skins and mash potatoes either by hand or in blender to make a thick purée. Add enough of the drained potato water to the potatoes to measure 2 cups. Add lukewarm water if needed to make 2 cups. The thicker the potato purée, the richer the starter. Cool mixture to 110°F (this is important).
2. Transfer the purée to a small crock, bowl, or glass jar. Whisk in the flour, sugar, and yeast until smooth.
3. Cover mixture with clean cloth or lid and set on kitchen countertop for at least 48 hours and up to 5 days. The mixture will begin to bubble and have a mild yeasty/sour fragrance. If the mixture is flat and has changed to a dark color, it cannot be used. Discard and start again.
4. Begin to build up the amount of starter you have by mixing in 1 cup of flour, 1 cup of water, and a pinch of sugar every 2 to 3 days. This is what is called "feeding" the starter to keep it active.
5. To use for a sourdough bread recipe, stir and remove starter needed for the recipe. To replenish the starter it is used, add equal amounts of water and flour i.e., if you use 1 cup of starter add 1 cup flour and 1 cup warm water.

# SOURDOUGH BREAD

***(Chleb na zakwasie)***

***Bread leavened only with sourdough may result in a thicker, less palatable bread than most people are accustomed to today. The addition of some yeast makes for a light, tender bread.***

5½ to 6 cups unbleached flour
One ¼-ounce package active dry yeast
1½ cups water
3 tablespoons sugar
1 teaspoon salt
3 tablespoons butter
1 cup Sourdough Starter (above)
Cornmeal

1. Bring unbleached flour to room temperature.
2. Combine 3 cups of the flour and yeast in bowl. In a small saucepan heat the water, sugar, salt, and butter just until till warm (110° to 115°F). Add to flour mixture. Mix together briefly and then add Sourdough Starter. Mix with electric mixture for 2 minutes. Add remaining 2½ to 3 cups of flour and continue mixing for another 5 minutes. Bring dough to lightly floured work surface and knead until smooth and elastic about 5 to 10 minutes.
3. Place dough in well-greased bowl, turning the dough so that all sides are well greased. Use a pastry brush with some vegetable oil if necessary to make sure entire top is well greased. This prevents the top of the dough from drying out as the dough rises. Cover with a cloth and place in warm area. Allow to rise until double in bulk—1½ to 2 hours.
4. Place risen dough on kneading board and shape into 2 round loaves. Place on slightly greased cookie sheet sprinkled with a little cornmeal. Cover with a damp cloth and let rise another hour.
5. Preheat oven to 375°F. Place a 9 × 13-inch shallow roasting pan or something similar filled with ½ inch of water on the floor of a gas oven or the bottom shelf of an electric oven to humidify the oven. When ready to place the dough into the oven, quickly slash top of bread with an X using

a single edge razor. This helps excess gas escape and keeps the top of bread from cracking.

6. Place bread into the preheated, humidified oven. After 15 to 20 minutes remove pan with water and continue baking for another 15 to 20 minutes until brown. Remove from baking sheet and place on a rack to cool.

MAKES 2 ROUND LOAVES

# Rye Bread

***(Razowy Chleb)***

2½ cups rye flour
2½ cups unbleached white flour
1½ cups warm water (110° to 115°F)
Two ¼-ounce packages active dry yeast
1 tablespoon sugar
½ cup unsulphered molasses
2 teaspoons salt
2 tablespoons vegetable oil
Cornmeal

1. Bring flour to room temperature.
2. Place warm water in mixing bowl. Sprinkle yeast over water, allow to soften briefly and mix to dissolve. Add the sugar and stir.
3. Add the molasses, salt, and oil. Stir rye and white flour together and add to liquids. Mix together. If dough seems too wet, add more white flour a tablespoon at a time until dough is smooth and elastic. Place dough in well-greased bowl, turning the dough so that all sides are well greased. Use pastry brush with some vegetable oil if necessary to make sure entire top is well greased. This prevents the top of the dough from drying out as the dough rises. Cover with a cloth and place in warm area. Allow to rise until double in bulk—1½ to 2 hours.
4. Place risen dough on kneading board and shape into 2 round loaves. Place on slightly greased cookie sheet sprinkled with a little cornmeal. Cover with a damp cloth and let rise another hour.
5. Preheat oven to 375°F. Place a 9 × 13-inch shallow roasting pan or something similar filled with ½ inch of water on the floor of a gas oven or the bottom shelf of an electric oven to humidify the oven. When ready to place the dough into the oven, quickly slash top of bread with an X using a single edge razor. This helps excess gas escape and keeps the top of bread from cracking.
6. Place bread into the preheated, humidified oven. After 15 to 20 minutes remove the pan with water and continue baking for another 15 to 20 minutes until brown. Remove from baking sheet and place on a rack to cool.

MAKES 2 ROUND LOAVES

## Homemade White Bread

***(Biały Chleb)***

*When my mother brushed egg yolk on top of bread she used a homemade brush made of tying together the quill end of three or four good-sized white feathers she saved from plucking geese. Polish farm wives throughout the centuries have made pastry brushes from goose feathers.*

4 to 5 cups unbleached flour
1 small egg
2 cups milk
One ¼-ounce package active dry yeast
3 tablespoons sugar
4 tablespoons (½ stick) butter
1 teaspoon salt
1 tablespoon water
Vegetable oil
Handful of poppy seed

1. Bring flour and egg to room temperature.
2. Warm ½ cup of the milk in saucepan to 110° or 115°F. Measure accurately with thermometer. Too high a temperature will kill the yeast. Transfer to small bowl, stir in the yeast, and 1 tablespoon of the sugar. Let stand until mixture begins to foam or "proof." Some people call this "making a sponge."
3. Scald the remaining 1½ cups of milk with the butter in a saucepan. Pour into large bowl and allow to cool to 110° to 115°F. When sufficiently cool, add the yeast mixture, 3 cups of flour, remaining 2 tablespoons of sugar and the salt. Stir to blend completely. Mixture will be very sticky. Begin adding the additional 1 to 2 cups of flour until dough is manageable.
4. Turn dough out onto floured surface and knead, adding additional flour until the dough is smooth and elastic.
5. Completely oil the inside of a large clean bowl. Place the dough in the oiled bowl, turning it so as to bring the well-oiled side up. This prevents the top of the dough from drying out as the dough rises. Cover with a clean cloth or dishtowel. Allow dough to rise in a warm place, away from drafts until double in size—about 1 hour.

6. In the meantime, grease two 8½ × 4½-inch loaf pans. When dough has risen, punch it down. Cut dough into two equal parts, shape into loaves, and place in greased pans. Cover with cloth and let rise until double in size again—30 to 40 minutes.
7. In small bowl, whisk egg with the 1 tablespoon of water to make the egg wash. Brush over tops of risen bread and sprinkle with poppy seeds.
8. Preheat oven to 350°F. Place a 9 × 13-inch shallow roasting pan or something similar filled with ½ inch of water on the floor of a gas oven or the bottom shelf of an electric oven to humidify the oven. When ready to place the dough into the oven, quickly slash top of bread with an X using a single edge razor. This helps excess gas escape and keeps the top of the bread from cracking.
9. Place bread into the preheated, humidified oven. Bake loaves for 30 to 35 minutes or until golden brown and bread sounds hollow when tapped on top. Remove from pans onto racks and cool to room temperature before cutting.

TIMESAVER: If you have some old recipes from your grandmother's day that call for compressed yeast remember that today's active dry yeast (one ¼-ounce package) is equal to 1 cake of compressed yeast. Some people still like to use the compressed yeast although it may be harder to find. If you forget, most packages of active dry yeast have the equivalent on the back of the package.

MAKES TWO8½ × 4½-INCH LOAVES

## SUPERSTITIONS

It was inevitable that the process of preparing and eating bread was a special one filled with magical beliefs:

- ▶ When a new loaf of bread is cut, a sign of the cross is made over it.
- ▶ If a housewife lends or borrows the leaven for bread after the sun has set, the bread will not rise.
- ▶ The individual who is baking bread should not sit down until the bread is baked or it will fall.
- ▶ If your leavened dough does not rise, it means the leavening agent is broken. Steep the dough bin in blessed herbs. It will improve.
- ▶ Should a piece of bread accidentally fall to the ground, pick it up along with all the crumbs and kiss as if in apology.
- ▶ Whoever eats a piece of bread should never give from the same piece to another person because it will transfer his strength and health to the other person.

## PIEROGI

In eastern Poland during the period between the World Wars, there was a bread called *krzyże*. The exterior was a dough while the interior consisted of a filling made of 1 part flour to 3 parts potato. Polish food historians and ethnographers feel that pierogi is a close relative of *krzyże*.

Pierogi is a dumpling made from wheat, rye, or even barley flour that is filled various grains such as buckwheat groats, millet, lentils, or barley. They could be filled with potatoes, sweet cabbage, sauerkraut, grated beets or carrots, mushrooms, or ground meat, or with sweet ingredients such as cheese, poppy seeds, or fruit or any of the numerous combinations of the above. The stuffed dumplings are usually half moon shape, cooked in boiling water, and served up with a variety of toppings. In the Radom region of Poland, pierogi were called *pirog* and sometimes *papuski*.

The concept of a stuffed dumpling is known in many different guises throughout the world. At a Chinese restaurant you can order steamed pork or vegetable dumplings. The Russians call them *piroshki*, the Ukrainians call them *varenki,* and in Jewish cooking they are called *kreplach*. In Lithuania and northeastern reaches of Poland they are called *kołduny*. The Italians call them *ravioli* and even Polish ethnographer Łukasz Gołębiowki mentions ravioli in his *Domy i Dwory* which was published in 1884.

Up until the late 1800s, pierogi were considered a real delicacy in a country cottage. The dough for making pierogi requires a fair amount of flour as well as a fair amount of time to make—something many housewives didn't have since the round of work including house, children, and fields kept a woman going sixteen hours a day. In spite of that, each region of Poland had their favorite or special way of making pierogi. Cheese pierogi could be flavored with sugar or cinnamon. Others preferred pepper, chives, or onion in their cheese pierogi and liked to top it off with jam, sugar, butter, sweet cream, or sour cream. The same was true for the other types of fillings. Everyone had their particular preferences.

The traditional shape for pierogi is half round, but in Łowicz it was made completely round. In that region, the word *pierog* also meant a grain such as millet wrapped in a cabbage leaf, what many Poles call *gołąbki,* or stuffed cabbage leaves. Size varied, too. Some pierogis were made small and some, especially those stuffed with cabbage or sauerkraut, were so large as to completely fill a 12-inch plate. To complicate matters even further, pierogi were also made with yeast and baked instead of boiled in water. Baked pierogi made with grains such as millet were popular in the Łowicz region. Baked *pierogi* made from lentils, soybeans, mushrooms, and sauerkraut were also popular in the region known as Podlasie in northeastern Poland. The people from the Radom area made baked pierogi from grated beets. Boiled pierogi were known throughout Poland with the exception of the Śląsk and Kaszuby area.

Some Polish historians and writers claim that pierogi were brought to Poland from Russia to the Polish city of Sandomierz. That particular city had many political and commercial dealings with its close neighbor to the east and it's been suggested that perhaps a Russian princess who married into the wealthy Odrowąż clan taught her new family how to make pierogi. Pierogi made with a mixture of cheese and potato are, indeed, known as *ruskie*, or Russian pierogi, and are popular throughout the Lublin, Rzeszów, and eastern Mazowsze region. Wherever the origin, there is no dish more closely associated with Polish country cooking than pierogi.

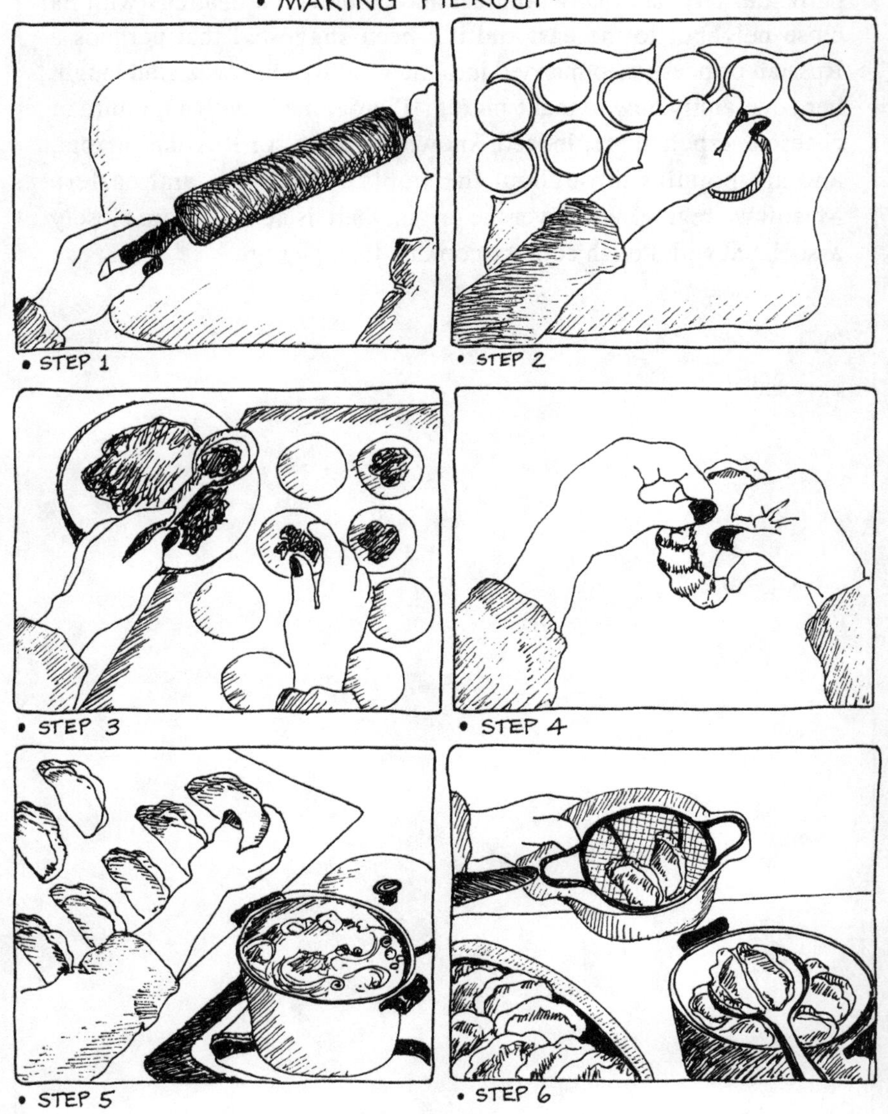
• MAKING PIEROGI •
• STEP 1
• STEP 2
• STEP 3
• STEP 4
• STEP 5
• STEP 6

# Pierogi Dough

*Preparing pierogi can be very time consuming and labor intensive when trying to make a large quantity. This recipe allows you to make the dough one day, the filling the next, and then put it together on the third day. This dough (which can easily be halved) freezes very well when tightly wrapped in plastic bags and kept frozen for no longer than a few weeks. I generally make the full dough recipe, use half and freeze the other half.*

6 cups all-purpose flour
½ cup (1 stick) margarine or butter, melted
2 eggs
1 teaspoon salt
One 16-ounce carton sour cream

1. Mix flour, melted margarine or butter, eggs, salt, and sour cream together on bread board or mixer with dough hook. Knead until firm. Allow to rest for an hour before using. May be refrigerated in plastic bag overnight. If so, bring to room temperature before using.
2. Divide dough into three sections. While working with one portion, keep others covered with an inverted bowl or in plastic bags to keep from drying out.
3. On lightly floured surface, roll out dough to ¼-inch thickness. Cut out 3-inch rounds with glass or biscuit cutter. Place a small spoonful of filling (recipes below) in center, fold over, and press edges firmly together. Be sure they are well sealed to prevent the filling from leaking out during boiling. If the edges refuse to seal, the dough may be drying out. Lightly moisten the edges of the dough with water and seal again.
4. As you work, place your raw pierogi on lightly floured surface and keep covered with clean dishtowel.
5. Drop the pierogi in large kettle of lightly salted, boiling water. The bigger the kettle the more pierogi you can cook at a time but they cannot be overcrowded. As you drop the pierogi into the kettle they will sink to the bottom. Stir them once lightly after dropping them in and watch for them to float to the top. Once they have done this, continue boiling gently for another 1 to 2 minutes.
6. Lift out with slotted spoon into a colander to drain. Some people rinse their pierogi under water while others, like myself, feel it is unnecessary.

Place the pierogi on a large buttered plate or platter, making sure the pierogi do not overlap each other. Serve immediately while hot with preferred toppings (see below). Some cooks like to allow the pierogi to cool and then fry them up in butter and serve them from the frying pan. Both methods are acceptable depending on who is watching their calories and cholesterol.

MAKES 12 DOZEN SMALL TO MEDIUM-SIZE PIEROGI

# Pierogi Fillings

## POTATO

½ cup finely chopped onion
2 tablespoons butter or bacon drippings
4 cups mashed potatoes
½ teaspoon salt
¼ teaspoon pepper

1. Sauté onion in butter or bacon drippings until golden. Mix in mashed potatoes. Allow to cool. Follow steps 3 through 6 of pierogi recipe.
2. Toppings include fried onions, bacon bits and drippings, sour cream or butter.

## SWEET CHEESE

1 to 2 pounds farmer cheese
1 large egg
3 to 4 tablespoons granulated sugar
¼ to ½ cups yellow raisins (optional)

1. Mix cheese, egg, and sugar until well mixed. Add raisins if desired. Follow steps 3 through 6 of pierogi recipe.
2. Toppings that can be used on the cooked pierogi include melted butter, sugar, or fruit and fruit syrup.

## POTATO AND CHEESE

½ cup finely chopped onions
4 tablespoons butter or bacon drippings
2 cups mashed potatoes
1 pound farmer cheese
1 egg
½ teaspoon salt
¼ teaspoon pepper

1. Sauté onion in butter or drippings until golden.
2. Mix together mashed potatoes with the cheese, fried onions, egg, salt, and pepper. Follow steps 3 through 6 of pierogi recipe.
3. Toppings that can be used on the cooked pierogi include fried onions, bacon bits and bacon drippings, sour cream, butter, or sugar.

## FRUIT

2 cups fresh or slightly thawed frozen blueberries, blackberries, cherries, etc.
2 tablespoons flour
Sugar

1. In medium-size bowl, mix berries and flour together very gently. Place the berries in the center of dough. Sprinkle ½ teaspoon sugar on top if berries are tart.
2. Follow steps 3 through 6 of pierogi recipe.
3. Toppings include sour cream, butter, or sugar.

## MEAT

*You can make meat pierogi from any leftover meat. My mother would make them from leftover ground turkey, chicken, or beef. Nothing was ever wasted.*

1 pound cooked, leftover roast beef with drippings
1 small onion, chopped fine
1 tablespoon vegetable oil
1 teaspoon salt
½ teaspoon pepper

1. Place cooked roast beef in food processor and pulse until beef is in small pieces, adding drippings to make mixture moist but not dripping wet.
2. Fry chopped onion in oil until golden. Remove from heat. Add minced roast beef, salt, and pepper and mix together.
3. Follow steps 3 through 6 of pierogi recipe.
4. Toppings can include leftover drippings, butter, or sour cream.

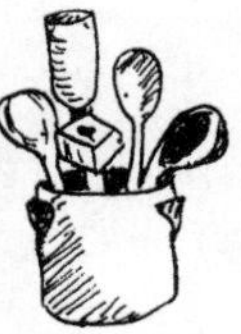

## SAUERKRAUT

*You can cook sauerkraut just to make pierogi or use leftovers. Do not use raw sauerkraut.*

3 to 4 cups cooked sauerkraut

1. Place sauerkraut in food processor and pulse until the sauerkraut is in small pieces. This makes it easy to fill the dough without long strings of sauerkraut getting in the way.
2. Follow steps 3 through 6 of pierogi recipe.
3. Toppings can include drippings or butter.

TIMESAVER: To freeze pierogis, place the boiled and cooled pierogi in airtight plastic bags or containers and freeze. When you are ready to prepare them, allow to come to room temperature. You can drop them into a pot of boiling water again if you like them boiled, or fry in a pan with butter and/or bacon drippings.

# Lazy Pierogi

**(*Leniwe pierogi*)**

*Polish Americans know lazy pierogi as a casserole of noodles, mushrooms, and sauerkraut. In Poland,* leniwe pierogi *is a mix of flour, eggs, and cheese made into dumplings and boiled. Everything rolled into one with less fuss and muss than the real pierogi.*

2 quarts water
2 teaspoons salt
1 pound farmer cheese
3 egg yolks
1½ cups all-purpose flour
3 egg whites, beaten

1. Place the water in a large cooking pot with 1 teaspoon salt on stove over low heat.
2. While water is slowly coming to a boil, combine cheese with egg yolks. Add the flour and remaining 1 teaspoon salt. In another mixing bowl, beat egg whites until stiff peaks form. Gently add beaten egg whites to cheese and flour mixture and stir lightly until well mixed. The dough will be sticky but should be soft and light. Divide into two portions. Place half of the dough onto a well-floured bread board or countertop and roll into a long roll, in the shape of a sausage. Cut off pieces at an angle, ¼ inch thick, with a sharp knife. Repeat this process with the other half of the dough.
3. Gently drop the dumplings in the boiling water two or three at a time until all have been placed in the pot. Stir very gently and within a few minutes they will float to the top. Boil very gently another minute. Carefully remove the dumplings in small batches from the pot with a slotted spoon into a colander and allow to drain briefly. Place on a well-buttered platter. Do not allow the dumplings to overlap one another as they will stick. Remove the rest of the dumplings in like manner. Serve while hot. In Poland the *leniwe pierogi* are drizzled with bacon drippings and bits of bacon. They can be reheated the next day in boiling water or fried on a well-greased frying pan.

SERVES 3 TO 4

## NOODLES

Flour from various grains was also made into a variety of noodles. The name of the noodle often varied from region to region but the names often suggest the method of preparation. *Krajane kluski* was a noodle made from dough rolled out flat and cut into thin strips. *Zacierka* was a piece of dough rolled with the fingers or rubbed against a grater. *Lane* were made from a thin wheat dough and egg, drizzled into soup or stew. *Drożdżowe* were made with yeast. *Kładzione* were drop dumplings made from a thicker wheat dough and egg mixture and dropped into a boiling soup or stew with a spoon. There were flat noodles cut into different shapes such as *łazanki* which were egg noodles cut into small squares. My mother liked to make *łazanki* for her mushroom soup on Christmas Eve.

# Egg Noodles

***(Kluski)***

*Remember the days before Formica countertops when everything was rolled out on the kitchen table on a large, hardwood pastry board? At our house it seemed there were always homemade noodles drying on the board.*

2¼ cups all-purpose flour
⅓ cup water
2 eggs
1 tablespoon vegetable oil
1 teaspoon salt

1. In large mixing bowl, combine 1 cup of the flour with the water, eggs, vegetable oil, and salt. With mixer at low speed, beat for 2 to 3 minutes. If you have a heavy-duty mixer with dough hook, gradually add the remaining flour to make a soft dough. If not, add rest of flour with a wooden spoon.
2. Turn the dough onto a lightly floured surface. Knead until smooth and elastic, about 10 minutes. Cover to prevent drying out and let dough rest for 30 to 45 minutes.
3. On lightly floured surface, roll out the dough into a large 18 × 20-inch rectangle, stretching the dough a little with each roll. As you roll and stretch, keep sprinkling lightly with flour both under the dough and over the top of the dough to keep it from sticking to the rolling pin or surface. Keep rolling until the dough is very thin. Let dry for about 30 minutes.
4. Cut the sheet of dough into 2- to 3-inch-wide strips. Making sure each strip is well floured, stack the strips one on top of the other and cut crosswise into ¼-inch "matchstick" widths. Separate the cut dough and place in single layer on floured surface to dry for at least 2 hours before using. Or dry completely, turning the noodles every day for 2 to 3 days and store in dry jars until needed.
5. Cook in boiling salted water until tender. Mix with cabbage, sauerkraut, cheese, poppy seeds, and so on.

MAKES 4 CUPS

# Egg Noodle Squares

***(Łazanki)***

***My mother always made these noodle squares for her mushroom soup on Christmas Eve.***

1. Follow the previous Egg Noodle recipe steps 1 through 3.
2. Cut the rectangle of dough into ½- or ¾-inch strips, depending on preference for size. Making sure each strip is well floured, stack strips one on top of the other and cut crosswise into small squares. Separate the squares and scatter them across a well-floured bread board. Allow to dry at least 2 hours before using. Or dry completely, turning the noodle squares every day for 2 to 3 days and store in dry jars until needed.
5. Cook in boiling salted water until tender. Add to soups, serve with meat, and/or gravies.

MAKES 4 CUPS

# Soup Dumplings

***(Kluski Kładzione)***

*One of the best and easiest ways to make noodles for soup, especially clear soups, is to drop them directly into the boiling broth. I love dropped soup dumplings with chicken broth. My mother had a large coffee cup that she used to make her drop noodles. I use a 2-cup glass measuring cup as the handle makes it easier to hold while stirring. This can be done quickly with a hand mixer, too.*

1 cup flour
1 large egg
¼ to ⅓ cup water
1 teaspoon salt
1 teaspoon parsley, dill, or chives (optional)

1. In 2-cup measuring cup or small bowl mix the flour with the egg, water, salt, and any optional herbs. Beat with a spoon until all flour is mixed, adding more water if needed to make a batter the consistency of thick cake batter.
2. With a regular kitchen teaspoon, pick up small portions (half a teaspoonful) of the batter and dip the spoon directly into the soup or broth. The batter will come away from the spoon. Repeat. Continue until all batter is used up.
3. Cook uncovered until dumplings float to the surface. Serve immediately. These dumplings do not improve with standing until the next day. *Note*: the addition of the dumplings will turn the soup cloudy. If all the soup you have made is not to be eaten at one sitting, you may wish to divide the soup in half and prepare only as much as you're going to eat.
4. If you are making dumplings to serve as side dish, drop the batter directly into a pot of boiling, lightly salted water. Cook uncovered until dumplings float to the surface. Remove with slotted spoon, place on greased platter with butter or oil, and serve. If using the next day, drain in colander and spread on platter until cooled. Refrigerate.

SERVES 2 TO 3

❖ LUCY'S HOUSEHOLD HINTS: Macaroni, flour, and buckwheat should be kept in a dry and airy place. To keep away insects, add one or two bay leaves.

## HOMEMADE BREAD CRUMBS

In all the years of my growing up I never saw my mother take the presence of bread on our table for granted. Growing up in the aftermath of World War I and experiencing World War II first hand, she knew what it was to be hungry. Bread was considered sacred and not a crumb or slice of it was ever wasted. If there was a slice or corner piece or crust left over she would place the bread in a paper bag that had small holes in it for circulation. When she had enough of these bread scraps, which by now were dry and hard, she would pull out her bread board and slowly crush the bread into bread crumbs with a rolling pin. Some of the bread was so hard she couldn't break it up with the rolling pin so she covered the bread with a dish towel and gave it a couple of good whacks with a hammer. It worked like a charm. When she was done, she would scoop up the various colored bread crumbs into a clean jar and place it in the refrigerator. She had her own bread crumbs for breading pork chops, fish, and *sznycle*, an oval-shaped hamburger coated with bread crumbs. She also used the bread crumbs to make a topping for fresh vegetables, especially cauliflower and the green beans that grew in our garden. This is a typical topping for vegetables in Poland and in culinary circles is called *vegetables polonaise*.

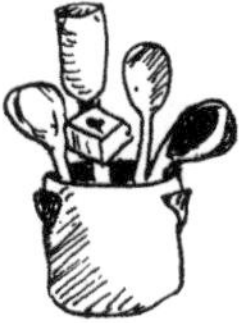

# Cauliflower Polonaise

***(Kalafior po polsku)***

*The amount of butter and bread crumbs depends on whether you are preparing a small or larger cauliflower or any other vegetable.*

1 whole cauliflower
4 to 8 tablespoons (½ to 1 stick) butter
4 to 8 tablespoons bread crumbs
1 teaspoon salt

1. Remove the large green leaves of cauliflower with a sharp knife. Cut the core to which they were attached flush with the head of cauliflower so that it rests evenly on the cutting board. Wash under running water.
2. Place the cauliflower in saucepan of boiling water with the right side up and core on bottom. Make sure entire head is covered with water. Cook the cauliflower 15 to 20 minutes or until tender.
3. While cauliflower is boiling, heat the butter in a small sauté pan until melted and hot.
4. Add bread crumbs and salt and mix together. Cook lightly until crisp.
5. When cauliflower is tender, remove from pot and allow to drain briefly. Place entire cauliflower right side up on round plate or platter. Spoon bread crumb mixture over cauliflower and serve. The browned bread crumbs contrast beautifully with the very pale cauliflower and looks pretty as a picture on the table!

SERVES 4 (SMALL HEAD) TO 6 (LARGE HEAD)

## SUMMER VEGETABLES

The latter part of July and August was a very intensive time in the kitchen and pantry, preparing foodstuffs that would take them through the difficult winter months and early spring. During this time housewives were sure there would be no unexpected guests or neighbors dropping by to gossip or exchange recipes. Everyone was busy getting ready for the cold time and making sure that everything from the kitchen garden and from the fields was marinated, dried, or pickled. One of Poland's favorite late summer vegetables is the cucumber. It is enjoyed both fresh and soaked in a brine as a pickle. Every Polish homemaker had her secrets for a tasty, crunchy pickle. Many recipes called for putting leaves such as oak, grape, black currant, cherry, or horseradish into the bottom of the jar which added additional flavoring and assisted with the fermentation process. Other recipes may call for fresh garlic or fresh horseradish root which makes the pickle more crispy. In my view, the best pickles are those made without vinegar. Adding vinegar to pickles speeds up the brining process but results in a different tasting pickle.

*Basket seller on the road. Illustration by Apoloniusz Kędzierski, 1885.*

# Auntie's Dill Pickles

***(Kiszone ogórki)***

*This is my Ciocia (Auntie) Stefa's recipe. I like these pickles after about three days, before fermentation is completed. When eaten before fermentation is completed they are generally referred to as half sour.*

1⅔ cups water
1 tablespoon salt
1 to 2 grape or black currant leaves, washed
1 whole branch dill
2 cloves garlic, cut in half
8 to 10 (3½-inch) thin cucumbers

1. Combine the water and the salt in a saucepan and bring to a boil. Allow to cool completely.
2. Wash a quart jar in hot water, rinse and dry well. Into bottom of jar place the washed grape or currant leaves, dill, and garlic.
3. Wash cucumbers and cut in half lengthwise. Pack cucumbers into the jar. Pour cooled brine over pickles so that it covers the cucumbers completely. Cover top of jar with clean cloth and tie with string at neck of jar or use rubber band. Place in warm area. Fermentation is ideal at 70° to 80°F and will be slower at cooler temperatures. Gas bubbles in the brine are a sign that fermentation is taking place.

MAKES 1 QUART

# Marysia's Dill Pickles

*This recipe from a friend makes a bigger batch of excellent pickles.*

4 to 8 quart baskets of small (4 to 6-inch) firm pickling cucumbers
3 to 5 stalks fresh dill
3 to 5 cloves garlic, sliced
½ slice rye bread
4 tablespoons salt
7 cups cold water

1. Wash cucumbers. Place one stalk of fresh dill and 1 or 2 cloves of garlic in bottom of clean 2- or 3-gallon crock. Place a layer of cucumbers on top. Place another layer of dill and garlic followed by cucumbers. Repeat the layering process until cucumbers are used up. Place the slice of rye bread on top.
2. Dissolve the salt in the cold water and pour the salt water into the crock covering all the pickles with water. Cover with a plate, bottom side up, which will fit into the opening. Place a canning jar filled with water on top to weigh the cucumbers down and keep them submerged.
3. Cover with a clean dishtowel and let stand at room temperature. Ready to eat after 3 to 4 days. Keep refrigerated.

MAKES 2 TO 3 GALLONS

# Cold Cucumber Soup

*(Chłodnik Ogórkowy)*

4 scallions, chopped
⅓ cup fresh dill
1 clove garlic, pressed
4 cucumbers, peeled, seeded, and coarsely chopped
3 tablespoons good quality olive oil
¼ cup lemon juice
1 teaspoon salt
¼ teaspoon pepper
5 cups plain yogurt or buttermilk
1 tablespoon fresh chopped dill as garnish (optional)

1. Combine the scallions, fresh dill, and garlic in bowl of food processor and pulse until finely chopped. Add the cucumbers, olive oil, lemon juice, salt, and pepper. Process until well blended.
2. Pour into a large bowl and whisk in yogurt or buttermilk until blended. Cover with plate or plastic wrap and refrigerate overnight. Serve cold with sprinkle of fresh dill on top if desired.

SERVES 6 TO 8

# Cucumbers in Sour Cream

*(Mizeria)*

*This is a vegetable dish that can be made very quickly while preparing other parts of a summer meal. The name* mizeria *(misery) suggests that it was a dish prepared by the poor. In the summer my mother would go out to the garden, pick some cucumbers and make a batch as part of our supper. When tomatoes started coming in she would slice up a few and add them last. Food doesn't get any better than this simple fare.*

2 thin cucumbers
1 teaspoon salt
2 to 3 tablespoons sour cream
1 teaspoon chopped fresh dill
1 tablespoon vinegar

1. Peel cucumbers and slice very thin into a medium-size bowl. Sprinkle salt over the cucumbers and mix. Allow to stand for 15 to 20 minutes to draw water from the cucumbers. Drain off liquid and squeeze out any remaining water in the cucumbers with your hands.
2. Place cucumbers back in bowl. Add sour cream, fresh dill, and vinegar. Mix together.

SERVES 2

❖ Lucy's Household Hints: In the event of loss of ice, meat can be preserved for a few days by wrapping the meat in nettle leaves, covering with a clean cloth and placing in a cool place.

# FEASTS & FESTIVALS

# Feasts & Festivals

Throughout the long year of struggling with the land to make ends meet, there was little time left in the life of a Polish farmer for fun and frivolity. Daily life was characterized by constant hard work to feed the family and get ahead. But there were the occasional family weddings and the special holy days associated with the church that provided some respite and relief in the day-to-day existence. Easter and Christmas were the high points of the entire year, but there were also smaller, yet highly significant, days on the calendar that brought joy and celebration into the lives of the people of Poland. And no day was looked forward to as much as the one on which the village celebrated the feast day of its patron saint.

From the beginning of Christianity, the church has venerated the persons who led a great life of holiness or suffered and died for the cause of God: the martyrs who died in persecutions, the virgins, the prophets and apostles, and all who are remembered for their good works. The Catholic saint's feast days first arose from the very early Christian custom of the annual commemoration of martyrs on the dates of their deaths. The names and dates of the individuals who were executed were carefully recorded. In the third century, bishops began also listing names of persons who did not reach the point of execution but died a natural death after having experienced persecution. These were holy people later canonized as saints. Most saints have specially designated feast days on a specific day of the year.

The practice of adopting patron saints harks back to the time of the building of the first public churches in the Roman Empire in the early days of Christianity—when most of them were built over the graves of martyrs. The churches were then given the name of the martyr and the martyr was expected to act as an intercessor for the people who worshipped there. Christians then began to dedicate churches to other holy men and women who were not martyrs but saints. Sometimes a church was named after a saint who had preached the gospel in the area and had died there, or perhaps a church was built where there had been miracles or visions of a particular saint. The cult of relics evolved during the Middle Ages and the building of a new church, more specifically the altar, required the relics of a saint. To this day a relic of a saint is placed inside the altar of each church and the church is named after that particular saint. Every church adopts its own special patron, becoming St. Stanislaus Church or St. John Kanty or St. Adalbert Basilica. There are hundreds of saints, sometimes hardly known to the rest of the world, but chosen for a particular reason by a new parish. Every church, parish diocese, ecclesiastical province, and every religious institution and community has its particular heavenly patron. In its long and venerable history of the acceptance of Christianity in 966 AD, and with a long list of its own saints, Poland kept these traditions of past centuries. The feast of the patron saint of a church was kept as a true holy day of religious solemnity by its parishioners and observed with great devotion and rejoicing.

In most circumstances, if the feast day of the saint fell on a weekday, the feast day was celebrated on the Sunday before or after the actual day of the liturgical feast on the calendar. Depending on the region and local tradition, the feast day celebration was begun on the eve of the feast day with vespers and lasted four days, culminating in the major celebration on a Sunday. This day was much anticipated and in Poland is called an *odpust*.

In Polish, the word *odpust* has two meanings. The first meaning is tied to religious practices and refers to an indulgence, that is, a way of fulfilling a penance for committing sins. Taking part in the religious observances on the church feast day gave the participant the opportunity to obtain indulgences for the forgiveness of sins. These church feast days and the chance to receive indulgences was very serious business and attracted a great many devout and faithful individuals. It also attracted numerous wandering salesmen selling devotional articles such as medals and prayer books, which were eagerly bought up by locals and visiting pilgrims. Not to be outdone, other merchants and tradesmen began setting up their own booths to sell not only religious objects, but sweets and souvenirs as well. Pretty soon it became an event that was important in the religious and spiritual sense, but also in the worldly sense of providing an opportunity to socialize, to meet new people, to hear some news, to look over the geegaws and trinkets in the booths, and have some fun. The word *odpust* began to mean both a church celebration and a time to be festive.

The religious aspect of the feast day focused on honoring the patron saint, seeking penance and reforming from sin. In preparation for the feast day, the pastor invited guest priests to hear confessions and assist in concelebrating a high mass called a *suma*. This high mass was held before noon, generally at 11 a.m., sometimes at 10:30. The church would be carefully cleaned and altars decorated with fresh flowers in preparation. The banners and flags of the various church society's and groups were removed from storage and dusted. The organist and choir practiced their music and songs—many of which were specifically devoted to the patron saint. The special day sometimes called for more than the organ and choir and an orchestra or ensemble of local musicians was organized to provide accompaniment to the mass and the all-important procession. The statue, large picture, or painting of the patron saint was carefully brought down from an altar and placed on a wheeled cart or special platform that would be carried on the shoulders of the bearers specifically chosen for this honor. It was the duty of the young unmarried girls to decorate this image with ribbons and flowers. The Holy Rosary Society, the Holy Name Society, and fraternal groups all prepared for this special day to honor their patron saint and celebrate their faith.

Władysław Reymont, winner of the Nobel Prize for literature for his masterpiece work titled *The Peasants*, describes an odpust in a small country village in the volume dedicated to Summer:

*It was the day of the local Feast - Saint Peter and Paul [...] and no sooner had the bells sent their merry peals over the countryside than all sorts of vehicles came rolling in through clouds of dust as far as the eyes could reach, with great crowds of people on foot. All the roads, lanes and field-paths were red with women's dresses or white with men's capotes [...] The pond was lined with women come to wash their feet clean of the dusty road, put their shoes on, and make themselves fit for church*

*[...] Several priests had come over from the nearer parishes. They at once took their places in confessionals, set up beneath the trees, and began to shrive the people.*"

While there were variations from church to church and region to region, at the completion of the high mass with its inspirational homily about the life of the saint, the parishioners participated in a procession that circled the church three times, weather permitting. It was the church organist who usually organized the order of the procession and there were variations on this, depending on the size of the parish community and the number of religious societies, etc., but essentially it consisted of the following: at the head of the procession was always an altar boy carrying a cross (either alone or sometimes assisted by two other altar boys, ringing bells); they were followed by all the religious clergy who had come to celebrate the occasion or maybe the musicians who kept up a steady stream of much-loved hymns while the voices of the entire procession sang out in joy and reverence; then men carrying the platform with the image of the patron saint; distinguished elders or members of an honor society carrying the banners and flags; the children in first communion clothes with the girls scattering rose petals and the boys carrying bouquets of flowers; the pastor or visiting priest carrying the Holy Sacrament in a monstrance covered by a *baldachim* (a canopy); the rest of the procession was composed of the remaining congregation, visiting pilgrims, men, women, and children. It was on these special feast days that the community would dress in their regional costumes or clothes. For instance, in Śląsk—a heavy coal mining region in Poland—on the feast day of St. Barbara, the men would proudly wear the special dress and regalia of the coalminers to pay tribute to their patron saint.

Each town, each village, each region had their particular way of celebrating the church observance. Much of it depended on the life of the saint and the role the saint had played in the life and times of the village. If it was the feast day of St. Anthony of Padua, the church would be decorated with lilies as the image of St. Anthony is often depicted with lilies. In the Kurpie region of Poland, on the Feast of St. Roch (August 16th), patron saint against pestilence and epidemics

*Banners and Feretories. Dębno, Zakopane region, 1990.*

*Procession. Dębno, Zakopane region, 1990.*

Votive offerings in the Kurpie region

and protector of cattle and friend of dogs, the parishioners brought gifts from nature to the altar in the form of bundles of wheat and flax and flowers. They also brought homemade candles affixed with small figures of domestic animals also made from wax as votive offerings.

After the mass, the parishioners processed out to a pasture beyond the village where sheep, cattle, and horses had been gathered. A bonfire was lit burning the green branches of the juniper bush with the addition of herbs blessed on Corpus Christi and the animals were driven through the gusts of smoke—first the sheep, then the cattle, then the horses—as a way of protecting them. During the entire proceedings, a drum kept up a steady beat. At the conclusion, the priest blessed the animals with holy water, concluding the event.

In Prostyń, in the Podlesie region of Poland in the year 1510, on the feast of the Holy Trinity, St. Anne is believed to have appeared to one of the village woman. Małgorzata, wife of Błażej, was instructed by St. Anne to tell village authorities to build a church dedicated to the Holy Trinity on the hill and a chapel in the place of her revelation. St. Anne left behind four wreaths made of herbs—three of them linked together as a sign of the Holy Trinity and the fourth one in her own memory. A church was built and named the Sanctuary of the Holy Trinity and St. Anne. The wreaths that St. Anne left during her revelation were encased in a special reliquary, a silver crown. For almost 500 years, during the celebration of the church feast day, anyone who chose to do so could approach the altar and be blessed by having the crown placed on their head. For centuries this kind of blessing on the feast day has been called the coronation.

This same church is also famous for its *kozy* (goats) often called *kozy prostyńksie* (the goats of Prostyń), small figures of goats made from dough. The history of the custom dates back to the 16th century and a famous Gothic sculpture representing the Holy Trinity that was sculpted by Veit Stoss or his pupils. The sculpture is believed to be the donation of Bishop Paweł Aligmunt Holszański, who presented it to Prostyń in connection with the creation of the parish. He sent his gift via boat on the Bug River since at that time water transportation was the safest method of delivery. According to legend, the arrival of the boat was first noticed by the goats who were pasturing on the

Kozy — Votive offerings in Prostyń

river meadows. They started bleating loudly and continuously and brought the arrival of the precious gift to the attention of the villagers. Another legend claims that the boat capsized on the swollen river and the sculpture was caught in the reeds of the riverbank. It was noticed by the goats who started bleating loudly to bring the villagers and the statue was miraculously saved from sinking to the bottom of the river. The goats of Prostyń were forever immortalized by the presence of *kozy* (goats) at the church feast day. These are figures of animals, chiefly goats as well as deer, made from wheat flour. The dough is shaped by hand into goat or deer figures that are boiled in water, baked hard, and decorated with red paint in stripes and dots. They are then taken to the church as votive offerings.

Another custom associated with feast days took place in churches dedicated to Św. Walenty (St. Valentine). Today St. Valentine is associated with lovers and sweethearts, but in church tradition, St. Valentine was patron saint of those suffering from epilepsy and nervous conditions. In some villages, parishioners brought votive offerings of wax figures formed by hand in the shape of arms, hands, jaws, but most importantly in the shape of a ball or circle, symbolic of the head. They were brought to the church on behalf of the sick, who were troubled with severe headaches, paralysis, neurosis, mental illness, and epilepsy. In the parish of Brodowe Łąki, there were also votive offerings in the shape of people but these were seen less often as the church forbade the use of wax votives in the shape of humans.

Initially, the wax votive offerings were made by the parishioners themselves but over time, the church warden would make them and lend them out in the church vestibule on the feast day for a small fee or even in exchange for food products, mostly eggs. With the votive offerings in their hands, or held in place on their heads with scarves (if designated to relieve headaches), the faithful processed around the altar three times, gathering dust from the wood of the altar and rubbing it on the hurting part of their bodies. At the same time they would pray for good health for themselves and those close to them and for a return to wellness; for peaceful sleep for the nervous, the weak, the constantly crying child; for the cessation of continuous headaches and buzzings in the head; and most importantly, for help for those suffering from epilepsy.

Whatever the region, the church feast day was richly celebrated in a spiritual sense and was also a much anticipated event that met the social needs of the community. The adults looked forward to it as a time to mingle socially, meet with others from the surrounding villages, and find out something new and interesting. It provided the young, unmarried men with an opportunity to meet young women from other villages and the young women, like young women everywhere, dreamed of meeting that someone special who would take them to the altar. If a young couple were already sweet on each other, it provided them with the opportunity to be together. Children eagerly looked forward to the entertainments and stalls full of trinkets and sweets that were not available at any other time of the year.

Those who had traveled some distance and wanted to stay to enjoy the outdoor festivities would sometimes partake of a meal at the local tavern. Some would find a spot under a tree and open their baskets to enjoy dinner in the open air: homemade bread and butter or cheese, hard-boiled eggs, tomatoes and cucumbers, a piece of homemade sausage, smoked ham or yeast pierogi made of buckwheat—all items that traveled well in the bumpiness of a horse-drawn wagon or carried by hand numerous miles. Those who lived locally went home for a special Sunday meal to celebrate the day.

Most church feast days were, and still are, celebrated each year on the same Sunday in a particular month. It became the custom in many parts of Poland, especially in the Śląsk region, for families who were separated from each other for whatever reason, to come home and reunite on the church feast day. This was especially true after World War II when families had been separated because of the war and brothers and sisters settled in different parts of Poland and children left home in search of work. Everyone would come back to the church of their childhood to celebrate the church feast day with the people who were important to them. The church feast day became a time of family reunion. And to celebrate the occasion, there was always a special midday meal after the high mass and procession. For days and weeks ahead of time, families prepared to host all the guests gathering together. Chickens were killed, breads and pastries were baked, and in the Śląsk region it wasn't unusual to kill a pig in order to properly host invited guests and returning family members. In this region the church feast day was as important as Christmas and Easter. The *obiad odpustowy* (the feast day dinner) consisted of chicken soup with homemade noodles; a meat dish of chicken, duck, pork or beef called zrazy or sometimes *roladami*. Side dishes included *śląskie kluski* or Silesian dumplings, salads such as cucumbers in sour cream, sweet cabbage, sauerkraut, or the much-loved red cabbage. This was finished off with a traditional fruit compote made from strawberries, pears, plums, or whatever fruit was in season. There would be hot drinks and homemade liqueurs and baked goods of yeast breads with poppy seeds or crumbs on top.

The mass and procession fed the soul and the dinner that followed filled the belly, but it was the merriment of the street vendors hawking their wares in loud voices, the beggars on the church steps seeking pennies in exchange for loud prayers, the carousel, the jugglers, the dancing bears, and the organ grinder with his monkey that fed and filled the senses.

There were monks in their cowls and nuns in their habits selling devotionals and holy pictures. There were the beggars, traveling from church fair to church fair. Among them roamed card sharps and thieves looking for the naive and easily taken yokel. It was a place alive with activity and anticipation and everyone—the young, the old, the poor, the rich—flocked to the streets to see and be seen. It was a place where each person sought that special something that would be a memento or souvenir of this very special day.

The very devout were perhaps looking for a holy picture or something to remember the day in a religious object. The selling of devotionals was not limited to the monks and nuns. Very often there were wandering peddlers selling large and small holy pictures. There were centers such as Bolima near Łowicz and Skulsk near Kalisz that were known for their religious oil paintings. Some artisans spent the entire winter painting and then took to the road in summer to sell their work themselves. Other artisans painted throughout the year and were taken up by peddlers called *obrazniki* to reach even the most remote villages and church fairs. The holy pictures varied in their subject matter. The most popular motifs were the Sacred Heart, the Blessed Mother, and the Last Supper. Equally popular were the various saints. St. Florian protected against fire; St. Barbara and St.

Agatha against lightning; St. John Nepomucen against flood; St. Martin against poverty. In later years, the holy picture sellers also sold less expensive forms of holy pictures in the form of black and white woodcuts produced by the Jesuit printing houses. These black and white paper holy pictures were cheaper than those painted on glass, wood, or canvas and subsequently enjoyed greater popularity at the smaller church fairs. Whatever the medium, the holy pictures were highly valued and hung in the best room of the house as a special purchase during odpusty.

Many of the merchants present at the *odpust* were on specific "church fair" tracks that followed all the festivals within a designated radius. These individuals made their living just from the items sold at the church fairs throughout the year. They had large inventories and had a cart or wagon and a horse. They were gone from home for weeks and months at a time until they ran out of things to sell or the church fairs ran out. There were those who sold herbs and potions for both man and beast. There were those who sold women's fripperies like hair ribbons and glass beads and small pieces of lace. Craftsmen from the bigger cities and towns brought their highly painted toys to catch the eyes of the children. Some of them were simply wandering peddlers selling their wares. Many carried their goods on their back in a basket or wrapped in a large cloth. They simply untied or opened their bundle directly onto a spot of grass and did the best they could. Local folk artists brought their homemade toys. Local women would set up a small stand to sell cool water and homemade blueberry juice as refreshment on a hot day. Another woman might bring the head of sunflowers to sell. Eating the interior of sunflowers seeds was a popular treat throughout all of Poland and people walking and nibbling on sunflower seeds was a common for a very long time but has now passed into oblivion with the loss of small individual farms.

For the children there were clay whistles in the shape of roosters and birds, celluloid windmills, wooden toys shaped like butterflies whose wings moved up and down when pulled along on string, small trumpets and drums, wooden wagons hitched to horses carved out of one piece of linden wood, simple clay figures of cats, dogs, and rabbits. There were rattles and toy hatchets, harmonicas, and recorders. One of the big attractions for boys was the wooden pop-gun.

Amateurs brought their own homemade toys to sell.

Young couples were more apt to look at baubles and bangles like rings for the fingers with "a stone that caught the light of the sun." For the hardworking housewife who had a bit of butter and egg money set aside there were ribbons of every color, threads for embroidery, needles and pins, strings of red beads to adorn the throat, hand mirrors, and paper flowers. She might stop by and look at the candles being sold by a local village woman or stop to talk with the man selling freshly brined pickles to talk recipes. She might linger at the religious statues made of plaster of Paris—something small perhaps to add to the home altar or a larger one for the *kapliczka*, the wayside shrine located in the front of the home or somewhere within the village boundaries, to replace the old one falling apart. Or if she had enough money, talk her husband into having their picture taken by the itinerant photographer. Photographers traveled the back country roads from church fair to church fair with canvases of painted backgrounds, chairs, and heavy photographic equipment. Much cherished, the family photograph took pride of place along with holy pictures in the central room of the Polish home.

The men, in lieu of looking at fripperies and toys, tended to wander off towards other males to watch the jugglers or the amateur troupe performing the life of the saint who was being honored that day, or go in search of the strong cider being sold directly out of a barrel or a pint of something like homemade beer or mead. One popular item that was sold was *kwas chlebowy*. This sour drink was made from dried rye bread and barley that had been crushed together, boiling water poured over the mash and allowed to sour in a barrel. After fermenting, the clear liquid on top was drawn off and additional boiling water added and then cooled. It was always made for special holidays and events and enjoyed as much as beer made from juniper berries.

The booths that caught everyone's attention, however, were the ones that offered traditional food. Who can ever forget the special taste of festival food? There was a dizzying array of goodies in each stall to choose from that drew the people like magnets. These included rings of soft pretzels called *obwarzanki* threaded on string and often worn around the neck by children who would snack on

•PIERNIKI•
as tokens of affection

them all day long. Soft pretzels have a history in Poland that dates back to the 15th century when King Jan Olbracht (reigned 1492-1501) gave the privilege of baking and selling white baked goods to the bakers of Kraków in 1496. They are still sold by street vendors everywhere in Kraków and are always found at church fairs and festivals throughout Poland. The traditional *obwarzanki* are about 3 to 4 inches wide, ¾ inch thick, and round in shape with a spiral twist.

There were honey spice cookies called *pierniki*, a perennial favorite with all age groups. Godmothers bought them for their godchildren, the elderly bought them because they were supposed to be good for the stomach and digestion, and they were a special favorite with young adults. These dark honey spice cookies appeared at small church fairs and local markets since the 17th century. Their shapes varied, often reflecting the life of townspeople and peasants, such as houses, roosters, geese, deer, and birds.

Among the most popular shapes at the church festival was the heart. The hearts varied in size, from tiny to very large. After baking, the plain heart-shaped cookie was decorated. Sometimes it was covered with a white glaze made from potato syrup and beaten egg whites which was applied hot over the *pierniki*. This same combination of ingredients, only thickened, also acted as an icing to decorate the top. White was the color most often used for icing. The baker used a funnel with metal shapes on the end such as stars, rosettes, or geometric pattern—all depending on the baker's repertoire—to make it as decorative and desirable as possible. Girls names like Hania, Zosia, Kasia, or messages such as "*Kocham cię*" (I love you) or "*Z serca*" (From the Heart) were written on the surface with white icing for a boy to give to a girl. For their sweethearts, the girls were more likely to buy a *piernik* that depicted a man on a horse. The couple would then enjoy sharing and eating the cookies together.

Another sweet made from honey and spices was *krajanka*, where the dough was layered between jams and covered with chocolate. Other cookies for sale were *pałeczki* made with poppy seeds and honey, and *makrony* or *makroniki*, a macaroon made chiefly with almonds. To the joy and excitement of the children, there were lollipops called *lizaki*, and sugar figures shaped as roosters with a spiral tail, chickens, and ducks. There were all types of candies: hard can-

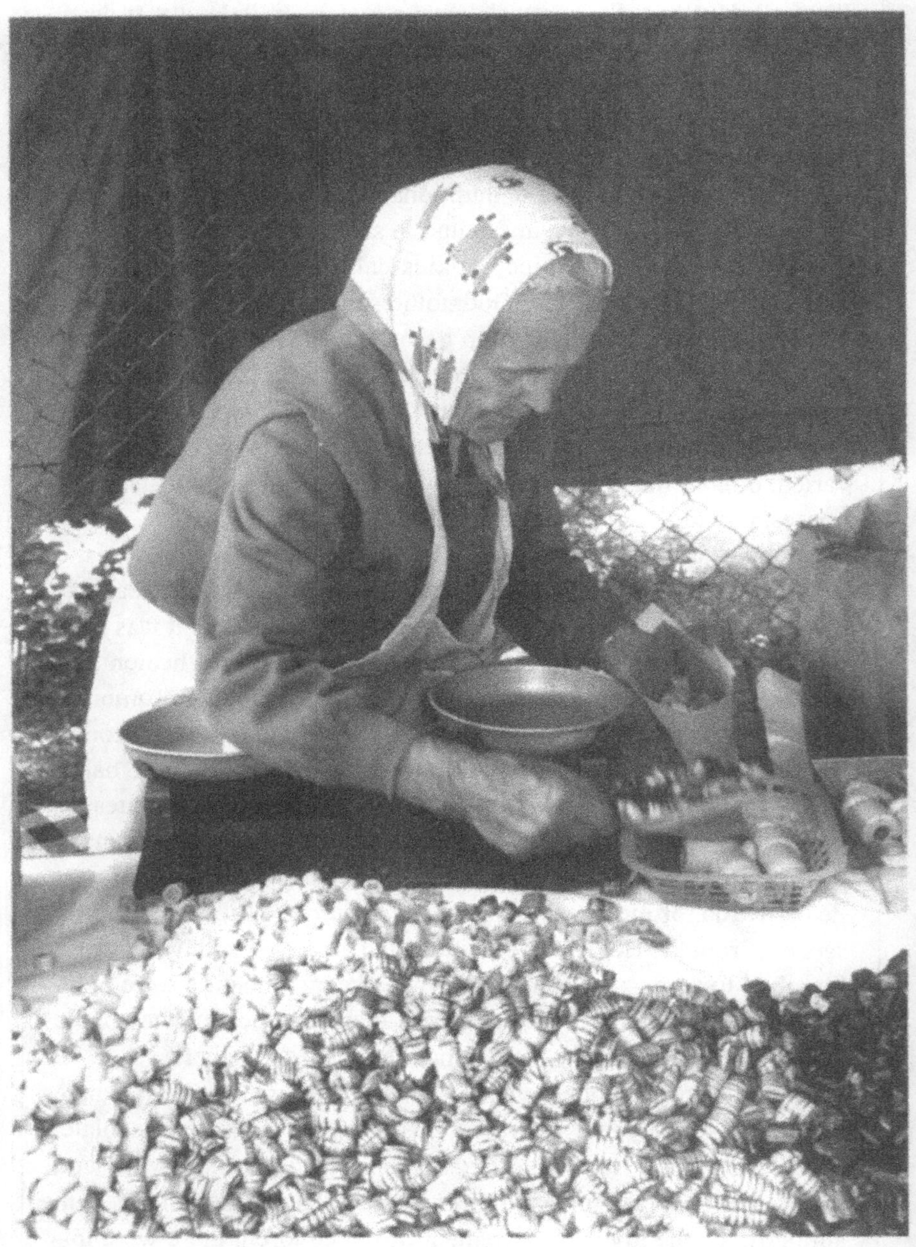

*Elderly woman with candy from Poronin.*

dies wrapped in a twist of paper, *cukierki ślazowe* (marshmallows), *landryki* (transparent candies in the shape of small pieces of glass), and *zozworki* made from ginger or mint. If the feast day was taking place in the Kurpie region, there would be special breads made from fine wheat in the shape of birds. *Andruty* were very popular in the Kalisz region. These were large, round flat wafers made from sugar and flour similar to the taste of a sugar cone which was sometimes spread with honey. Each region had its specialties, oftentimes seen and tasted only on the feast day of the church patron saint.

The feast day often concluded with an evening vesper called *nieszpory*. As daylight ended, and festivities concluded, the faithful traveled home, clutching their prized purchases with lots to think and talk about until the following year.

•PIERNIKI•

## Honey Spice Cookies

***(Pierniki)***

*Over the centuries these honey cookies filled with spices have maintained their popularity and continue to be a household's best "sweet" gift or offering when guests come to visit. This is a delicious variation of this popular cookie (see also page 135).*

1 cup buckwheat honey
2 eggs
½ cup molasses
4 cups all-purpose flour
1 teaspoon ground cinnamon
1 teaspoon ground cloves
1 teaspoon ground allspice
⅛ teaspoon ground ginger
1 tablespoon unsweetened cocoa
1 teaspoon baking soda

ICING
1 pound confectioners' sugar
3 tablespoons meringue powder
⅓ cup warm water

1. Heat the honey in a saucepan until it begins to boil. Allow to cool to lukewarm.
2. Beat eggs and molasses together.
3. Mix all dry ingredients together in a separate bowl.
4. Add the dry ingredients to the egg mixture a little at a time to mix thoroughly.
5. Pour in the warm honey and mix until smooth.
6. Chill the mixture in the refrigerator for a few hours.
7. Heat oven to 350°F. Turn mixture onto lightly floured surface and roll out to 3/16 inch thick. Cut into desired shapes.
8. Place the cookies onto a baking tray covered with parchment paper without overcrowding and bake for 12 minutes. Allow to cool.

(*continued next page*)

9. **Make icing:** In large bowl, beat confectioners' sugar, meringue powder, and water until stiff. Spoon into decorating bags and utilizing a small plain tip, pipe along the edges of the cookies or write names on the surface. (Keep any icing in the bowl tightly covered to prevent drying out. If the icing becomes too stiff a little warm water can be added to thin out for better piping consistency.)

MAKES APPROXIMATELY 32 COOKIES USING 3-INCH TO 5-INCH COOKIE CUTOUTS

# Silesian Dumplings

***(Śląskie kluski)***

*You will enjoy these dimpled dumplings that catch the gravy of whatever meat you are serving. They are traditionally made in the Śląsk region of Poland for church feast days and are a relative to* kopytka *(p. 62) only shaped differently. They are traditionally made with the addition of potato flour but regular wheat flour works just as well.*

2 teaspoons salt
4 cups cooked and riced baking potatoes (about 4 potatoes)
1 cup potato flour
1 egg

1. Place 3 quarts of water in a large cooking pot with 1 teaspoon salt and slowly bring to a boil.
2. Meanwhile place potatoes in a bowl or mound on countertop, kitchen table, or dough board. Add the flour and remaining 1 teaspoon salt. Make a well in the center and add the egg. Work the mixture slowly with hands until it forms a soft dough. If the mixture is too dry to come together, add a tablespoon of water at a time. Knead lightly. Divide the dough in half. Flour your counter or dough board lightly to keep the dough from sticking and roll each half into a long roll about 1½ inches thick.
3. Cut the ropes into 1-inch pieces. Roll a piece in the palm of your hand (like making a meatball) and make a deep indentation in the top with your thumb. Continue until all the dough has been formed.
4. Drop the dumplings in the boiling water until they cover the bottom of the pot. Do not overcrowd. Stir gently to keep dumplings from sticking to the bottom of the pot. Within a few minutes the dumplings will rise to the surface. Boil gently another 2 minutes. Remove the dumplings with a slotted spoon into a colander and allow to drain briefly. Place on well-buttered platter, careful not to let the dumplings overlap one another and serve.

NOTE: If you have made a double batch, drizzle the cooked dumplings with some of the meat sauce that will be accompanying the dumplings or pour melted butter, bacon drippings, chopped parsley, caramelized onions, or whatever you wish over the dumplings and place in warm oven while cooking the rest of the dumplings as above.

SERVES 4

# Hard Candy

***(Twarde cukierki)***

*Small chunks of hard candy flavored with anise loom large in the memories of adults when they remember the church festivals of their childhood. Other popular flavors included lemon, cinnamon, and mint. Food coloring is optional as many recall the candy looking "clear, like shards of glass."*

Confectioners' sugar
1¾ cups granulated sugar
½ cup water
½ cup light corn syrup
Flavoring (*see choices opposite page*)
Food coloring (*optional; see choices opposite page*)

1. Generously dust a jelly-roll pan with confectioners' sugar and set aside.
2. Grease a marble slab or jelly-roll pan with thin layer of oil or butter.
3. Place granulated sugar, water, and corn syrup in heavy saucepan and gradually heat until sugar dissolves. Bring the syrup to a boil and bring to 310°F, using a candy thermometer to measure temperature and stirring constantly.
4. Remove the pan from heat and add chosen flavoring and coloring. Mix well and pour onto the prepared marble slab or jelly-roll pan and use a spatula to fold the edges to the center several times till slightly thickened (the syrup should be slightly cooled and not runny).
5. Working very quickly, cut the hardening candy into strips with oiled scissors as soon as it begins to cool and before it hardens too much. Then using the same oiled scissors, cut each strip into ¼ or ⅜-inch small pieces (or whatever size pleases you) and immediately throw onto the jelly-roll pan dusted with confectioners' sugar to coat them and prevent sticking. After dusting and cooling completely shake off excess sugar by placing in strainer and store in tight container. (If making more than one flavor, store each flavored candy separately.)

| FOOD COLOR | ESSENTIAL OIL FLAVORINGS* |
|---|---|
| black | 1 teaspoon anise oil |
| blue | ¾ to 1 teaspoon clove oil |
| yellow | 1¼ to 1½ teaspoons lemon oil |
| red | 1 to 1¼ teaspoons cinnamon oil |
| clear | ¼ to ½ teaspoons peppermint oil |
| orange | ½ to ¾ teaspoons sassafras oil |
| light green | 1 to 1½ teaspoons spearmint oil |
| dark green | 1¼ teaspoons wintergreen oil |

*NOTE: Essential oils are the most concentrated flavoring and are available from candymaking supply stores. Extracts are less concentrated so if you have to use those adjust amounts accordingly.

# LOLLIPOPS

***(Lizaki)***

*Sugar was an expensive commodity in old Poland and any sweet was considered a luxury. Lollipops were a perennial favorite with children at church fairs. These can be made free form or through the use of molds which are available at candy making supply stores.*

2 cups granulated sugar
¾ cup light corn syrup
½ cup water
Several drops oil of cinnamon, peppermint, or flavor of choice
Several drops of food coloring of choice
Lollipop sticks

1. If using heat proof lollipop molds, oil lightly and place lollipop molds on foil with sticks in place. Or grease a marble slab with flavorless vegetable oil. Or cover 2 baking sheets with aluminum foil, shiny side up.
2. In a heavy 3-quart saucepan, combine sugar, corn syrup, and water. Heat to boiling. Cook, without stirring, until mixture reaches 300°F on a candy thermometer or hard-crack stage. Stir in flavoring oil and food coloring of choice.
3. Fill the molds with hot syrup. Or if using a marble slab or cookie sheets covered with aluminum foil, use a large spoon to pour 4 pools of syrup into free form lollipop shapes, about 2-inch circles. Quickly place a lollipop stick into each pool about one-third of the way in.
4. Continue to pour four lollipops at a time, until only a little syrup is left. To make sure the sticks are secure, spoon a few drops of the remaining syrup over each stick where it meets the lollipop.
5. Set aside to cool completely. When completely cool, remove lollipops from molds. If using a marble slab, use a metal spatula to gently loosen the lollipops from the surface; if using aluminum foil, gently peel the lollipops from the foil. Place each in its own small plastic bag and tie.

MAKES ABOUT 16 TO 20 SMALL LOLLIPOPS

# Macaroons

***(Makaroniki)***

*Almonds were considered a real treat in early Poland, and reserved for baking on special occasions. Unlike in the homes of nobles and kings, coconut did not play a large role in the kitchens of the country folk. In times of war, when items like almonds—a luxury in the best of times—were unheard of, browned and crushed oats were substituted for the almonds.*

4 egg whites
1½ cups confectioners' sugar
1½ cups finely ground almonds
2 teaspoons lemon juice
1 teaspoon almond extract
2 tablespoons flour
Almond slivers

1. Preheat oven to 350°F. Beat egg whites until frothy.
2. Gradually add confectioners' sugar and continue beating between additions until incorporated into a stiff batter.
3. Slowly add the finely ground almonds into the batter. Then add the lemon juice, almond extract, and flour.
4. Line baking sheets with parchment paper. Place 1 tablespoon (using measuring tablespoon) batter on parchment paper for each cookie. Top with slivered almonds.
5. Bake for 15 to 16 minutes until a delicate golden color. Cool. Store in a tightly covered container.

MAKES APPROXIMATELY 32 COOKIES.

# MERINGUES

**(*Bezy*)**

*Meringues flavored with cocoa, coffee, and various extracts are popular on St. Valentine's Day as a dessert. The superfine sugar can be made in your own food processor using regular granular sugar and pulsing ¼ cup at a time until superfine.*

- 3 egg whites
- ¼ teaspoon cream of tartar
- ¾ cup superfine sugar (castor sugar)
- ¼ teaspoon almond, vanilla, or peppermint extract or other extract of choice

1. Preheat oven to 200°F. Bring egg whites to room temperature.
2. Beat egg whites at medium speed in large bowl until foamy.
3. Add cream of tartar and continue beating until soft peaks form.
4. Slowly add sugar, a few tablespoons at a time, making sure the sugar dissolves into the egg whites and you obtain stiff shiny peaks. Test this by rubbing a small amount of the batter between your fingers. If it feels gritty it needs additional beating. Add flavoring of choice.
5. Line cookie sheet with parchment paper. Drop batter by large spoonfuls onto the cookie sheet using a pastry bag or two spoons.
6. Bake for 1½ hours. The outsides should be nice and crisp and the insides should be soft like marshmallow. Turn off oven and allow cookies to cool completely in oven for several more hours or even overnight.

MAKES ABOUT 10 LARGE MERINGUES OR 20 SMALL ONES.

# Baked Yeast Pierogi

***(Pierogi w Ciasto)***

*Many individuals traveled to church fairs on foot or by horse-drawn wagon and brought along their own lunches for the journey. Baked pierogi travel well as they can be wrapped in paper or clean cloth when cool and require no heating or utensils—just eat with your fingers and wash down with a cooling drink.*

Dough

1 package active dry yeast
¼ cup lukewarm water (110°F)
2 teaspoons sugar
¼ cup butter
1 cup milk
4 to 5 cups all-purpose flour
1 teaspoon salt
3 egg yolks, at room temperature
1 egg white

Filling

8 ounces fresh cremini mushrooms, sliced
4 cups water
1 large onion, finely chopped
2 tablespoons oil
2 cups buckwheat groats
1 teaspoon salt
½ teaspoon pepper

*Make dough:*

1. Sprinkle yeast on the warmed water. Add sugar and allow to "proof" for a few minutes. Melt the butter in the milk until it reaches 110°F.
2. Mix together flour, salt, egg yolks, and milk mixture. Add yeast mixture. Dough will be crumbly. Gather dough together into a ball.
3. Oil the sides and bottom of a medium bowl. Place dough in the oiled bowl and turn to coat the dough with oil. Cover with plastic wrap to keep from drying out and refrigerate for at least an hour.

(*continued on next page*)

*Prepare filling:*

4. In saucepan, cook mushrooms in the water for 15 minutes. Scoop out mushrooms with a slotted spoon and set aside. Keep mushroom water hot. (There should be 4 cups water; if not, add hot water to equal 4 cups.)
5. In large 6 quart saucepan, fry onion in oil until translucent about 5 minutes. Add buckwheat groats and stir until all the buckwheat is coated with the oil. Add the hot mushroom water and season with the salt and pepper. Cover and cook 15 minutes or until all the mushroom water is absorbed by the groats.
6. Chop the mushrooms very fine or run through food processor. Mix the chopped mushrooms with the buckwheat. Allow to cool.

*Assemble pierogi:*

7. Grease two cookie sheets. On a floured work surface, roll out half the dough into a circle about ¼ inch thick. Cut circles with 4-inch biscuit cutter or empty 1-lb. coffee can.
8. Place packed, heaping tablespoon of buckwheat filling in center of each circle. Fold dough over the filling and seal edges. Place on greased cookie sheet, leaving enough space between to allow to rise and not touch each other. About 10 pierogis will fit comfortably on a cookie sheet. Gather remaining dough scraps together, roll out, and cut some more circles and fill. Repeat process with other half of dough.
9. Allow pierogi to rise in draft-free place until double in bulk, about 1 hour. Heat oven to 350°F.
10. Bake in preheated oven for 20 minutes. Brush with egg white and bake 5 or 10 additional minutes until golden brown.

**VARIATION:** Refrigerated crescent rolls can be a quick and easy replacement for the dough for these flaky pierogi.

MAKES 18 TO 20 BAKED PIEROGI

## Last Note

The people of Poland have also celebrated this custom:

When returning or lending a bowl or pot, never return or lend it empty. Put in a piece of bread or a handful of flour.

Over the years the origin and meaning of this custom has been lost to us. I like to believe that it was a symbol of the Poles' mutual giving and sharing with one another; that no matter how small the offering, it was always given with the thought and genuine feeling of "may your bowl or plate never be empty, may you never go hungry."

# Sources

**The Baker's Catalogue**
**P.O. Box 876**
**Norwich, Vermont 05055-0876**
**(800) 827-6836**
**www.kingarthurflour.com**

A great source for fine tools, ingredients, and equipment for the home baker. Carries the much sought-after Boles□awiec pottery bowls that are made in Poland as well as poppy seeds, honey, and fine variety of wheat, rye, and multigrain flours, and compressed yeast.

**Christmas Wafers Bakery-OCO**
**P.O. Box 99**
**Lewiston, New York 14092-0099**
**(716) 754-2399**
**Fax (716) 754-2824**

Christmas wafers, cards, and books. Their motto is "Dedicated to preserve, perpetuate and propagate sacred Christian traditions." Offers *A Polish Christmas Eve* by Rev. Czesław Michał Krysa, a 264-page book on Polish Christmas traditions ($26.95). A must for anyone trying to preserve Christmas traditions. Mail order only.

**Polish Bookstore and Publishing**
**135A India Street**
**Brooklyn, New York 11222**
**(718) 349-2738**

You can buy books as well as dried and marinated mushrooms, soups, pickles, jams and preserves and delicious chocolate from Poland. A cornucopia of the best of Poland.

**Polish Art Center**
**9539 Joseph Campau Boulevard**
**Hamtramck, Michigan 48212**
**(313) 874-2242**
**(888) 619-9771**
**www.polartcenter.com**

This store has everything you need. The most comprehensive store I know containing Polish books, cards, craft supplies, art, jewelry, traditional Polish costume—everything under one roof. A regular treasure trove of Polish heritage.

**Polish American Journal**
**P.O. Box 328**
**Boston, New York 14025-0328**
**(716) 312-8088** or **1-800-422-1275**
**E-mail: info@polamjournal.com**

If you are interested in news from Poland as well as what's going on in the Polish American community in the United States you'll want to subscribe to this monthly newspaper. It is dedicated to the promotion and continuance of Polish American culture.

**SACO Foods Inc.**
**6120 University Avenue**
**Middleton, Wisconsin 53562**
**(800) 373-7226**
**SacoFoods@aol.com**

If you love buttermilk pancakes as much as I do and you don't always have fresh buttermilk on hand, you'll enjoy this dry buttermilk powder. Just add water and add to your favorite recipe.

**Triple Oaks Nursery and Herb Garden**
**P.O. Box 385**
**2359 Delsea Drive**
**Franklinville, NJ 08322**
**(856) 694-4274**

Polish owned and operated. The nursery has all the herbs and flowers you might want for your garden while the gift shop is loaded with items from Poland, books, butter lamb molds and Polish pottery. Carries *pisanki* kits and classes on making your own *pisanki*.

# Books

***A Polish Christmas Eve*** by Rev. Czesław Michał Krysa. CWB Press, Lewiston, New York, 1998.

Everything you want to know about a Polish Christmas Eve: traditions, recipes and song as well as memoirs of Polish Americans celebrating this beautiful holiday.

To order send to Christmas Wafers Bakery on page 289.

***Polish Heritage Cookery*** by Robert and Maria Strybel. Hippocrene Books, Inc., New York, 1993.

If you can't find the recipe you are looking for anywhere, you will find it in this book. It is the most extensive Polish cookbook ever published in English with over 2,000 recipes. A must for lovers of Polish cooking.

***Eat Smart in Poland*** by Joan and David Peterson. Ginkgo Press, Inc., Madison, Wisconsin, 2000.

A guidebook for travelers who want to get to the heart of Poland's culture through its cuisine. Includes an alphabetical listing of menu entries in Polish, with English translations, to make ordering food easy as well as helpful phrases for use in restaurants and food markets.

# Bibliography

Baranowski, Bohdan. *Życie codzienne wsi miédzy wartą a pilicą w XIX Wieku*. [Everyday Village Life between the Warta and Pilica]; Warszawa: Państwowy Instytut Wydawniczny, 1969.

Bochdanowicz, Janusz. "Pożywienie w Pracah Polskiego Atlasu Etnograficznego," [Food in the Polish Ethnographic Atlas]; In: *Pożywienie Ludności Wiejskiej*. Kraków; Muzeum Etnograficzne, 1973, pp.53–60.

Bochenheim, Krystyna. *Przy Polskim Stole*. [At the Polish Table]; Wrocław: Wydawnictwo Dolnośląskie, 1998.

Bursztą, Jozef (Ed.). *Kultura Ludowa Mazurów i Warmiaków*. [Culture of the People of Mazury and Warmia]; Ośrodek Badań Naukowych Imienia Wojciecha Kętrzyńskiego w Olsztynie, 1976.

Chętnik, Adam. *Pożywiennie Kurpiów*. [Food of the Kurpie]; Nakłdem Polskiej Akademji Umiejętności skład Główny w Księgarni Gebethnera I Wolffa. Kraków, 1936.

Ćwierczakiewicz, Lucyna. *Porządki Domowe*. [Household Hints]; Warszawa: Księgarnii Gebethera i Wolffa, 1887.

Ćwierczakiewicz, Lucyna. *365 Obiady za 5 złoty*. [365 Dinners for 5 cents]; Nakład Jana Fiszera. Lwów, 1911.

Ćwierczakiewicz, Lucyna. *Obiady, Ciasta i Konfitury*. [Dinners, Baked Goods and Jams]; Rzeszów: Krajowa Agencja Wydawnicza, 1991.

Dekowski, Jan Piotr. "Przemiany Tradycyjnego Poźwienia Wiejskiego na Obszarze Polski Środkowej." [Changes in Traditional Food Consumption in Central Poland]; *Prace i Materiały Muzeum Archeologicznego i Etnograficznego w Łodzi. Seria Etnograficzna Nr 20;* Łodź: 1979, pp. 171–218.

Dekowski, Jan Piotr. "Z Badań Nad Pożywieniem Ludu Łęczyckiego." [Research on Food Practices among the People of Łęczyki]; *Prace i Materiały Muzeum Archeologicznego I Etnograficznego w Łodzi. Seria Etnograficzna Nr 8;* Łodź: 1964, pp. 185–197.

Dekowski, Jan Piotr. "Z Badań Nad Pożywieniem Ludu Łowickiego." [Research on Food Practices among the People of Łowicz]; *Prace i Materiały Muzeum Archeologicznego i Etnograficznego w Łodzi. Seria Etnograficzna Nr 12;* Łodê: 1968, pp. 5–205.

Dekowski, Jan Piotr. "Pożwienia Ludu Radomskiego." [Food of the People of Radom]; *Prace i Materiały Muzeum Archeologicznego i Etnograficznego w Łodzi. Seria Etnograficzna. Nr 7;* Łodź: 1963, pp. 103–127.

Estreicherówna, Maria. *Życie Towarzyskie i Obyczjaowe Krakowa w Latach 1848–1863.* [Social Life and Customs in Cracow during the years 1848–1863]; Literackie: Kraków, 1968.

Gajek, Józef, ed. *Polski Atlas Etnograficzny.* [Polish Ethnographical Atlas]; Insytut Historii Kultury Materialnej: Warszawa, 1964.

Gerlich, Halina and Gerlich, Marian. *Sacrum Rodzina Tradycje.* [Sacred Family Traditions]; Śląsk. Katowice, 1995.

Gloger, Zygmunt. *Encyklopedia Staropolska, Tom I–IV.* [Encyclopedia of Old Poland, Volumes I–IV]; Warszawa: Wiedza Powszechna, 1985.

Gołębiowski, Łukasz. *Domy i Dwory.* [Houses and Manors]; Lwów: A. Kaczurba, 1884.

Gołębiowski, Łukasz. *Lud Polski: Jego Zwyczaje, Zabobony.* [The Polish People; their Customs, Superstitions]; Warszawa: Drukarnia A Gałęzowskiego, 1830.

Hensla, W. and Pazdura, J. (Eds.). *Historia Kultury Materialnej Polski Tom II, III, IV.* [History of the Material Culture of Poland. Volumes 2,3,4]; Zakład Narodowy Imienia Ossolińskich. Wrocław, 1978.

Iwaskiewicz, Maria. *Gawędy o Jedzeniu.* [Chats about Food]; Wydawnictwo Kultura Życia Codzienniego "Watra". Warszawa, 1969.

Jarosińska, Izabela. *Kuchnia Polska i Romantyczna.* [The Polish Kitchen and Romance]; Wydawnictwo Literackie. Kraków, 1994.

*Kalendarz domowy Babci Aliny.* [Home Calendar of Grandma Alina]; Kraków: Trans-Krak, Firma Wydawnicza, 1997.

Kalkowski, Jan. *Podróże Kulinarne.* [Culinary Travels]; Warszawa: Wydawnictwo Spółdzielce, 1984.

Kolberg, Oskar. *LUD. Jego zwyczaje, sposób życia, mowa, podania, przysłowia, gusła, zabawy, pieśni, muzyka i tance. Tom 5,10,24.* [The People. Their traditions, manner of living, speech, proverbs, customs, witchcraft, entertainment, songs, music and dance. Volumes 5, 10, 24]; Kraków: Polskie Towarzystwo Ludoznawcze, w drukarni Universytetu Jagiellonskiego, 1871–1890.

Kossak, Zofia. *Rok Polski.* [The Polish Year]; Wydawnictwo "Pax". Warszawa, 1958.

Kowalska-Lewicka, Anna (Ed.) *Pożywienie Ludności Wiejskiej.* [Food of Country People]; Kraków: Muzeum Etnograficzne w Krakowie, 1973.

Kowalska-Lewicka, Anna. "Traditional Cheese-making in Poland." *Ethnologia Europea.* Volume II. 1968–1969. pp. 238–243.

Łozińscy, Maja i Jan. *Wokół Stołu i Kuchni*. [About the Table and Kitchen]; Warszawa: Wydawnictwo Tenten, 1994.
Magiera, Jan. "Wielkanoc w Sądeczyźnie." [Easter in Sądecz]; *Wisła*, 1904. pp. 227–281.
Michalakówna, Barbara. "Pożywienie." [Food.] In: *Kultura Ludowa Wielkopolska Tom 2*. [Culture of the People of Great Poland]; Józef Burszta, Ed. Wydawnictwo Poznańskie. Poznań, 1964.
Odachowska-Zielinska, Ewa. *Porady Babuni, czyli o urokach życia w dworku polskim*. [Grandma's Helpful Hints or Life's Superstitions in a Polish Manor]; Warszawa: Wydawnictwo "Watra." 1990.
Saloni, Aleksander. "Lud Przeworski." [People of Przeworsk]; *Wisła*, 1898, p. 49.
Sumców, Mikołoj. "Starodawne Sposoby Przyrzàdania Chleba." [Old Methods of Preparing Bread]; *Wisła*, 1890, pp. 639–657.
Świtała-Trybek, Dorota. *Święto i Zabawa: Odpusty Parafialne na Górnym Śląsku* [Holy Day and Merry-making: Church Feast Days in Upper Silesia]; Wrocław: Polskie Towarzystwo Ludoznawcze, 2000.
Sztabowa, Wera. *Krupnioki i moczka czyli gawędy o kuchni śląskiej*. [Tales From a Silesian Kitchen]; Wydawnictwo Śląsk, 1985.
Topolski, Jerzy. *Ogrodnicztwo*: In *Kultura Ludowa Wielkopolski Tom 2*. [Gardening: In Culture of the People of Great Poland]; Poznań: Wydawnictwo Poznańskie, 1964, pp. 267–298.
Wojcik, Halina. "Rzeszowskie Łyżniki Schodowane." [Tiered Spoon Racks in Rzeszów]; *Polska Sztuka Ludowa*, Vol. 4 1968, pp. 199–208.
Zadrożyńska, Anna. *Powtarzać Czas Początku*. [Retelling Beginning Times]; Warszawa: Wydawnictwo Spółdzielcze, 1985.
Ziółkowska, Maria. *Szczodry Wieczór, Szczodry Dzień*. [Abundant Evening, Abundant Day]; Warszawa: Ludowa Spółdzielnia Wydawnicza, 1989.

# INDEX

# INDEX TO ILLUSTRATIONS AND PHOTOGRAPHS

## THE COUNTRY KITCHEN



### FALL

**WINTER**



**SPRING**



**SUMMER**

**FEASTS & FESTIVALS**

www.ingramcontent.com/pod-product-compliance
Lightning Source LLC
Jackson TN
JSHW011353130125
77033JS00023B/665

* 9 7 8 0 7 8 1 8 1 2 9 4 8 *